Electronic Services Networks _____

ELECTRONIC SERVICES NETWORKS

A BUSINESS AND PUBLIC POLICY CHALLENGE

Edited by
Margaret E. Guerin-Calvert
and
Steven S. Wildman

HD
9999
.I492
E44
1991

THE ANNENBERG
WASHINGTON PROGRAM
Communications Policy Studies
Northwestern University

PRAEGER

New York
Westport, Connecticut
London

Library of Congress Cataloging-in-Publication Data

Electronic services networks : a business and public policy challenge
/ edited by Margaret E. Guerin-Calvert and Steven S. Wildman.
      p.   cm.
   "The Annenberg Washington Program [in] Communications Policy
Studies, Northwestern University."
   Includes bibliographical references and index.
   ISBN 0-275-93527-2 (alk. paper)
   1. Information services industry—Congresses. 2. Audiotex
services industry—Congresses. 3. Electronic data interchange—
Congresses. 4. Telecommunication—Congresses. 5. Computer
networks—Congresses. 6. Information networks—Congresses.
I. Guerin-Calvert, Margaret E. II. Wildman, Steven S.
III. Northwestern University (Evanston, Ill.). Annenberg Washington
Program in Communications Policy Studies.
HD9999.I492E44   1991
384.3'3—dc20   91-4627

British Library Cataloguing in Publication Data is available.

Library of Congress Catalog Card Number: 91-4627
ISBN: 0-275-93527-2

First published in 1991

Praeger Publishers, One Madison Avenue, New York, NY 10010
An imprint of Greenwood Publishing Group, Inc.

Printed in the United States of America

The paper used in this book complies with the
Permanent Paper Standard issued by the National
Information Standards Organization (Z39.48-1984).

10 9 8 7 6 5 4 3 2 1

To Preston, who has helped more than he knows,
and to Kate, who makes life fun.

M.E.G.C.

To Susan, Brittany, and Jason—
for inspiration and
understanding.

S.S.W.

Contents

Tables and Figures

Preface

This book is the outgrowth of shared interests—between the editors, among the editors and the many authors who contributed papers to this book, and among that set of individuals and a broad and diverse group of academics, businesspeople, and policymakers. The shared interests include a desire—at times, an obsession—to try to understand the operations and implications of certain industry structures involving electronic services networks for the performance of industries and their effects on the ultimate consumer. Electronic services networks, or ESNs, are networks of terminals and computers (or switches) connected by various types of telecommunications links that are used to process transactions, the most fundamental of commercial activities. These networks have developed and spread rapidly over the last three decades and are now a significant influence on industry structures and commercial practices in financial industries, manufacturing, and the service industries, including transportation.

The issues addressed in this book concerning these networks are among the most hotly debated in both academic and policy circles. Many are of immediate practical concern to the businesses involved. Yet, to date, work on these issues has been hampered by the fact that the relevant literature on ESN issues is widely scattered and poorly cross-referenced. One of our objectives in putting this volume together was to collect in one place the best of current thinking on these electronic networks. A second motive for this book was the shared belief that the literature and research on network industries had not dealt adequately with the information-processing characteristics of ESNs that set them apart from the physical transportation networks to which they frequently are compared. In many respects, the use of electronic linkages and remote terminals seemed to raise the prospect that the industry structure could be more flexible and responsive to market conditions than physical networks such as pipelines with their high fixed costs and limited routing flexibility. Yet many of the same policy problems such as access, pricing, and bias against competitors that occurred in these networks were arising in ESNs as well. The editors of this book, in their (different) roles (at different times) as consultant, policymaker, or academic, found that they were continually confronting what appeared to be essentially similar problems in a wide array of ESNs. Discussions with others revealed that the case law, the literature, and the folklore all tended to concentrate on the physical networks. In large part, many seem to assume that all networks, including the full range of ESNs, are pipelines, for purposes of policy analysis.

We raised and reraised these issues with each other and with colleagues in an effort to model the problems and the processes. Our effort to collect thoughts, theories, and empirical insights into the issues resulted in a conference on ESNs sponsored by the Annenberg Washington Program in February 1990. We asked the authors of papers presented at the conference, and included as chapters herein, to go beyond the current literature and the current cases to develop more general theories of networks. In addition, we encouraged authors of papers focused on particular industries using ESNs to explore the implications for ESNs in general and to give their insights into the workings of these networks in particular industry settings. These papers have benefited from intense, lively, and critical discussion by both discussants and the active audience of practicing attorneys, policymakers, and academics. The result, we believe, is a collection of writings that provide the most thorough review of ESNs available to date and a more complete understanding of the complex issues and policies required for efficient and effective operation of ESNs. In many respects, we regard this as an extraordinarily useful starting point. Here is set down, in a single place, in a form not previously provided, what we (taken collectively as the authors in this book and others who have been generous with their comments and advice) know about the structure and operation of ESNs. This collection also points out many avenues of additional research and identifies policy issues that are likely to keep us engrossed, and at times aggravated, for years to come.

We have many people to thank for the advice and support they provided over the year or so in which this book took shape. Without the support, both financial and administrative, of the Washington Annenberg Program of Northwestern University this book would not have been possible. In particular, we are grateful to Newton Minow, its director, and to Yvonne Zecca, associate director, for their support of our vision, first of the ESN conference and then of this book. We owe an equal debt to the authors in this book, who have contributed substantially of their time and talent in drafting and redrafting their respective chapters. We also would like to thank the participants in the Annenberg conference for their stimulating, and at times provocative, contributions to the substantive discussion of network issues. Jade Eaton is deserving of special thanks for remarkable encouragement of the editors' efforts to bring this book to fruition. Special thanks also to our colleagues at Economists Incorporated and more recently at Northwestern and the Department of Justice. Steve Wildman wants to express his personal thanks to the Ameritech Foundation for financial support that funded release time for editing and writing for this volume. We also thank James Dunton, executive editor at Praeger, for his support in this endeavor.

Finally, our special thanks to supportive spouses and children, who tolerated absences, long phone calls, and abstracted looks when particularly complex or aggravating details stymied the editors' ability to leave the book or the chapter alone.

Introduction

There has been a general recognition at least since Machlup's (1962) pioneering empirical study that the information sectors in the United States and other economically advanced nations account for a substantial and growing fraction of national income. However, through the 1960s, computers and the profusion of new and enhanced telecommunications technologies were viewed primarily as new and improved tools to perform standard computational and communication tasks more effectively and at lower cost. Since the 1970s, there has been a growing realization that the new information technologies also bear the seeds of an economic and social transformation potentially as far-reaching as that wrought by the industrial revolution. Daniel Bell's *The Coming of Post-Industrial Society: A Venture in Social Forecasting* (1973) is probably the best known and most influential of the early statements of the new perspective on communication technologies. In the 1980s, this perspective was reflected in the recognition and elevation of the "communication infrastructure" to the status of a major policy concern, in academic studies of the effects of new communication technologies on various industries (see, e.g., Faulhaber et al., 1986), and in the proliferation of books in the last half of the decade advising businesses on how to use telecommunications to enhance profits and disadvantage competitors (e.g., Keene, 1988; Davis, 1987; Stalk and Hout, 1990).

Of course, recognizing that new technologies have the potential to transform economic relationships is not the same as understanding the logic inherent in the emerging economic structures. It is difficult to anticipate the exact forms in which the many potentials of new technologies will be manifest. For this reason, studies of the new order must wait until its contours have begun to take shape.

We think it is now clear that what we are calling the electronic services network (ESN) has emerged as an important and fundamental new economic structure spawned by advances in information technology. ESNs are networks of terminals and central computers or switches linked by any of a variety of telecommunication technologies that are used to process transactions and to facilitate the process of transacting in a variety of ways. In the process they are changing transactional relationships. As transacting is fundamental to any economy that has risen above autarchy, it should be clear that a technology with the potential to alter transactional practices has the potential to transform economic relationships more generally.

ESNs are now integral components of the structures of a number of manufacturing and service industries, including various transportation and financial services. Several industries using ESNs are studied in this volume. In some of these industries, such as airlines, the vast majority of transactions are now handled in some form by networks. Others, like foreign currency exchange, where forty percent of all transactions are processed by a Reuters network (Bremner and Rothfeder, 1990), are headed in the same direction. Furthermore, it appears that the spread of this network form of organization is still in its accelerating growth phase. New applications in service industries are being introduced continuously, and the growth in vendors of electronic data interchange (EDI) software and equipment for manufacturers and retailers has been explosive in recent years. ESNs are even being marketed to the home through PRODIGY, the IBM-Sears joint venture, and by a number of smaller companies that compete with PRODIGY, usually with specialized regional and local shopping services. Peapod Delivery Services, an Evanston, Illinois, company that developed and operates a computerized grocery-shopping and -delivery service in the northern Chicago suburbs, is an example of the latter.

The chapters in this volume explore the economics of these new networks and the business and public policy issues they raise. ESNs have been studied before, but typically as features of the industries or firms that employed them. Here the focus is on the networks themselves. Analyses of ESNs to date have tended to rely heavily on analogies to the older and better-understood physical transportation networks such as pipelines, railroads, highway systems, and electricity grids, building on important parallels between the new networks and their physical counterparts. For example, the older networks are vital components of the economic infrastructure, and it appears that ESNs will one day have similar status, if they don't already. Both types of networks also affect commercial practices and economic structures by reducing transaction costs and making possible transactions and transactional relationships that would not be feasible without them.

The differences between the older networks that mostly move people and goods and the new networks that transmit and process information are also important, however. The telecommunications links between the terminals of ESNs often are much less likely to be constrained to one or a few routes than, say, are railroads and pipelines. These ESNs are therefore more flexible structures that can more easily expand and contract capacity in response to changing market conditions. While the older networks dramatically reduced the importance of distance as a barrier to commerce, ESNs are deployed primarily to reduce the informational constraints on transacting. Numerous lawsuits and regulatory actions over access to ESNs are testimony to the effectiveness of these networks in reducing transaction costs. Access would not be a matter of significant policy concern if the benefits of using a network were not substantial.

Market power and access to network services have been the subjects of fairly extensive study in both the academic and policy literatures on physical networks, such as electric utility transmission grids and railroads. It is tempting simply to extrapolate the results of this research to the related policy issues in ESNs. To do so, however, substantially overstates the similarities of the two types of networks and provides inadequate insight into the fundamental issues involved in ESNs. Moreover, the rapid and extensive deployment of ESNs in a wide array of industries and the crucial role played by ESNs in many of these means that incorrect or incomplete characterization of the important economic features of ESNs could lead to public policies that are fundamentally flawed and potentially destructive of important market-generated innovations.

The studies reported in this book represent a shared effort to develop new theoretical and empirical frameworks for understanding the structure and implications of ESNs. Where possible, the chapters build on the existing literature on the physical networks. In many cases, however, the authors started anew by "dismantling" the network and examining its basic components. They posed basic questions concerning the nature of the services provided, the economic rationale for the network's existence, and the mode of the network's operation, which provided greater insight into the nature of ESNs. The chapters and the book as a whole, nonetheless, share a common goal with the literature on physical networks: to understand the basic economics of networks and their effects on transactions and economic relationships.

This book is divided into two parts. The six chapters in Part I present fairly general theoretical perspectives on the economics of different types of ESNs, their effects on the industries and markets that employ them, and the policy issues they raise. The five chapters in Part II all focus on the working of ESNs in specific industries. ESNs examined include automatic teller machine (ATM) networks, computer reservation systems (CRSs), real estate multiple-listing services (MLSs), and electronic data interchange (EDI) networks in several industries. The theory/industry analysis distinction between the two sections is one of degree rather than a distinction in kind. The industry studies of Part II are all informed by economic theory and the theoretical analyses in Part I are all grounded in observations of real-world industries. Richard Gilbert's chapter, in particular, which begins Part II, bridges the two approaches. Gilbert develops an elaborate and general model of network pricing that he applies to automatic teller networks. The common theme linking the two parts is the attempt to develop sound business and policy perspectives on ESNs.

Relationships among the structures of ESNs, the nature of the services they provide, and the conditions under which they develop are examined by Steven Wildman and Margaret Guerin-Calvert in Chapter 1. They examine ESNs from a transactions cost perspective and conclude that network structures and the services provided with individual networks are determined in large part by the costs and market/industry structures of the industries that employ them. Of particular importance are differences in transaction costs and coordination costs. Their taxonomy of ESNs should provide a useful starting point for readers not already familiar with these networks.

While the organizational structures of firms and markets influence the applications of communication technologies, the influence must be reciprocal. Ajit Kambil's study complements that of Wildman and Guerin-Calvert by examining the influence of communication technologies, including ESNs, on the organizational structures of markets and firms. Specifically, he tests, with a large data base of manufacturing industries, the hypothesis originally advanced by Malone et al. (1987) that, because they lower transaction costs, the new communication technologies will promote greater reliance on markets to coordinate economic activities and less reliance on vertically integrated hierarchies, such as firms that encompass two stages of production. Kambil's regressions provide support for this hypothesis. He finds that his measure of vertical integration (or reliance on intrafirm transactions) fell over time for those industries that invested the most in information technology.

The recent wave of network mergers in the ATM industry makes Nicholas Economides's chapter particularly relevant to a very current policy concern. The structure of the ATM industry is rapidly being transformed by mergers of local and regional networks to form larger networks with, potentially, a national reach. The credit card industry went through a similar period of consolidation some years ago. Yet, we find that a few banks are resisting this trend. The causes and effects of network consolidations currently are a matter of considerable importance to banking regulators because of their potential for affecting the vigor of competition among banks. Economides models the incentives of firms with private networks to promote compatibility with other networks to make possible transactions across them. He shows that firms' incentives to join or to refrain from joining shared networks are affected by the structure of demand for the products of the component networks and their individual market shares. His work is also applicable to the incentives of joint-venture shared networks, where such networks are considering a merger of two or more shared networks.

A number of ESNs facilitate transactions by making it possible for consumers to search among the products of competing sellers more effectively. Real estate MLSs, which permit home buyers to screen property listings on-line, and airline computer reservation systems, which travel agents use to identify and book flights from network terminals, are common examples. It is commonly assumed that market prices fall as consumers become better informed about the options of different sellers. From this perspective, the decisions of some industries to invest in technologies that facilitate consumer search seem counterintuitive, unless firms' costs are also reduced. Wildman builds on the economic literature of consumer search to model the process of network search facilitation. He shows that, in some cases, search facilitation reduces prices, but that in other cases prices may rise even if the competitive structure of an industry is not affected. The model is then employed to examine the conditions under which consumers benefit and lose from search facilitation and the implications of search facilitation for economic efficiency.

In shared networks, by definition, firms must cooperate to develop, operate, and expand the network. In many, if not most, cases, however, the participants in a shared network are competitors at some level of the industry. Dennis Carlton confronts the business and policy problems raised when maximum network benefits can be realized only through the development and operation of shared, rather than private, networks. The inherent tension between cooperation and competition raises, according to Carlton, some of the most interesting and complex antitrust issues. He raises and addresses several key business and policy issues. For example, is it possible for one firm to develop and operate a network and for all of the firms in the industry to benefit equally from access to the network? Will firms make the investments required to develop networks if they are not allowed to employ practices that appear anticompetitive from a purely static, short-run efficiency perspective? When is government intervention appropriate? He concludes with a policy recommendation on which there is likely to be relatively uniform agreement: there are sufficiently important differences among ESNs that the policy issues should be addressed on a case-by-case basis. This advice is supported by the industry studies in Part II.

Steven Salop's chapter concludes Part I. This chapter and Richard Gilbert's, which begins Part II, illustrate very vividly the direct applications of economic theory to current network policy problems. Salop begins where Carlton leaves off—firms have agreed to cooperate and have developed a shared network. Salop then considers in the context of networks with joint products whether competitive pricing for the products of the network is compatible with cooperation at the network level. He finds that for products such as ATM services, competitive prices set by each of the network members are compatible both with sustainable network operation and with economic efficiency defined to be the maximization of the total of consumer and producer benefits. He argues that consumers benefit from competitive market pricing of network services (as opposed to prices set jointly by firms participating in a network) because quality and service options are better.

The chapters in Part II look closely at the economic and policy histories of ESNs in certain manufacturing and service industries. It is no accident that the case studies in this section include automatic teller machines (ATMs), computer reservation systems (CRSs), and multiple listing services (MLSs). These three three-initial ESNs have all been the subjects of intense private and public scrutiny, lawsuits, and regulatory actions. Each involves some degree of sharing, whether of information, of technologies, or of ownership and control. Each contributes importantly to the production and sale of products or services in related industries; and the relationship between access and competition has figured prominently in the policy debates concerning each of them. The case studies provided by Gilbert; Guerin-Calvert and Noll; Annan; and Lopatka and Simons are all outgrowths of the litigation and policy work in these areas.

Gilbert, like Salop, considers the pricing of network services by joint-venture ATM networks. Unlike Salop, he concludes that self-regulated networks may behave efficiently. He argues that self-regulated shared networks have an incentive to select pricing mechanisms that promote economic efficiency. The disagreement between Salop and Gilbert over the likelihood that self-regulated networks will price efficiently illustrates the importance of subtle differences in the assumptions underlying their models.

Margaret Guerin-Calvert and Roger Noll and Richard Annan provide thorough descriptions of the CRS industries in the United States and Canada and review the economic analyses and policies that have been developed in the debates over CRSs in these two countries and in Europe. Noll and Guerin-Calvert's analysis precedes Annan's both in its location in the book and in the historical development of CRS policy. Their chapter assesses developments in the CRS industry in the United States, the effect of the CRS industry's conduct and performance on the newly deregulated airline industry, and the private and public policy responses to the substantial competitive concerns raised by three eras of CRS growth in the United States. Annan follows by exploring the relationship between U.S. CRS policies up to 1987 and the more recent developments in CRS policy in Canada and in Europe. Noll and Guerin-Calvert conclude that the policy tools employed thus far have not been effective in dealing with what they perceive to be the U.S. industry's problems. Annan concludes on a somewhat cheerier note and highlights the potentially significant role that can be played by combining private and public solutions to large network problems.

John Lopatka and Joseph Simons address the access issues that have been raised concerning MLSs—asking in the context of the MLS and real estate what conditions can be legitimately imposed on competitors seeking access to the services of a shared network. Lopatka and Simons review the historical development of the MLS in the context of problems faced by the real estate industry and consider the role and relevance of various rationales for excluding competitors, such as the need to ensure the quality of the network services. They conclude that access restrictions found to be anticompetitive by the courts have valid efficiency justifications.

In contrast to the networks that were the foci of the first four chapters in Part II, each of which has been the subject of numerous complaints of anticompetitive conduct, Robin Allen, in the last chapter, studies the development of electronic data interchange (EDI) networks, none of which has been the subject of significant legal or regulatory action. She argues that this is because the tasks to which EDI networks are applied and the situations in which they develop do not lend themselves to competitive abuse. She concludes that any competitive problems that may arise are likely to be very short-lived because the competitors, customers, and suppliers of firms controlling networks will generally have viable options to pursue. Allen's study is a useful counterweight to the preceding studies of MLSs, CRSs, and ATMs. It demonstrates that it would be a mistake to conclude that complaints of competitive abuse (if not actual anti-competitive acts) are endemic to ESNs.

Taken as a group, the studies in this volume demonstrate the incredible variety of the applications of ESN technology and the complexity of the policy and business strategy issues these networks raise. Clearly no single analytical framework is sufficient for understanding all ESN industries and there is no single policy that is appropriate to all ESNs. Our hope is that this book, as a package of carefully chosen analytical frameworks and studies of different industries, will provide the reader—whether businessperson, academic, or policymaker—with greater insight into the nature of ESNs, the benefits they make possible, and the policy issues they raise.

Part I

Economics and Policy Perspectives

Electronic Services Networks: Functions, Structures, and Public Policy

Steven S. Wildman and Margaret E. Guerin-Calvert

As computer and telecommunications equipment and services have become more flexible and less expensive, there has been a growing movement to combine these technologies in telecommunications-linked networks of computers and terminals used to facilitate commercial transactions. In some industries, such as airlines, where over ninety percent of all travel agencies rely on computer reservation systems (CRSs) for ticketing and flight selection, network transactions now dominate commercial activity. While development of these electronic services networks (ESNs) has been motivated by the impressive gains in transactional efficiency they often produce, accumulating experience with these networks has shown that they sometimes are catalysts for dramatic and unanticipated changes in commercial practices and industry structures. The potential for this technology to alter the competitive balance among the firms in an industry is of obvious concern to businesses and is at the heart of the concerns sometimes voiced by policymakers that the technology may be used to weaken competition within an industry to the detriment of consumers.

ESNs are a relatively new form of business organization and our understanding of them is still very incomplete. Both business leaders and policymakers have much to gain from a better understanding of the economics of these networks. Other chapters in this book examine various issues raised by ESNs, such as the design of pricing and access policies that further public policy objectives, the conditions under which private networks combine to form larger shared networks, and the effects of ESNs on the structures of markets and industries using them. ESNs vary considerably from industry to industry and even within industries in the functions they serve and the ways in which they are organized. This chapter examines factors that contribute to this variation.

We begin in the next section with a general taxonomy of ESN functions. As we shall see, ESNs' functions vary considerably from industry to industry. We explore the reasons for this variation in the third section. This analysis complements the electronic markets and hierarchies framework of Malone et al. (1987), which forms the basis of Ajit Kambil's study in Chapter 2 of the effects of information technology on industry structure. Where Malone et al. and Kambil are concerned with the implications of ESNs and other information technologies for the choice of markets vs. hierarchical structures, such as firms, in order to coordinate economic activities, we ask how the characteristics of goods and services and the organizational features of firms and markets influence the applications of ESN technology.

We examine a number of characteristics of ESNs that may be loosely characterized as structural in the fourth section of this chapter. These include differences in forms of ownership, rules governing access by nonowners, the locus of control over network operations within the structure of an industry, the range of products serviced with a network, and the development of gateways to link different networks. The structural characteristics of ESNs differ considerably from industry to industry, and sometimes within an industry. We conclude that in most industries a variety of ownership and organizational structures is possible. The structures that emerge reflect differences in the level of concentration at different stages of an industry, the nature of demand for ESN services, economies of scale in processing and transmitting information, and the idiosyncracies of individual networks' histories, among other factors. We briefly consider the policy implications of this analysis in the last section of the chapter.

This chapter was written to stand on its own as a self-contained piece of analysis. However, it is also our hope that it will provide perspective and background on ESNs useful to readers of the following chapters who are not already familiar with the technology and its diverse applications.

ELECTRONIC SERVICES NETWORK

Transaction Processing

The record-keeping and accounting activities of a large and rapidly growing volume of commercial transactions are now automated through network-linked computer applications, generally known as electronic data interchange, or EDI. For example, General Motors is linked to many of its major parts suppliers through a common EDI network. EDI makes it possible for General Motors to order parts on-line and, once the order has been placed, to monitor on a continuous basis a supplier's progress in filling the order. The network automatically carries out much of the record-keeping and generation of documents, such as invoicing, that otherwise would have to be performed manually and coordinated with voice and/or written communication. IBM has developed a similar network linking it with the larger resellers of its products. The ability to process these transactions on ESNs may produce a substantial cost savings relative to the costs associated with paper, voice, or in-person transactions. In addition, it makes possible improved coordination between buyer and seller that can produce additional efficiencies, such as the reduced delivery times and inventory costs associated with "just-in-time inventory" strategies for ordering and inventory management.[1] While most of the larger (and older) EDI networks were developed as customized applications of computer and telecommunications technology, companies such as IBM and Digital Equipment Corporation are now actively promoting generic versions of the hardware and software.

ESNs may also be used to process and coordinate a series of transactions among a seller and its suppliers initiated by a seemingly simple request from a customer. This is the case with automatic teller machine (ATM) networks, for example, where a number of transactions occur in response to the request of a bank customer for cash at an ATM terminal. The network processes simultaneously the transaction between the consumer and the ATM deployer (which may or may not be the customer's bank), the transaction between the consumer and the financial institution that holds her account, transactions between both financial institutions and the organization that operates the network's central switch, and a possible transaction between the ATM deployer and the customer's bank. A point-of-sale (POS) network may process a similar set of transactions in response to a customer's request at a POS terminal that her checking account be debited.

Facilitation of Search and Evaluation

A real estate multiple-listing service (MLS) is an example of an ESN used to facilitate prepurchase search and evaluation. For home-buyers, the process of first identifying and then comparing potentially acceptable homes may be both time-consuming and expensive. An MLS reduces the cost of prepurchase search and evaluation by making it possible to both gather and evaluate information on different houses on the market from a terminal in a broker's office. Since the electronic listings are updated continuously, they are more accurate and up-to-date than printed real estate listings. Furthermore, the search algorithms provided with these services make it possible to prescreen houses in the database quickly for a variety of characteristics. While the MLS typically does not eliminate the need for the buyer to inspect houses personally, it saves time and expense by narrowing the pool of houses that must be searched the old-fashioned way. On-line searching typically reduces the time required for buyers to identify suitable properties and often results in better matches of buyer preferences with the characteristics of homes available.[2] Once a buyer has selected a house and has agreed upon terms with the seller, she may also use an on-line mortgage service to compare the lending terms of different mortgage companies.[3]

The data-gathering features of ESNs may be very simple or highly complex. In its simplest form, sellers simply list the availability and prices of their products on the network. The early computer links between American Hospital Supply (AHS) and its hospital customers are an example. The hospitals used dumb terminals supplied by AHS that were linked to AHS mainframes to check prices and place orders for products carried by AHS. Buyer search is facilitated when multiple sellers participate in a network because buyers can then use the network to compare sellers' prices and the characteristics of their products.

The ability to use a network to sort and process data in other ways becomes more important as the number of sellers and buyers using the network increases and as the number of product attributes important to buyers increases. For example, air travelers flying between two cities may compare the flights of different airlines in terms of departure time, number of stopovers, elapsed time, locations of unsold seats, and ticket price. All of this information may be accessed, processed, and displayed on a terminal within seconds of a query from a travel agent. If requested, flights may also be ranked according to weights the traveler assigns to different flight characteristics. Search is typically more accurate, more comprehensive, and quicker with a CRS than when an agent uses printed guides and phone calls to airlines to identify flights and check their availability. Similarly, an MLS enables home-buyers to quickly identify houses for sale and to compare them on a number of important characteristics such as price, architectural style, numbers of bedrooms and bathrooms, and floor space.

When the advantages of on-line searching over other types of search are very large, there may be circumstances in which a firm or firms controlling a network are able to profit from biasing the network's search and display algorithms in favor of their own products or services and against those of their competitors who may also be represented on the network. Biased displays have been a focal concern in the ongoing debate over the rules governing CRSs (Guerin-Calvert and Noll, this book, Chapter 8; Guerin-Calvert, 1989a), and it is easy to visualize the same issues arising in other industries, such as financial securities, where the use of on-line services as an aid to search and purchase is increasing.[4]

Product Delivery

At first glance, an ATM network would appear to illustrate product delivery in an almost trivial sense. The customer wants to convert funds in a bank account to cash, which the terminal delivers on the spot. However, the cash is not actually delivered via the ATM network. The cash is delivered via surface transportation beforehand. The electronic network merely releases it, an act that facilitates the exchange. Hence ATM networks are essentially transaction processing networks. Given the electronic nature of ESNs, the only products that can actually be delivered are information products that can be encoded for electronic transmission. Computer database services, such as CompuServe, and

LEXIS, the on-line legal search and retrieval service, are familiar examples of ESNs that deliver a product. In each case, a subscriber to the network uses a terminal to access information stored in a distant mainframe. The information may be accessed on-line or downloaded to the user's terminal from which the user may print it, and so retain it on a tangible medium. The database may merely be made available, as are most databases on CompuServe, or assistance in processing the data may also be provided. The assistance provided by LEXIS for tracing legal precedents is a good example of the latter. Electronic delivery saves on the time and material costs of physical transportation. When electronic delivery is combined with algorithms to increase the effectiveness with which information is accessed, the value of the product to the buyer increases as well.

The cost characteristics of electronic delivery are different from those of other modes of information delivery, particularly the physical delivery of information in printed media. As Rosse (1978) has shown for newspapers, there are important economies of scope and scale in delivery due to the large fixed costs of maintaining a distribution network. The incremental cost of delivering a larger newspaper to the home (or a larger magazine to retail outlets) may be relatively insignificant once the distribution network is in place. Thus, it is advantageous to sell the same broadly targeted magazine or newspaper to many readers, knowing few will read all, or even most, of the material inside. However, when information is delivered electronically, delivery costs are approximately proportional to the amount of information delivered; so there is a substantial cost penalty for information delivered but not used. Therefore, one would expect to find information delivered electronically to be more narrowly targeted to what buyers want. Thus, a subscriber to a journal published electronically selects from the table of contents (or a subject index) only those articles she wants to read, in contrast to printed journals that deliver all the articles in every issue, regardless of whether they are read.

DETERMINANTS OF ELECTRONIC SERVICES NETWORK FUNCTIONS

Most ESNs serve only one or two of the functions just described. This is illustrated in Table 1.1, which lists the functions of several familiar ESNs. None of these networks serves all three ESN functions, although there is no barrier inherent in the technology that would prevent it. The fact that ESNs are used to service widely varying needs in different commercial contexts testifies to the flexibility of the underlying technology and this form of network organization.

ESNs differ in the functions they serve for several reasons. First, and almost trivially, information products are the only products that can be provided over ESNs. Thus, only ESNs used to facilitate transactions in information products will be used for delivery. Hence, airline transportation, the primary product whose sale is facilitated by CRSs, is not actually provided over the ESN. Among

Table 1.1
Electronic Services Networks' Functions

Networks	ESN Functions		
	Process Transactions	Facilitate Search and Evaluation	Delivery
ATM	X		
POS	X		
GM EDI	X		
CRS	X	X	
CompuServe		X	X
LEXIS			X
MLS		X	

the ESNs listed in Table 1.1, only LEXIS and CompuServe facilitate transactions in information products that can be encoded for electronic transmission. The classification of LEXIS as specialized to product delivery reflects the peculiar nature of its product. LEXIS provides access to the texts of case law and regulatory decisions. By its very nature, there can be no competing products among which to search. (There are, however, other services, both electronic and hard copy, that compete with LEXIS to make the law more accessible.) In the context of the current discussion, the special algorithms LEXIS provides for searching legal databases may be considered either as components of the delivery process or as part of the product delivered.

CRS are used to process transactions and to facilitate search, which is not typical for ESNs. Most ESNs serve one, but not both, of these functions. Much of the differentiation among ESNs in their search facilitation and transaction-processing capabilities reflects interindustry differences in the buyer-seller relationships that ESNs service. The following equation for the net benefits, *NB*, of an ESN (benefits after costs are subtracted out) provides a useful starting point for exploring the implications of differences in transactional relationships for the services provided with ESNs.

$$NB = gN - K$$

NB is equal to the product of the average increase in the gains from trade per transaction, *g*, times the number of transactions, *N*, minus the cost of the network, K. K represents the total costs incurred in installing, maintaining, and running a network over the course of its useful life. (For convenience, we are ignoring the complications introduced by discounting costs or benefits late in the life of the network relative to costs and benefits realized earlier.) N is the number of transactions facilitated by the network during its operating life. And g is the average amount by which the sum of buyer and seller benefits from the transaction is increased by network facilitation. Here, g could include the value of search time saved and a buyer's valuation of a better match of her preferences with the characteristics of available products when an ESN is used to facilitate search, or it could reflect the per-transaction value of improved speed and accuracy and reduced paperwork when an ESN is used to process transactions. The gross benefits of the network are g times N.

In general, ESNs will be used to facilitate transactions for products and services for which a network can generate positive net benefits. (Of course, some mistakes will be made, resulting in a few ESNs with negative net benefits.) If we set NB equal to zero, representing an ESN that provides benefits just sufficient to cover its costs (zero net benefits), then the net benefits equation describes a curve in g,N space that is convex to the origin and asymptotically approaches each axis. This is illustrated by the solid curve labeled "$gN = K_0$" in Figure 1.1 for a network with costs K_0.[5] Industries or markets with g,N combinations on or outside of this schedule (above and to the right) can profitably employ ESNs. ESNs are not cost-justified for industries or markets inside of this schedule (below and to the left). The zero net-benefits curve depicts a trade-off between the volume of transactions and increased gains from trade determined by the requirement that the network produce aggregate benefits sufficient to cover its costs.

Despite the increasing use of networks to facilitate transactions, most trans-

Figure 1.1
Gains-from-Trade and Volume Contributions to Network Costs

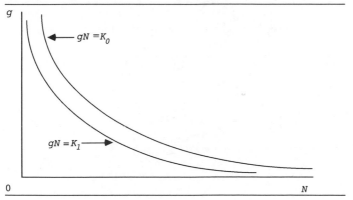

actions are still carried out the old-fashioned way without electronic assistance. However, as information technologies become more flexible and their costs fall, ESNs will be used to facilitate an ever-larger proportion of transactions.[6] This is illustrated by the schedule of break-even g,N combinations labeled "$gN = K_1$" in Figure 1.1, which is interior to the schedule for $gN = K_0$. Industries and markets with g,N combinations between these two lines would also find it profitable to develop ESNs to facilitate transactions if the cost of the technology fell from K_0 to K_1.

ESNs differ considerably in the relative contributions of increased gains from trade and volume of transactions to network benefits. Table 1.2 gives our rough estimates of the relative importance of these two sources of benefits for the ESNs listed in Table 1.1. The classification of MLSs as high gains from trade and low volume is fairly obvious. Even in major metropolitan areas, the number of houses sold is small enough that properties sold are listed in daily papers. However, the value to a buyer of a better match of her wants with the characteristics of houses on the market may be worth thousands or tens of thousands of dollars. The improved search capabilities of CRSs relative to search with airline guides and phone calls may be worth a few hundreds of dollars at best to most business travelers. On the other hand, most bank customers probably would not be willing to pay more than a few dollars for the convenience of ATM and POS networks. Finally, while the efficiency gains from EDI have been estimated as high as $200 per car for auto manufacturers, this is spread over a large number of transactions for each car.[7]

Malone et al. (1987) and Kambil (this book, Chapter 2) argue persuasively that communication technologies, by lowering transaction costs, affect choices among alternative institutions for governing vertical relationships among firms.

Table 1.2
Gains-from-Trade and Volume Comparisons

Volume of Transactions	Gains from Trade		
	High	Medium	Low
High		CRS, ATM	EDI, POS
Medium		LEXIS, CompuServe	
Low	MLS		

Lowering transaction costs favors markets over more hierarchical control structures like long-term exclusive contracts and vertical integration. It must be the case, however, that the relationship between the organization of vertical relationships and applications of communication technology is a reciprocal one. There is little to be gained from search facilitation when buyers and sellers pair off in stable and exclusive long-term hierarchical relationships. If there are benefits to ESNs in these situations, it must be for processing transactions. Therefore, we should expect to see ESNs employed for transactions processing, but not for search facilitation, when circumstances favor the development of tight buyer-seller hierarchies.

We know from the work of Williamson (1975, 1985) and others who have followed his lead in developing the transactions cost (or markets and hierarchies) framework that hierarchical coordination structures are more likely to be employed when at least one of the parties to a transaction would be vulnerable to various types of nonperformance by the other party in a market setting. Firms may feel vulnerable relying only on the market to coordinate vertical relationships for a variety of reasons, including the possibility that the value of assets employed in a relationship may depend on the durability of the relationship,[8] the possibility that the complexity or other attributes of a product or service may make it difficult to evaluate its quality prior to purchase, and the possibility that the unpredictability of future circumstances may make it impossible to write contingent contracts that adequately protect one or both of the parties in an ongoing transactional relationship against attempts by the other to renegotiate the terms of trade. Hierarchies link the fates of the transacting parties so that both suffer if either violates an initial understanding.[9] Therefore, we would expect the need for close coordination between an auto maker and the manufacturers of parts designed for its cars to give rise to tight buyer-supplier relationships like those between GM and its specialized suppliers.[10] Given the volume of ongoing transactions between GM and its suppliers and the long term nature of these relationships, it is natural that an ESN employed in this setting would be dedicated primarily to processing these bilateral transactions. Furthermore, the network itself may be a specialized investment that further cements the hierarchical relationship between the transacting parties.

Networks will be used to facilitate search only in settings in which buyers can benefit from comparing the wares of different sellers prior to purchase. Therefore, search facilitation presumes market coordination. The two are not synonymous, however. Search is costly in terms of time, personal energy, and other resources. Buyers search when the differences (including price) in the products of different sellers are large enough to justify the effort. If products are homogeneous and priced competitively, buyers will search very little because price differences will be small.[11] There will be little profit in investments in search facilitation under these conditions unless the volume of transactions is so large that arbitraging even small margins is profitable. Thus, we have the paradox that ESNs are mostly likely to be specialized to processing transactions in conditions where markets are inefficient mechanisms for coordinating vertical relationships *and* when they are most efficient.

ESNs are used for search facilitation when products are differentiated in ways important enough to buyers to make search worthwhile. Houses and commercial real estate listed on an MLS and airline tickets are cases in point. There may also be substantial gains to electronic search facilitation when products are homogeneous but changing market conditions give rise to frequent changes in market clearing prices, resulting in substantial, though temporary, spreads between high and low price offers. Examples are securities and commodities exchanges. In these cases, ESNs increase the efficiency of the arbitrage process.

Of course, the fact that an ESN is a valuable aid to search does not mean that buyers can acquire enough information on-line to select the product to be purchased. This is clearly the case in real estate. Information on the MLS is used to narrow the range of choices, but the final decision is almost always made following a personal inspection by the buyer. This is because some of the information critical to choosing a home, such as hard-to-express esthetic aspects of style or view, cannot be effectively represented electronically. This, and the fact that in most cases the home-buyer must be evaluated by a lender, means an MLS will not be used to process the transactions it facilitates. The situation is different for airline tickets and financial instruments, however. In both cases, a network may provide enough information for a buyer to make a selection on line,[12] and the network may also be used to process the transaction.[13]

STRUCTURAL DIFFERENCES AMONG ELECTRONIC SERVICES NETWORKS

Important Structural Features

Structural differences are differences in the ways that ESNs are organized and controlled. Here we describe five structural features that, in addition to the network services provided, are significant indicators of the nature of transactional relationships serviced. These structural features may also affect the performance of ESNs with respect to traditional competition policy concerns.

First, ESNs may be either *private or shared*. A *private* network is owned and controlled by a single firm. Ownership and control are exercised jointly by two or more firms in a *shared* network. Citicorp's network of hundreds of ATMs in and around New York City, which is owned and operated by Citicorp, is an example of a private ESN. Most ATM networks are joint ventures with from a few to hundreds of banks, and thus are shared. Other examples of shared ESNs include VISA and MasterCard, and some of the European and U.S. computer reservations systems, which are joint ventures with several airline partners.

Both private and shared networks may be either *open or closed*. A *closed* network provides services for its owners and their customers (or suppliers) only. A network is *open* if competitors to the owners can use it as well. Most computer reservations systems are open because they enable travel agents to book flights offered by other carriers in addition to those of the host airlines. Citicorp's ATM network was closed and private, until it joined the nationwide Cirrus system in early 1991. Now it is open and private.

Location of network control within the structure of an industry is a third important structural feature. ESNs may be controlled by buyers, as is General Motors' EDI network; controlled by suppliers, as are the networks linking American Hospital Supply with its hospital customers and IBM with computer remarketers; or provided and controlled by independent third parties as is the case with the grocery EDI networks described by Allen in Chapter 11.

ESNs differ dramatically in the *number of products and services* they handle. Some, like ATM networks, which until recently were dedicated to processing cash requests, handle only a single product or service. Others, like CompuServe and PRODIGY, may facilitate hundreds or thousands of different types of transactions. Many ESNs have expanded the range of products and services facilitated as they matured. Computer reservation systems, for example, originally were used only to select and book flights. Now they can be used to purchase lodging, rental cars, and an array of other travel-related services. Similarly, ATM networks have traditionally been employed for banking services, but the capabilities of some recently have been expanded to dispense airline tickets and movie tickets.

Finally, an ESN may serve as a point of access, or *gateway,* to other networks. CompuServe is the classic example of a gateway service, having been designed explicitly to serve this function. However, gateways may arise less formally. For example, one member of a regional shared ATM network may also be a member of a national shared system and serve as a gateway for all of its members to networks in other parts of the country.

Determinants of Network Structure

We have seen—and the following chapters will make this even clearer—that network structures vary widely. Here we consider five sets of factors that theory and experience with network industries suggest are important influences on network structures. We are not offering a grand, all-encompassing theory of network structure. Economists have yet to produce a grand theory of industrial organization and it would be presumptuous to offer one for networks. However, much of the variation in network structures can be explained in terms of variation in these five factors and interactions among them. Specifically, we consider the structural implications of (1) the nature of the demand for network services, (2) organizational features of the industries and markets that develop ESNs, (3) events unique to the histories of different networks, (4) economies of scale in information processing and transmission, and (5) the capabilities of communication technologies at the time a network first develops. The following discussion of these factors is selective and limited to what we believe to be the most important ways these factors affect network structure, either individually or through their interactions with each other. We focus most heavily on demand considerations, because much of what is interesting in the economics of ESN development arises from the ways the various demands for ESN services interact with the other factors.

Demand Factors

For economists, the term network has come to apply to much more than the physical and electromagnetic pathways, such as electricity grids, railroads, and telephone systems, that commonly come to mind. There has been growing recognition over the past ten to fifteen years that product systems coordinated by technical standards, such as personal computers and software, television receivers and broadcasting equipment, and ATM cards and ATM terminals, have networklike qualities in that changes in individual components must be coordinated to maintain the integrity of the product system. In a very real sense, the users of a product system are connected by their reliance on a common set of product standards. Intense work on the economics of "network industries" over the last decade has produced new insights and a better understanding of the way that these industries function. Critical to this understanding is the concept of network externalities, described by Katz and Shapiro (1986) as "demand-side economies of scale."

A product or service is characterized by network externalities if its value to an individual user increases with the number of users. A product's value to its users may increase as their numbers grow for a variety of reasons that apply to ESNs as well as to other types of network technologies. At the most basic level, the firms sponsoring a network technology are most likely to continue to support it with replacement parts, service, and improvements if it is widely used. The quality and variety of network components may also increase with the size of the network because a larger installed base makes the development of more and higher-quality components both feasible and profitable. The same logic suggests that larger networks are also likely to carry more products and services than are smaller networks. Transactions in a product or service will be serviced on a network as long as the additional revenue generated covers all additional costs incurred in doing so. In general, the larger the base of network customers with access to a product or service, the larger the incremental revenue gain will be. For example, a comparison of the gateway services that facilitate access to computer database services shows that CompuServe, the one with the most subscribers, also offers, by far, the largest selection of network services. Finally, for many communication purposes the value of a network increases with the number of individuals using it. Telephone networks and computer bulletin board services exemplify this last type of network externality.[14]

When network externalities are large, large networks have significant advantages over smaller networks, all else being equal. In this case, small networks are not likely to be features of a competitive equilibrium unless they can serve niche markets for consumers with specialized needs not easily met with networks designed to cater to the needs of the majority of consumers. The relationship between the scale of operation required to realize most of the positive externalities of a network and the minimum efficient scales of the firms that use it may significantly influence both network and industry structure. If networks continue to generate positive network externalities well beyond the scale otherwise required for efficiency in the firms using them, firms will have a strong incentive to collaborate to form shared networks. Another possibility is for one of an industry's firms, or a firm outside the industry, to specialize as a supplier of network services through a network open to other firms and their customers.

Related to network externalities are possible complementarities among networks, which Economides examines in depth in Chapter 3. (See also Matutes and Regibeau (1988) and Economides (1989a).) A shared network created by combining two or more preexisting private networks may be more valuable to its users than any of the private networks by themselves, not because users benefit from being part of a larger user group, but because the individual networks are consumption complements to each other.[15] (The same increase in benefits may also be realized if the networks remain private but are open to each other's customers.) The ATM example used by Economides in Chapter 3 illustrates this perfectly. Each of two banks that combine their ATM systems improves the value of its ATM network to its customers because they value the convenience of being able to use their ATM cards at a larger number of ATM stations in more locations. The banks may be able to capture part of the increased value of their networks by raising their prices for ATM services. Thus, as with network externalities, network complementaries may be an incentive for the creation of larger networks—in this case through the joining of smaller networks. However, as Economides demonstrates, this depends critically on the structural characteristics of the markets served by the networks. If one network has a much larger customer base than the other, the fact that the first network would provide the second with access to many more potential customers than the second could make available to the first in return could make creation of a shared network unattractive to the first network.

Network structure is also influenced by transaction complementaries, a concept introduced by Ayres (1985) and applied to ESNs by Salop in Chapter 6. Two products (or a number of products) are transaction complements on a network when the use of the network to facilitate transactions in both products reduces the costs of arranging and executing transactions for them by more than would be possible if separate networks facilitated transactions for each product. Transaction complementarity is thus an incentive to include the products of numerous sellers on the same network.

There are at least three types of transaction complementarity—joint-purchase complementarities, search complementarities, and economies of scale in information processing. Products are joint-purchase complements if the nonprice costs of transactions for them are lower when they are purchased from a common source. A commonplace example is the selection of products stocked by grocery stores. Grocery shopping is easier when it is possible to buy many of a household's food and household products in a single trip to a single store instead of going to several stores to purchase different items. Similarly, there may be transactional savings from using a common network to facilitate transactions in a variety of network services that may be of value to a single user. Gateway services, such as CompuServe and GEnie, may be viewed as services developed primarily to reduce the transaction costs of network services by making it possible to use a single protocol to access a large number of computer networks.[16] Here, the savings is the extra time that would be required to dial-up and log-on to the various computer networks individually.

Airline computer reservation systems have taken advantage of joint-purchase complementarities by expanding into other travel-related services such as lodging, insurance, and rental cars. Transactional complementarities are also a reason for including the flights of different airlines on the same CRS when their route structures are complementary. For example, the routes of two airlines are complements if a traveler flying from San Francisco to Chicago and then from Chicago to Green Bay has to book flights with both airlines to do so. It is easier to make both reservations on a single CRS than to use a separate CRS for each flight. Search complementarities, discussed immediately below, are also a reason to include airlines with competitive route structures (flights serving the same city pairs) on the same CRS.

Products that are substitutes in consumption may be search complements on a network if buyers engage in costly and time-consuming search before selecting a product, and if it is also possible to reduce buyer search costs significantly by making information about the products available on a network for on-line inspection. Buyers benefit because their search costs fall and because search facilitation enables them to find products better suited to their tastes. Unlike joint-purchase complementarities, which are an incentive to include different kinds of products on a network, search complementarities are an incentive to include numerous products of the same type on a network (e.g., the different real estate properties listed on an MLS). Of course, a single network may be used to facilitate transactions in both search and joint-consumption complements, as is the case with CRSs, where all airlines' flights, whether complements or substitutes, are listed together.

Finally, economies of scale in processing capacity in mainframe computers, switches, and transmission facilities may provide the incentive to use a single network to facilitate transactions in different products—whether search complements, joint-purchase complements, or neither—if no single product generates transactions volume sufficient for efficient scale. For example, economies of scale in both switching capacity and in transmission have been an important force driving the movement to combine private ATM networks into larger, shared networks. Whether economies of scale by themselves are motivation enough to form shared ATM networks is not clear, however, because the component networks are also complements to each other.

Organizational Features of Industries and Markets

We have examined already some of the ways in which the organizational features of markets and industries affect network structures in our discussion of the ways organizational features interact with demand characteristics. We observed that if some firms are much larger than other firms in the same market, the larger firms may not want to join with smaller firms in shared networks for fear of losing customers. Network externalities increasing over a range extending beyond the minimum efficient scale for firms (excluding network considerations) was also seen to be a factor encouraging the development of shared or open networks. In some cases, however, firms utilizing a network may gain a competitive advantage by excluding other firms to prevent them from sharing in the network's benefits. To see how this might work, assume that a range of firm sizes is consistent with efficiency in all facets of a firm's operation (production, distribution, promotion, etc.), with the exception of network facilitation. Further assume that the largest firms in the market are large enough to realize all positive network externalities with private, closed networks and that the smallest firms cannot achieve this scale by combining. Then the largest firms could gain a permanent competitive advantage relative to the smaller ones by excluding them from their networks.

A related example shows that if no firm is large enough to fully exploit network externalities with a private network, but if some subset of the market's firms can, then the members of the subset can create for themselves a permanent competitive advantage by forming a shared network closed to other firms if the excluded firms cannot combine to form a network with comparable network benefits. Consider a market with three equal-size firms, A, B, and C. Two firms are required to realize full network benefits. Then A and B might combine to create a network in which C is not allowed to participate. A and B would then have the advantage of being able to offer their customers network benefits that C could not match.

The identities of firms originating and controlling networks may also reflect their relative sizes in the market the networks serve. If a high volume of transactions is required to realize network benefits or scale economies, larger firms may be better positioned to develop networks. For example, the largest airlines, American and United, were the first to develop CRSs. Both had already done extensive work to computerize their internal reservation systems and a CRS was a natural extension of this work.

Differences in market structures at different stages of an industry may determine in part which of the vertical stages of an industry introduces and controls a network. Networks may fail to develop when network externalities are strong and every firm is small relative to the market because each firm may see itself as powerless to move the market toward adopting a network it introduces. Each, fearful of the consequences of failure, may wait for other firms to sponsor a network. Besen and Johnson's (1986) case studies of standard-setting in broadcast industries (where network externalities are likely to be important) suggest that firms with large shares at the most concentrated stage of an industry are most influential in determining the standards the industry adopts. This observation is consistent with the argument that larger firms at more concentrated stages of an industry should be more influential in setting standards because large firms internalize more network externalities and because a single firm carries more weight in a concentrated market. This logic should apply to the sponsorship and control of ESNs as well.

Economies of Scale in Information Processing and Transmission

Economies of scale in information processing are similar to the demand factors discussed above in their effects on network structures. Cost savings due to scale economies are an incentive to form shared or open networks when scale economies in information processing are significant and continue beyond what otherwise would be the minimum efficient scale for firms. Similarly, some firms may find it strategically advantageous to exclude other firms from their networks when scale economies are important.

Unique Events in Network History

One of the striking findings of the literature on network industries is that established networks may be locked-in against competition from new, technically superior networks when network externalities are strong (Farrell and Saloner, 1985). Users of established networks may be reluctant to switch to a new network because they know that, even if it is technologically superior, it will have to grow substantially before it can offer benefits comparable to what is provided by the established network. Each user might rationally decide to wait for the new network to grow before joining it. However, if all users follow this strategy, the established network is locked-in. This argument should apply to the three types of transaction complementarities discussed as well.

When established networks may be locked-in, events that influence the order in which different networks are launched may determine which survive in the long run. Unless it falters, the first network in a market has an advantage that builds on itself. Since network benefits are greatest for larger networks, new users will gravitate to them and their advantage over smaller networks will grow. For example, the current structure of the U.S. CRS industry may have been predetermined by the failure of a travel agent association–computer company venture to produce an operational CRS before the three largest airlines had each introduced and implemented independent CRSs. Had the travel agents'

CRS become established first as an industry-wide CRS, the airlines might not have developed theirs.

Capabilities of Communication Technology

Here, we merely point out what should be obvious: that network structures are influenced by the nature of the communication technology employed, and that this is determined in large part by the capabilities of the technology available at the time a network is developed. For example, CRS might have developed differently if the flexible and powerful PCs we now have were available when these systems were developed. It is now possible to utilize CRS services with a personal computer and a modem. The CRS would be a much more flexible system if travel agents or vendors were not locked-in to investments in dedicated CRS terminals. It is almost certainly the case that the majority of the computer database services now available would not exist were it not for the millions of PCs that are used to access them.

IMPLICATIONS FOR ELECTRONIC SERVICES NETWORK POLICY

The preceding analysis of ESN functions and structures provides no simple answers to the policy problems raised by ESNs. However, the framework set out should be useful for distinguishing situations in which competition problems are a legitimate concern from situations in which competitive abuses are unlikely. Access restrictions and the efficiency implications of the rules self-regulating ESNs devise to govern relations among their members are the primary public policy concerns with ESNs today. Access restrictions can be a problem only if the firms controlling an ESN are in a position to place competitors at a disadvantage either by excluding them or by granting access on discriminatory terms. Our analysis of determinants of ESN structure suggests that this is possible only when the provision of ESN services is characterized by significant network externalities, transaction complementarities, network complementarities, or economies of scale. If careful study of a network fails to show that it has at least one of these properties, exclusion is not likely to be be harmful to competition.

Finding that an ESN is characterized by one of these properties does not mean that access should be mandated, however. Exclusion may actually be socially beneficial (1) if it is necessary to ensure the quality of network services, which Lopatka and Simons argue in Chapter 10 is the rationale behind MLS restrictions, (2) if excluded firms constrain the prices of firms using the network, which Wildman shows in Chapter 4 is possible in some circumstances, or (3) if the supracompetitive profits produced by exclusionary practices are necessary to induce firms to undertake the risky investments required to develop networks in the first place, a topic addressed by Carlton in Chapter 5. Clearly, there is no single policy applicable to exclusion in all network industries, and perhaps not to all ESNs within any given industry. A case-by-case approach to policy development is thus recommended.

The history of ESN development within an industry may provide some guidance with respect to assessing the need for restrictive practices to ensure investments in networks. The history of CRSs in the United States, for example, shows that actors at different stages of the industry tried to develop CRSs at different times. CRSs have also developed under very different regulatory restrictions in different countries. Furthermore, CRSs in the United States were a natural outgrowth of the early work by the largest airlines to computerize their internal reservation systems. In combination, these observations suggest that the CRS was probably an inevitable development and that access restrictions probably were not needed to ensure that it developed.

Our analyses of ESN structures and functions provide but modest guidance for developing policy on the rules of self-regulating shared networks. If the benefits of network participation are small, then an ESN will contribute little to the ability of firms in a market to maintain the discipline required to collude effectively. However, if the networks confer substantial benefits on participating firms, the threat of expulsion or discriminatory treatment may serve to increase market discipline.

The analysis of the relationship between industry structure and ESN functions is useful for identifying situations in which competitive problems are unlikely to arise. When a network is used to process the transactions between buyers and suppliers linked together in long-term, high-volume relationships, it is more appropriate to view the firms so linked as components of a larger unit that may compete with other similar hierarchically organized collections of firms that produce the same final product. Efficiencies due to networks in these situations make the larger unit more competitive and promote economic efficiency.

NOTES

Steven Wildman's contribution to this chapter was supported by a grant from the Ameritech Foundation. Margaret Guerin-Calvert's contribution to the chapter was done while she was at Economists Incorporated and the views herein are not necessarily those of her former colleagues at Economists Incorporated or those of the U.S. Department of Justice, where she is currently employed.

1. Early estimates were that EDI would save the American auto industry about $200 per car (Mitchell and Heywood, 1985).

2. The economics of prepurchase screening is examined in depth in Chapter 4.

3. If the lender is Citicorp, mortgage applicants may also have their credit checked electronically.

4. In fact, the developer of a network system for comparing and purchasing securities has sought financial backing from a major securities dealer with the promise that displays would be biased in favor of securities sold by the dealer (Miller and Winkler, 1988).

5. In dealing with a generic network, we are ignoring the fact that network design and costs will vary with the characteristics of the transactions being facilitated.

6. For example, the first EDI networks were custom engineered for large firms or industry associations. Now firms that could not have afforded custom-designed networks can implement EDI with generic technologies developed by companies like IBM and DEC.

7. A single customer's order from a dealer may be translated directly into orders from automotive suppliers through electronic data interchange.

8. See Klein et al. (1978) for elaboration on this theme.

9. Kambil provides a more detailed review of the markets-and-hierarchies framework in Chapter 2.

10. See Monteverde and Teece (1982b) for a discussion of these relationships.

11. Sellers may also have similar prices if they are able to collude effectively. This could also eliminate the incentive for buyers to search.

12. In the case of networks used to facilitate trades in financial instruments, choices among competing offers may be made automatically on the basis of decision algorithms written into the software governing the network's operations.

13. This is a fairly new feature in networks facilitating transactions in financial securities (Bremner and Rothfeder, 1990).

14. This brief summary of factors contributing to network externalities does not do justice to the extensive literature on this topic which has developed over the last ten years. For two excellent reviews of the economics of network industries and the nature of network externalities see Besen and Johnson (1986) and Besen and Saloner (1989).

15. Two goods, such as coffee and cream, are complements in consumption if they are valued more highly when consumed jointly than when consumed separately.

16. For example, CompuServe makes available approximately 14,000 features and services, many of which are also available on a stand-alone basis. The CompuServe user eliminates the hassles of subscribing to each service she wants individually and of having to use different phone numbers and log-on procedures for each of them.

2

Information Technology and Vertical Integration: Evidence from the Manufacturing Sector

Ajit Kambil

The effects of electronic services networks (ESNs) and other new information technologies (ITs) on firm structures and industry competition are central issues to managers, as well as to researchers in information systems and organization studies. While information technology currently constitutes less than ten percent of total capital stocks, it is rapidly increasing as a proportion of a firm's total capital equipment stock. This transformation in capital investments and the widespread adoption of information technologies are already observed to have major impacts on industrial organization, market structure, and competition in various industries (Clemons and Row, 1988; Cash and Konsynski, 1985).

Many organization and information systems researchers predict that improved and lower-cost information technologies, which enable new applications in the areas of ESNs, computer-supported cooperative work, and computer-aided design and manufacturing, will radically alter the coordination of economic activity (Malone et al., 1987; Johnston and Lawrence, 1988) and transform industry and firm structure. These changes may lead to the development of "postindustrial" or "network" organizations (Drucker, 1988; Huber, 1984; Antonelli, 1988) characterized by reduced levels of hierarchies, by a shift to flexible specialization from mass production that permits increased customization of products and services, and by increased use of teams and lateral coordination mechanisms both within and across organizations. In addition, these organizations will undertake to contract externally for a larger fraction of the goods and services previously produced within the boundaries of the firm. To date these predictions are primarily based on anecdotal evidence or case studies of information technology impacts on organizations. This does not enable us to establish clearly generalizable links between the increased use of information technology and specific organizational changes.

This paper develops a framework within which to analyze the impacts of IT on the structure of organizations and empirically examines the impact of IT on the choice of markets and hierarchies as alternate modes of economic organization. Specifically, it examines the impact of IT investments on vertical integration in the manufacturing sector of the economy. The analytic framework is based on the transaction cost economics paradigm as originally developed by Oliver Williamson, and later applied by Thomas Malone et al., to assess the effects of IT on organizations. Williamson (1975, 1981, 1985) identified transaction costs as a key determinant of organizational structure. Malone et al. (1987) have shown how IT can be used to reduce transaction costs and alter the proportional mix of markets and hierarchies in an economy. Although both markets and hierarchies are likely to become more efficient through the use of IT, Malone et al. (1987) predict a proportionally greater shift to the market mode of coordinating economic activity. Increased shifts to the market mode of coordination are also enabled by ESNs used to create "electronic markets." Examples of such markets include airline CRSs and hospital products distribution systems (e.g., American Airlines SABRE, and Baxter's ASAP systems).

This chapter consists of four main sections. The second section defines markets and hierarchies and uses the transaction cost paradigm to model the role of IT in altering the relative cost advantages of the different modes of economic organization. This is used to develop the hypothesis that vertical integration will decrease with increased investments in the utilization of new information technologies. The third section presents the data, methodology, and results of an empirical test of the information technology and vertical integration relationship. The final section presents conclusions and outlines areas for future research.

MARKETS AND HIERARCHIES: A TRANSACTION COSTS PERSPECTIVE

Markets and hierarchies constitute alternative and extreme modes of economic organization. Markets coordinate economic activity through a decentralized price system that is used by economic agents to allocate resources for the manufacture and exchange of goods. Prices are assumed to serve as sufficient statistics for resource allocation. In contrast, hierarchies rely on managerial decisions or the "visible hand" (Chandler, 1967) of managers to explicitly direct resource allocation under the managerial span of control. The real economy shows elements of both modes of economic organization and the use of various intermediate structures such as long-term contracts, joint ventures, franchising, and "value-added partnerships" (Joskow, 1987; Johnston and Lawrence, 1988). The transaction costs perspective views the choice of markets or hierarchies as governance structures for transactions to be a key economic problem. The lack of fit between particular transactions and their governance structures leads to economic inefficiency and poorer economic performance. Thus, firms will organize to economize on both production and transaction costs.

This section defines transaction costs and outlines the main features of the transaction cost paradigm. This is used to evaluate the relative cost advantages of markets and hierarchies and to identify reasons for market failure. Next the effects of ESNs and other new information technologies on transaction costs are modeled to develop the hypothesis that increased utilization of new information technologies and ESNs will lead to decreases in vertical integration.

Transaction Costs

Transaction costs are the costs of governing an exchange of goods or services between separate economic agents. Williamson (1975) identifies two types of transaction costs: ex ante and ex post costs. Ex ante costs are the costs of searching, drafting, negotiating, and safeguarding a contract, and ex post costs are those incurred due to correcting or adapting to contract misalignments and the costs of setting arbitration mechanisms or effecting secure commitments. Transaction costs arise as a consequence of bounded rationality and potentially opportunistic behaviors on the part of economic agents. Bounded rationality assumes limitations in human cognitive capabilities, and the presumption of opportunism assumes that individuals will mainly act in their own self-interest.

The bounded rationality concept identifies the mind as a scarce resource which cannot plan for all future contingencies. Hence "human actions will be intendedly rational but only limitedly so" (Simon, 1961). Given the bounded rationality constraint, the information-processing costs of planning, adapting, and monitoring transactions must be taken into account when designing organizations to govern and execute specific transactions.

The opportunism assumption highlights the need to safeguard against self-seeking behavior after a transaction by devising appropriate contracts before the execution of the transaction. The costs of devising such contracts or safeguards against opportunistic behavior may also be minimized by choosing an appropriate governance structure.

The magnitude of transaction costs is determined by three key transaction attributes: *asset specificity, uncertainty,* and the *frequency* of the transaction. *Asset specificity* refers to the degree of customization of an asset to a particular transaction. As asset specificity increases, the utilization of the asset results in specialized practices and processes that increase the costs of redeploying the asset. Transaction costs increase from asset specificity due to the costs of planning and safeguarding the utilization of the specialized asset. Four sources of asset specificity identified by Williamson are site, physical, human, and dedicated asset specificity. An input that is available at one site but very expensive to move to another location is site-specific: for example, smelters are usually located close to the mine to reduce raw-material shipping costs. Physical asset specificity refers to the specialization of an asset for a single purpose, such as the customization of a machine tool to only produce one type of product. Human asset specificity refers to specialized knowledge or skills of particular employees. Dedicated asset specificity arises from the use of a general-purpose tool for just a single purpose. Malone et al. (1987) identify time specificity as another category of asset specificity—especially when a resource is perishable.

Transaction costs increase with *uncertainty* due to increased planning, communications, and information retrieval and acquisition requirements. Williamson (1985) identifies three key types of uncertainty. The first is the state-contingent form that arises from the unpredictability of environmental changes and other factors that make it difficult to predict the outcome of a particular transaction. The second form of uncertainty arises from poor communications, which limits the ability of decision-makers to know about relevant concurrent events. Finally, the third form of uncertainty arises based on the strategic behaviors of the parties in the transaction.

In contrast, increased *transaction frequency* can reduce the likelihood of opportunism and the magnitude of the associated transaction costs. If highly idiosyncratic or asset-specific investments are frequently transacted between two parties, it reduces the opportunity for both parties to engage in opportunistic behavior. This is because both parties have a high degree of interdependency, and neither gains from opportunistic behavior in the long run. Thus the degree of interdependency and frequency of transactions can reduce transaction costs.

In addition to the above factors, Malone et al. (1987) identify product complexity as a factor that increases transaction costs. As product complexity increases, the information required to support the sale of the product increases, thus increasing the costs of the transaction.

Markets versus Hierarchies: Relative Costs

The market mode of coordination economizes on production costs. Specifically, markets permit buyers to select from a wide variety of goods and services, and markets also aggregate demand across multiple buyers, enabling producers of goods and services to achieve economies of scale or scope. In contrast hierarchies generally restrict buyers to specific producers, limiting choice in terms of goods and services. This generally allows neither aggregation of demand nor the creation of production volumes sufficient to exploit scale and scope economies. Hence, markets generally have lower production costs than hierarchies. However, markets are not always perfect, and the costs of search, specification, and safeguarding of a transaction can often exceed the production cost advantage of markets. This encourages the use of hierarchies, which are then likely to have lower total costs (production plus transaction costs). Williamson (1975) identifies four specific sources of ''market failure'' leading to internal hierarchies. These are discussed below.

Bounded Rationality

When uncertainty and complexity exceed the bounded rationality of individuals, the information-processing cost of determining all possible future states is expensive and computationally prohibitive. By organizing into a firm, each individual does not have to specify contingent contracts with every other individual in the economic system. Instead, by specifying incomplete contracts based on general principles, including shared goals and norms, parties to the contract can focus on events as they unfold instead of attempting to specify contingent contracts to protect against opportunism in all possible future transactions. Thus internal organizations serve to minimize the negative effects of bounded rationality.

Opportunism and Small Numbers

Hierarchies economize over markets by reducing transaction costs in three ways. First, shared objectives and incentives of an organization reduce transaction costs by removing many incentives for subgroup gains. Second, internal organizations can be more efficiently monitored and audited to prevent opportunistic behavior. Finally, hierarchies have various advantages over markets in dispute resolution.

Information Impactedness

A third cause of market failure is asymmetric information between economic agents, allowing agents to misrepresent information at the expense of another party. Again, common objectives and monitoring systems in hierarchies remove incentives and opportunities for gains through misrepresentation of information to other parties.

Atmosphere

The fourth advantage of hierarchies over markets is primarily sociological rather than economic. Markets encourage calculating relations that are transaction-specific between parties. These contracts are not presumed to carry over from one set of transactions to another. Hierarchies, on the other hand, are better able to satisfy the "quasi-moral" involvements among the parties. Recurring relations may therefore satisfy the sociological requirements of individuals. Thus, when all other conditions are equal between internal and market modes of coordination, Williamson argues that the former will be the preferred choice.

Williamson's market failures framework provides reasons for vertical integration by firms to coordinate economic activity. When all other conditions related to production costs are equal between markets and hierarchies, the latter will be the preferred choice due to their transaction cost advantage. Vertical integration is defined as the combination of two or more technologically separable stages of production or distribution under common organizational control through common ownership. The market failures framework thus implies the existence of an efficient boundary for firms, contingent on both their transaction attributes and production costs.

The transaction cost paradigm as developed by Williamson provides a framework with which to analyze the trade-offs between markets and hierarchies. Williamson's key insight is that it is not the interrelationship between technologies of successive stages of production that leads to vertical integration (increased use of hierarchies); rather, it is the sum of production and transaction costs associated with different modes of coordination that determines the degree of markets and hierarchies in an industry. Levy (1985), Joskow (1985), and Caves and Bradburd (1988) have shown that models emphasizing transaction costs have considerable explanatory power as determinants of vertical integration.

Malone and Smith (1984) and Malone et al. (1987) reestablish the linkage between technology and the firm and industry structure. Specifically, they outline how IT applications can be used to mitigate the effects of bounded rationality and opportunism and reduce transaction costs. They forecast that increased IT utilization will lead to an overall shift in the economy toward the market modes of coordination, as well as the increased use of both electronic markets and electronic hierarchies which are enabled by ESNs.

Modeling the Effects of New Information Technologies

Two reasons are given for why increased utilization of new ITs will lead to an overall shift to the market mode of coordination. First, ESNs and other IT applications can lower the cost of communications and of coordinating economic activity in both markets and hierarchies. This reduces the overall importance of transaction costs as a determinant of firm structure. Thus the production cost advantage of alternative models of organization will dominate over governance costs as the key determinant of organization design. Since markets generally have a production cost advantage, there will be a proportionally greater shift toward markets. Second, different types of IT applications can be used to overcome specific sources of market failure and reduce the magnitude of transaction costs associated with the market (Brynjolfsson et al., 1988). Four types of IT impacts are given below.

First, decision support systems, executive support systems, and other applications that support individual analysis can be used to extend the individual decision-maker's rationality and to allow him or her to analyze more complex and uncertain future business scenarios. These enable individuals to specify and plan for a larger set of contingencies. In addition ESNs and knowledge-based systems can also be used to distribute information and expertise inexpensively to many users. Thus IT can reduce the costs associated with planning, information search, communication, and analysis to overcome limitations arising from bounded rationality.

Second, ESNs and other IT applications can be used to reduce the threat of opportunism. Credit checks using the Dun and Bradstreet or TRW databases and accounting information systems are examples of how these technologies can be used to gather critical information and lower the costs of safeguarding against opportunistic behavior by individuals or businesses.

Third, ESNs and database applications can also be used to reduce information impactedness. For instance, information services such as Citishopper and CitiTravel allow individuals to compare a particular vendor's prices against nationwide prices on goods and services and reduce threats from information impactedness. New on-line videotext services such as PRODIGY provide users with consumer reports which reduce the costs of search and likelihood of information impactedness.

The impact of ESNs and other IT applications on the fourth source of market failure, social atmosphere, is unclear. Certain applications of technology can reduce the quality of work life by reducing the flexibility allowed workers to schedule and structure their working and social relationships. In contrast, other applications of information technology, such as telecommuting, computer conferencing, and electronic mail, can be used to increase the workers' control over their professional and social relationships, thereby enhancing the quality of their work life.

Electronic Markets and Electronic Hierarchies

While the above reasons motivate an overall increased shift toward the market mode of coordination, Malone et al. (1987) predict the increased use of ESNs will create more "electronic markets" and "electronic hierarchies." Examples of electronic markets include airline reservation systems such as SABRE and APOLLO, markets for foreign exchange, stocks, bonds, and bills, and the AucNet system in Japan for trading used automobiles. Electronic markets enable multiple buyers and sellers to transact electronically without having to be collocated. While early electronic markets such as airline reservation systems were biased to favor one supplier, Malone et al. (1987) suggest that competition among suppliers and legal forces will lead to the development of unbiased electronic markets. However, unbiased markets are likely to provide large amounts of information that can overwhelm the information-processing capabilities of individuals. Thus they suggest these electronic markets will eventually evolve to personalized markets that provide individuals with artificial intelligence tools to selectively filter information.

Electronic hierarchies use ESNs to more closely integrate business processes within and across organizations. Examples of electronic hierarchies include the use of interorganizational networks to link General Motors with its key parts suppliers. Electronic hierarchies enable organizations to implement "just-in-time" inventory systems and integrate design and manufacturing processes to reduce product development times. Electronic hierarchies arise in situations characterized by high asset specificity or uncertainty where bilateral arrangements between managers and quicker information exchange can reduce transaction costs.

Shifts to Markets: Reduced Vertical Integration

The framework developed above states that new IT applications will generally facilitate the increased use of markets to coordinate economic activity. This shift should result in a decrease in hierarchical control and vertical integration. While recent articles and studies have shown a decrease in firm size, as well as vertical disintegration (*Rise and rise of America's small firms,* 1989; *Is your company too big?* 1989), they have not explicitly explored the effects of IT investments on vertical integration. The next section empirically examines the relation between vertical integration and IT as it concerns the manufacturing sector of the U.S. economy.

Summary

In summary, the transaction cost paradigm provides a framework for analyzing the effects of IT on the choice of alternative modes of economic organization. As ESNs and other IT applications enable cheaper communications and reduce transaction costs there will be an increased shift to market modes of coordination as firms seek the production cost efficiencies of markets. This will lead to corresponding decreases in vertical integration.

INFORMATION TECHNOLOGY AND VERTICAL INTEGRATION

The determinants and extent of markets and hierarchies (and especially the degree of vertical integration) have been empirically examined in numerous studies. (See Tucker and Wilder, 1977; Levy, 1985; Monteverde and Teece, 1982a; and Joskow, 1985.) However, no prior empirical studies have systematically addressed the potential effects of IT investments on vertical integration.[1]

Related studies (Brynjolfsson et al., 1988; Brynjolfsson et al., 1989) examine the effects of IT on markets and hierarchies by using employment categories to create indicators for market coordination. The ratio of salespersons to managers was used as an indicator of the degree of market coordination. As this ratio increases the degree of market coordination increases. In addition the effects of IT on average establishment and firm sizes were examined. These studies determined that increases in IT stocks were correlated to increased market coordination as well as decreases in average firm and establishment sizes.

This study directly investigates the relation between IT stocks, investments, and vertical integration in the manufacturing sector of the economy. A series of regressions was run on panel data of vertical integration, IT, and other capital stocks for the manufacturing sector of the U.S. economy over the period

1975 to 1985. This was done to identify the direction and magnitude of the relationship between IT and vertical integration. This section further describes the data and methodology used in this study and presents results of regression models used to test the IT and vertical integration relationship.

Information Technology and Vertical Integration Data

Measures for the independent variables: *IT stock, IT investments,* and *total equipment stock* were constructed from the national income and product accounts data on industry investments provided by the Bureau of Economic Analysis (BEA). The data-gathering methodology is described in Gorman et al. (1985).

The BEA database provides total annual investments (excluding leased equipment) in 27 asset categories for various industries at the two-digit standard industrial classification (SIC) code level. Nominal investments were converted into constant-dollar or "real-dollar" investments by multiplying investments in each asset category by their associated quality-adjusted price deflators. The asset category "office, computing, and accounting machinery" was used to construct figures for IT investments and stocks. The sum of all equipment categories was used to determine the total annual capital investments and stocks. Estimates of capital stocks from annual investment data were derived by using the procedures described by Gorman et al. (1985).[2]

Vertical integration is defined as the act of combining two or more stages of production under common ownership (Gort, 1962) where a stage consists of a continuous process or separate operation used in the production of a particular good or service. Stages of production are separable if they can be performed successfully under separate ownership. An indicator for the vertical integration construct measures the extent to which separable stages of production exist under common ownership or managerial coordination. Hence it should monotonically increase as the number of stages of production under common ownership and control increases.[3]

This study operationalizes the *vertical integration* construct through the use of a modified value-added-per-firm/total-sales-per-firm ratio. This indicator, originally proposed by Adelman (1955) and later modified to the current version by Tucker and Wilder (1977), is constructed from value-added-by-manufacture and value-of-shipments[4] data from the Census of Manufacturers, provided by the Bureau of the Census, and the Annual Survey of Manufacturers produced by the Department of Commerce. As more activities are undertaken in-house rather than external to the firm, the value-added/shipments ratio will increase. Hence the index will increase monotonically with increases in vertical integration.

The data was categorized by SIC codes (at the two-digit level) into twenty different manufacturing industry categories. (See the appendix to this chapter.) The natural logarithms of capital equipment stocks and investments were taken in order to interpret these variables in terms of their percentage-effects on vertical integration. In addition, dummy variables were used to adjust for any omitted independent variables in the regression models testing the IT–vertical integration relation. These were specified for each industry sector to account for industry-specific effects, and other dummy variables were included for each year to control for any time-specific effects such as recessions.

Methodology

The data was analyzed by using least-squares regression on pooled cross-sectional and time-series data.[5] Two basic regression models were specified to explore the relationships between IT stock, total capital equipment stock, and vertical integration over the period 1975–1985. This period marks a rapid change in the proportion of IT stock to total equipment stock. This ratio rose to over 8 percent after remaining at less than 2 percent during the previous decade. (See Figure 2.1.) The period also marks the development of departmental and end-user computing, improvements in data communications, and adoption of new applications such as decision support systems and ESNs which can be used to reduce transaction costs.

Since lags are commonly observed in the assimilation of new technologies into the operations of a firm, the two basic specifications allow for and examine

Figure 2.1
Ratio of IT Stock to Total Capital Equipment Stock

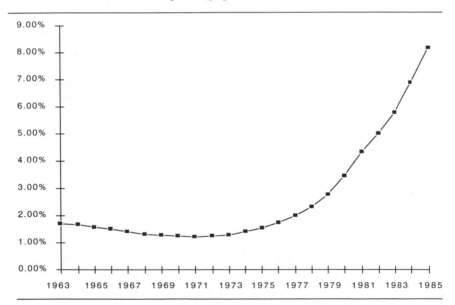

Based on National Income and Product Accounts data for industry investments as provided by the Bureau of Economic Analysis.

the effects of lags in IT on vertical integration. Delays between the acquisition of IT and its impact on industry and firm structure can arise from the time required to train users, develop software, and set up and test equipment. The basic models are discussed below.

Model 1: Current and Lagged Effects of Information Technology Stock

This specification examined the effect of both current and previous levels of IT stock on the vertical integration index. As discussed earlier, dummy variables were used to adjust for any important missing information in the model. These variables also account for changing cross-section and time-series intercepts due to omitted variables specific to different industries at different times. This restricted covariance multiple regression model is illustrated below:

$$\text{m1: } VI = \beta_o + \beta_1 LITST(X) + \beta_2 LEQST + \Sigma \beta_i S_i + \Sigma \beta_j T_j$$

VI $\quad$ = value-added/shipments ratio

LITST(X) = natural logarithm of IT stock

X $\quad$ = 1,2,3,4 refers to the number of years by which the data is lagged

LEQST $\quad$ = natural logarithm of the total equipment stock

S_{20-39} $\quad$ = dummy variables for the 20 industries

T_{75-84} $\quad$ = dummy variables for the 11 years of the study

The framework developed earlier predicts that the current level of vertical integration will be negatively correlated to either current or previous levels of IT stock. Thus we expect a negative coefficient for the LITST. In contrast we expect vertical integration to be positively correlated to the levels of total equipment stock, LEQST. The latter reflects the firm's total investments in specialized assets for production. Vertical integration should increase in proportion to increased specialized investments in a firm, as the latter leads to greater transaction costs. Thus we expect a positive coefficient for LEQST.

Model 2: Partial Adjustments Model

This specification tests a partial adjustments model to better understand the effects of lags on vertical integration. It assumes that vertical integration will not fully adjust to more recent investments in IT stocks. This is because we expect delays in the time required to assimilate the technology. Including more than one of the lagged stock variables in specifying a partial adjustment model would lead to significant multicollinearity.[6] Instead, the current level of IT stock and recent annual IT investments LITFL and LITFL1 were included in the model given below:[7]

$$\text{m2: } VI = \beta_o + \beta_1 LITST(X) + \beta_2 LITFL + \beta_3 LITFL1$$
$$+ \beta_4 LEQST + \Sigma \beta_i S_i + \Sigma \beta_j T_j$$

LITFL   = natural logarithm of most recent years of IT stock investments
LITFL1 = natural logarithm of previous years of IT stock investments

In contrast to the current effects model, explicitly including recent IT investments (LITFL and LITFL1) in the partial adjustments model should result in a larger negative coefficient for current IT stock (LITST). In the latter model the effects of more recent IT investments on vertical integration are more effectively separated from the effects of prior investments. Specifically, the model accounts for the fact that the level of vertical integration is unlikely to have fully adjusted to the recent investments, LITFL and LITFL1. Due to this parameter estimates of LITFL and LITFL1 should be small and positive as new IT investments are unlikely to immediately reduce the level of vertical integration. This is because we expect delays and lags in the time required to effectively integrate technology into the operations of the firm. The positive parameter estimates for LITFL1 and LITFL2 should also decrease in magnitude with the lags. This reflects the fact that as IT investments are effectively integrated into the operations of the firm they are likely to enable more marketlike modes of coordination.

Autocorrelation

Examination of the Durbin Watson statistic in the initial regressions showed substantial positive autocorrelation for both models. The presence of autocorrelation can result in inflated estimates of the precision-of-parameter values in the model. This in turn can lead to the acceptance of an incorrect model specification. A generalized differencing method was used to correct for problems of overestimation posed by autocorrelation. Both models were transformed by this procedure.[8]

Results

The results of the models transformed by generalized differencing are summarized in Tables 2.1 and 2.2. The results show that the relationship between vertical integration and the IT stock and total equipment stock variables is in the direction hypothesized by the transaction cost model. However, the relationship between the current level of vertical integration and the current IT stock is statistically insignificant. In contrast, vertical integration is negatively correlated to lagged values of IT stock and coefficients for LITST(X>0) are statistically significant. Comparing the results of lagged models shows that an IT stock lag of two years has the largest impact on the vertical integration indicator. After the two-year lag the impact of IT stock on the dependent variable declines in magnitude and statistical significance. As expected, the results imply that the firm does not fully adjust its structure to IT as soon as it is acquired. The pattern of results implies that technology acquired in the most recent two years, excluding the current year, has the greatest impact on struc-

Table 2.1
Current and Lagged Effect Model

Dependent Variable: Vertical Integration Index

X=	0	1	2	3	4
LITST(X)N	-0.019	-0.030	-0.031	-0.024	-0.023
	t=1.134	t=2.50	t=3.15	t=2.60	t=2.67
		*	**	*	*
LEQSTN	+0.096	+0.106	+0.104	+0.093	+0.090
	t=3.325	t=4.11	t=4.37	t=4.07	t=4.03
	**	**	**	**	**
R^2	0.94	0.94	0.94	0.94	0.94
DURBIN WATSON	1.83	1.85	1.84	1.85	1.84

* significant at 0.05 level (two-tailed test)
** significant at 0.01 level (two-tailed test)

Table 2.2
The Partial Adjustments Model

Dependent variable: vertical integration

VARIABLE	COEFFICIENT	T-STATISTIC
LITST	-0.045 **	3.449
LITFL	0.027 **	3.867
LITFL1	0.018 **	2.593
LEQST	0.0537 *	2.020
R^2	0.953	
DURBIN WATSON	1.76	

* significant at 0.05 level (two-tailed test)
** significant at 0.01 level (two-tailed test)

ture. The delays are likely to arise from the time required to learn the uses and capabilities of the technology, as well as the time required to restructure work patterns and relationships.

The regression results showed that the magnitude of the IT stock coefficient was small (ca. 0.02) in comparison to the positive coefficient (ca. 0.1) associated with total equipment stock. However, IT stock has increased more than 600%, compared to 40% for total equipment stock in the period 1975–1985. Thus despite the smaller IT stock parameter estimate, the impact of IT on vertical integration is likely to be larger in magnitude than the impact of total capital equipment investments for the 1975–1985 period.

The partial adjustments model also affirms the hypothesis that learning effects are operating in this situation. As expected the current value of IT stocks (LITST) has a negative coefficient, and recent investments (LITFL(x)) have smaller positive coefficients reflecting delays in structural adjustments to new IT investments.

Industry and Time Dummy Variables

Parameter estimates on the dummy variables (see Kambil, 1989) are not included since a reparameterization of the model by using a different combination of dummy variables to represent the twenty industries and eleven years is likely to result in different signs. This is because the parameter estimates are made relative to the value of the intercept term representing the twentieth industry and eleventh year.

However, as expected, most of the industry dummy variables are statistically significant for both models (see Kambil, 1989), suggesting that there are omitted variables unique to these industries that account for a particular industry's level of vertical integration. In contrast, the majority of the time dummy variables are not statistically significant, since their standard errors are larger than the parameter estimates for their coefficients. Results also showed that time dummies are not substantially different from zero, and do not significantly increase the explanatory power of the model.[9] The time dummies are included to increase the theoretical meaningfulness of the models and account for any annual shocks in the vertical integration index not directly related to IT stocks, total capital stocks, or other industry-specific variables.

Summary

These results show that the relationship between vertical integration and the IT stock in previous years is statistically significant and consistent with the predictions of the transaction cost models. Lags of up to two years in IT stock showed the largest impact on vertical integration and statistical significance. The results suggest that it takes up to two years to adjust to the new technology. The second model confirmed this result by showing that recent investments in IT have limited effects on reducing vertical integration. Total equipment stock variables were also positively related to vertical integration, consistent with the transaction costs approach.

The next section summarizes results, presents conclusions, and outlines areas for future study.

CONCLUSIONS

The impact of ESNs and other new ITs on markets and hierarchies was modeled by using a transaction costs framework. IT was hypothesized to reduce transaction costs and encourage a shift from hierarchies to markets. An empirical examination of the relationship between vertical integration and IT stocks and flows found evidence for this hypothesis. The degree of vertical integration is found to be negatively correlated to current and previous values of IT stocks. Related studies of the effect of IT on markets and hierarchies also provide support for this result (Brynjolfsson et al., 1988).

The decline in vertical integration was greatest two years following investments in IT. Thus IT stocks lagged by two years had the greatest impact on the current level of vertical integration, suggesting delays in the effects of IT on firm structure. We expect that this delay arises from the time required to learn how to utilize new technologies, as well as that required to redesign business processes. The use of the partial adjustment model to examine the lag structure also confirmed the above learning effect.

During the period 1975–1985, IT stocks rose more than 600 percent, compared to 40 percent for total equipment stocks in the same period. Thus despite the smaller IT stock parameter estimates, the impact of IT on vertical integration is likely to be larger in magnitude than the impact of total capital equipment investments for the 1975–1985 period. Given the trend of increased investments in IT, we expect an acceleration in the 1990s of the trend toward vertical disintegration, and the increased use of markets.

Future Research

This chapter has generally presumed a dichotomy between markets and hierarchies. However, various intermediate forms exist for economic coordination. For example, Williamson (1985) identifies trilateral and bilateral modes of governance as alternative mechanisms for coordinating economic relations relevant to different contexts. These mechanisms are likely to play increasingly important roles in the governance of new organizational forms enabled by ESNs. These new organization forms enabled by IT include "network organizations" (Antonelli, 1988) and value-added partnerships (Johnston and Lawrence, 1988) that use a variety of mechanisms to coordinate key economic activities across firms. Future research should clarify features of different modes of governance and emerging organizational forms to systematically identify how IT affects structural choices in different business contexts. In addition, the managerial processes and IT applications that are critical to the efficient and effective implementation of new coordinative mechanisms must be identified.

ESNs also enable the implementation of electronic markets and electronic hierarchies. Barriers to entry in providing electronic markets can arise from network externalities and economies of scale and scope. These barriers to entry reduce the contestability of markets and allow current producers in the marketplace to exercise greater price discrimination and monopoly power. Inefficiencies can also arise from other strategic behaviors by owners of electronic markets and participants in electronic hierarchies. These include the use of restrictive contracts with market participants and the use of informational advantages to effectively monitor or distort market signals (Kambil, 1989). Regulatory and other policy mechanisms to ensure the integrity and efficient functioning of electronic markets and electronic hierarchies merit further study.

APPENDIX

Explanation of variables:

ITST = the total IT stock in an industry in any one year

EQST = the total equipment stock in an industry in a particular year

ITFL = IT investments in a given year

The prefix L refers to a log transformation of the variable. The suffixes 1–4 indicate the number years the variable has been lagged. The suffix N indicates that the variable has been transformed by using a generalized differencing method to correct for autocorrelation. The variables S_{20-39} are dummy variables representing different manufacturing industries. These industries are listed below:

S_{20} = Food and Kindred Products

S_{21} = Tobacco Manufactures

S_{22} = Textile Mill Products

S_{23} = Apparel, Other Textile Products

S_{24} = Lumber and Wood Products

S_{25} = Furniture and Fixtures

S_{26} = Paper and Allied Products

S_{27} = Printing and Publishing

S_{28} = Chemicals and Allied Products

S_{29} = Petroleum and Coal Products

The variables T_{75-84} represent time dummies for the years 1975 to 1984.

NOTES

The author would like to thank Professor Thomas Malone, Professor Ernst Berndt, and Erik Brynjolfsson for their helpful comments and insights in the development and specification of the econometric models.

1. See Kambil (1989) for a critique and review of prior research and alternate theories for vertical integration.

2. The derivations employed modified Winfrey tables to determine the percentage of equipment stocks annually retired from service due to age. The Winfrey tables assume a normal distribution for equipment service lifetimes centered around their ex-

pected average lifetime. Based on BEA estimates, the average life of IT was taken to be eight years. Average lifetime for non-IT stock was estimated as twelve years.

3. Kambil (1989) provides a detailed review of features of indicators for vertical integration.

4. The value of industry shipments is defined as the amount received on net receivable selling value, f.o.b. plant, after discounts and allowances and excluding freight charges and excise taxes. Value added by manufacture is derived by first converting the value of shipments to the value of production by adding in the ending inventory in finished goods and work in process and subtracting the beginning inventory. The cost of materials, supplies, containers, fuels, purchased electricity, and contract work is subtracted from the value of production to obtain the value added by manufacture. The change to reporting all inventories by the last in, first out (LIFO) method in 1982 makes value added by manufacture not strictly comparable to that prior to 1982. Time dummy variables used to account for measurement changes were insignificant (see Kambil, 1989).

5. See Pindyck and Rubinfield (1976) on covariance models.

6. Multicollinearity can increase the standard error of variables and reduce their statistical significance. It can also reverse the signs on parameters of highly correlated explanatory variables, making it difficult to interpret the effect of a particular explanatory variable on the dependent variable.

7. This specification was suggested by Professor E. Berndt and Erik Brynjolfsson.

8. This method transforms the models into ones where successive error terms are independent. This transformation is illustrated below:

For m1: $VI = \beta_o + \beta_1 LITST + \beta_2 LEQST + \Sigma \beta_i S_i + \Sigma \beta_j T_j + E$
$VIN = VI - p*LAG1(VI)$
$LITSTN = LITST - p*LAG1(LITST)$
$EN = E - p*LAG1(E)$

The transformed equation is

m1: $VIN = \beta_o + \beta_1 LITSTN + \beta_2 LEQSTN + \Sigma \beta_i S_i + \Sigma \beta_j T_j + EN$

9. F-tests were used to compare models with and without the time dummies; see Kambil (1989).

3

Compatibility and the Creation of Shared Networks

Nicholas Economides

Many networks start out as self-contained private (or proprietary) networks. It is often the case that over time private networks link up to form shared networks. However, this does not always happen. Until Citicorp joined the nationwide Cirrus system in early 1991, both outcomes could be seen in different automatic teller networks in the New York City area. Citicorp's extensive network of automatic teller machines (ATMs) was private and essentially restricted to use by Citicorp's customers only, while the New York Cash Exchange (NYCE) network was a shared joint-venture network of a number of banks. In this chapter, I develop an economic model to explore the incentives for private networks to form shared networks. The model has broader applications to product systems generally. More specifically, this chapter explores the incentives for private networks to adopt compatible specifications so that transactions across networks are feasible and at no extra cost due to incompatibilities.

A private network can vary its degree of compatibility with another private network. In general, an adapter is required for transactions across networks, and each private network contributes to the cost of the adapter through its choice of specifications. It is shown that, even in the absence of binding agreements, full compatibility (zero adapter cost) will emerge at equilibrium provided that the demands for each of the potential transactions are of the same size. Various degrees of incompatibility and limitations of access across private networks will emerge when this condition does not hold. In particular, when demand for hybrid (across networks) transactions is small, all private networks prefer to have incompatibility and restrict access across the networks. If only one private network has a large demand (because of good reputation or high quality of service) then it will opt for incompatibility while the smaller private network desires compatibility.

The next section introduces the terminology and analytical framework required to examine the incentives for compatibility. An example is presented that captures the intuition underlying the formal analysis and illustrates the primary findings of the formal analysis developed in the remainder of the chapter. The formal model is introduced in its simplest form in the third section. In the following sections, I discuss the symmetric case, where the demand for (hybrid) transactions across the private networks is equal to their internal transactions demands, followed by the asymmetric case, where the demand for hybrid transactions falls short of the demand for transactions within the private networks. The model is elaborated to allow for the bundling of services within private networks and the possibility that different adapters are required for different hybrid transactions. I conclude the formal analysis by showing that the conclusions of the previous analyses extend to a model that allows for sequential decisions, with the decisions on specifications taken at an earlier stage than the decisions on prices.

BASIC FRAMEWORK

Many complex goods are composed of simpler *elementary goods,* which in many cases are sold separately. For example, the good "phone call from X to Y" requires use of phone appliances at X and at Y as well as the use of a network that allows the transmission of signals from X to Y. This network may include the local networks of locations X and Y plus a long-distance network. Note that each of the elementary goods is complementary with the other, since their combination allows the consumer to purchase the *composite good* that he desires, the phone call from X to Y.

The elementary goods can be thought of as *components* and the composite goods as *systems.* For example, consider a personal computer that is composed of a central processing unit (CPU), a video monitor, and a keyboard. Each of these three elementary goods can be considered a component and their combination is a system.

In general there will be a number of elementary goods of each type. Elementary goods of the same type are obviously substitutes. The different combinations of elementary goods create systems that are also seen by the consumers as substitutes. IBM and Compaq CPUs are substitutes. So are IBM and Compaq monitors. And the four systems (pure IBM, pure Compaq, and the two hybrids) are also substitutes for each other.

The ability of all elementary goods (or components) to be combined costlessly with all elementary goods of a different type to produce functioning composite goods (or systems) is defined as *full compatibility.* Compatible elementary goods can be thought of as constituting a *network.* Consider the composite good "cash withdrawal through an ATM." It is composed of at least two elementary goods that are complementary with each other—the use of the ATM and the use of the services of a bank from which the funds are withdrawn. Full compatibility of all elementary goods means that a cash withdrawal from any bank by using any ATM is feasible. Thus, under full compatibility, "there is an ATM network." Of course, it is the *vertical* connection between ATMs and banks and *not a horizontal* connection between ATMs that constitutes the (vertical) network.[1] Thus, the existence of a (vertical) network is contingent upon compatibility between complementary elementary goods.

This chapter will analyze the conditions under which full compatibility and thereby networks will emerge from the noncooperative behavior of firms—that is, without binding agreements between the firms. Thus, firms are assumed to consider only their individual incentives in making compatibility decisions and not the collective industry-wide interests. Parties are allowed to agree on compatibility specifications, but the agreements are based on the individual incentives of the parties rather than their collective interests. Firms are not allowed to enter into agreements with punishments for deviation from them.

A significant proportion of the existing literature on compatibility has focused on the issue of "network externalities," a catchall term for positive consumption or production externalities. For example, in a network externalities framework, the buyer of the last unit of a good has a higher benefit than the buyer of the first unit because the sale of the earlier units has created some benefits in a related dimension. The large sales of VHS video recorders/players and the implied demand for VHS tape rentals has created over time large VHS tape libraries that benefit the later buyers of VHS players. Similarly, later buyers of Lotus 1-2-3 find already-trained personnel and can reap higher benefits. In a world of network externalities, it pays manufacturers that arrive late in the market to adopt the specifications of the existing network or at least to make their product compatible with the existing network specifications. For example, Microsoft Excel, arriving late in the spreadsheet market for MS-DOS computers that was dominated by Lotus 1-2-3, is able to read 1-2-3 files. Borland's Quattro, also arriving late in the same market, is able to both read and write 1-2-3 files. The complementarity between the pair of goods that exhibit network externalities is self-reinforcing. Thus, the large tape libraries of VHS tapes increase the value and sales of VHS players; the high sales of VHS players create an even higher demand for larger VHS tape libraries.[2]

Although the existence of network externalities can easily explain the expansion of an existing network and the adherence of latecomers to old standards, it is not sufficient to explain the creation of a shared network out of preexisting private networks.

Suppose there are two types of elementary goods, A (standing, for example, for ATM) and B (standing, for example, for bank), and each firm produces a good of each type. To start with, consider the case of two elementary goods of each type. Elementary goods of different types can be combined in a 1:1 ratio to create composite goods that are demanded by consumers. Suppose there are two firms, $i = 1, 2$, and firm i sells products A_i and B_i.

In Figure 3.1, the composite goods are denoted by double-pointed arrows. Ownership is denoted by boxes enclosing the products produced by the same firm. The elementary goods produced by the same firms are readily and cost-lessly combinable yielding systems A_1B_1 and A_2B_2. If each firm decides to make its products *incompatible* with the products of the opponent, then only these two composite goods will exist. This is shown in Figure 3.1a. Then there are two incompatible private networks. Alternatively, when both firms decide to make their elementary goods fully compatible with those of the opponent, the hybrid products A_1B_2 and A_2B_1 also become available as in Figure 3.1b. Now there are four composite products available to the consumer. This is a "shared" network. The shared network is created by the decisions of firms to make their elementary goods compatible with those of the opponents.

In what regime will firms have higher prices and profits? Economides (1989a) discusses this question in the context of differentiated goods. For example, ATMs can be at different physical locations while banking services are differentiated in features of variety such as pricing schedules, deposit requirements, locations, risk, etc. It is shown that under fairly general conditions,[3] firms will have higher prices and profits under compatibility. The intuition for this result is relatively simple. Imagine that good A is computer CPUs, good B is monitors, and firm 1 is IBM. Suppose that we are in the world of incompatibility of Figure 3.1a and IBM contemplates a price increase in its computer system A_1B_1. Similarly, suppose IBM contemplates the same price increase in the price of its CPU (A_1) in the world of compatibility. Equal price increases create equal demand responses as long as the demand for hybrids is of the same size as the demand for single-producer goods. But now, in the case of incompatibility, IBM's demand response is in units of systems, while in the case of

Figure 3.1
Network Compatibility Relationships

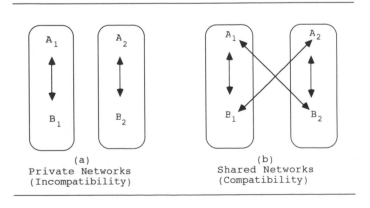

(a)
Private Networks
(Incompatibility)

(b)
Shared Networks
(Compatibility)

compatibility IBM's demand response is in units of CPUs. Multiplying with the corresponding prices, we see that the value (profit) response is higher in the case of incompatibility. In the world of compatibility, only sales of CPUs are lost as a result of the price increase and therefore the profit loss is smaller. This prompts IBM to set a *lower price* in the regime of incompatibility where *demand appears (to IBM) to be more elastic*. Profits follow the direction of prices, so that higher profits are realized in the regime of full compatibility. Higher profits lead more firms to enter in the market under compatibility. Thus, under compatibility there will be more varieties available to consumers for two reasons: first because more firms will operate in the market, and second because all the cross (hybrid) combinations are available under compatibility that are not available under incompatibility. It is evident that the standardization implied by compatibility is in no conflict with lots of varieties being available at equilibrium. Therefore, comparing a shared network with a collection of private networks, we find a larger number of competitors, a much larger number of composite goods, and higher prices in a shared network.

Firms are usually active participants in the decision processes that define the degree of compatibility in the marketplace. Thus, a comparison of the two regimes, the regime of compatibility (shared network) and the regime of incompatibility (private networks), is not sufficient to determine which will emerge. One needs to analyze how the individual decisions of the firms result or do not result in full compatibility and the creation of shared networks. This chapter explicitly models the decisions of competing firms on the choice of compatibility, and thus the creation of shared networks.

In general, there will always exist some technologically feasible way to make two components work together as a system through the addition of an adapter, interface, or gateway. Of course, the required adapter can be extremely expensive and therefore not used, but the possibility of its use exists in general. Thus, the degree of compatibility of two components is measured by the cost of the adapter that is required to allow them to function together as a working system. Full compatibility means that an adapter of zero cost is required. Varying degrees of incompatibility are reflected in the size of adapter costs.

Component-producing firms can choose the specifications of their components to make them compatible or incompatible in some degree with the complementary components produced by competitors. Owners of private networks can use technical specifications or other means to restrict access to the elementary goods of their network by outsiders. In this sense, any incompatibilities introduced are nuisance incompatibilities, designed to limit competition. They are not technologically necessary.

Some readers may already be wondering how it could possibly be that any firm would have an incentive to introduce or tolerate incompatibilities. The previous discussion may lead some readers to conclude that compatibility is obviously the equilibrium. This is not true. One needs to recognize that there are two potentially opposing incentives in the combination of two private networks and the creation of a shared one. The first incentive is the increase in demand that accompanies the merger of private networks. It is a strong incentive for the creation of a shared network. For example, if originally there are two banks, each with its private and distinct ATM network, the unification of the networks will allow access to bank 1 from ATMs owned by bank 2, thereby creating an increase in demand for the banking services of bank 1. The second incentive is more subtle. Remember that the ownership structure does not change as the networks become shared. A merger of two private networks can increase competition between the owners of these two networks. Prices of banking services and of ATM services are not obviously guaranteed to rise as a result of the combination of the two private networks. A significant part of the rest of this chapter analyzes the balance of these two incentives. I show that when the demand incentive is strong—that is, when the demand for hybrid transactions is strong relative to the demand for transactions within the private networks, then the demand incentive outweighs the competitive effects of compatibility and firms prefer compatibility. However, when the demand for hybrids is small, the potential demand gain from the creation of a shared network is overshadowed by the concurrent increase in competition. Then each private network will prefer to be inaccessible and separate from other private networks.

THE STARTING MODEL

Suppose that there are two elementary goods of each type, A_1, A_2, B_1, and B_2. For concreteness, consider A_1 and A_2 to be competing ATMs and B_1 and B_2 to be competing banks. Assume that composite goods A_1B_1 and A_2B_2 require no adapters, but hybrid goods A_1B_2 and A_2B_1 require adapters of cost R. R is the extra cost of doing business across the private networks. Let the prices of elementary goods A_1, A_2 be p_1, p_2 and of goods B_1, B_2 be q_1, q_2 respectively. Then the four composite goods in the market are available at the prices shown in Table 3.1.[4]

Each firm can affect the price of an adapter through its choice of specifica-

Table 3.1
Composite Goods and Corresponding Prices with No Bundling

Composite Good	Price
A_1B_1	$p_1 + q_1$
A_1B_2	$p_1 + q_2 + R$
A_2B_1	$q_1 + p_2 + R$
A_2B_2	$p_2 + q_2$

tion of components. It will be assumed that each firm can contribute positively to the cost of the adapter but cannot decrease the cost attributed to incompatibilities introduced by other firms. A simple functional form exemplifies this assumption. Let x, $x_h \geq x \geq 0$, reflect the cost attributed to incompatibilities introduced by firm 1 and y, $y_h \geq y \geq 0$, reflect the cost of those attributed to firm 2. Then $R = x + y$. Thus, I assume that an incompatibility introduced by one firm cannot be wiped out by the other firm. Incompatibilities can be introduced in many dimensions of technical specifications, and it is hard for one firm to anticipate and counteract each incompatibility introduced by the opponent.[5] It will be assumed that adapters are produced by a competitive sector and sold at cost.[6]

The demand for each of the four products A_1B_1, A_1B_2, A_2B_1, and A_2B_2, is a function of its own price, the price of the composite good that differs from it in the second component, the price of the composite good that differs in the first component, and the price of the composite good that differs in both components. We can write these demand functions as follows:

$$D^{11} = D^{11}(p_1 + q_1,\ p_1 + q_2 + R,\ q_1 + p_2 + R,\ p_2 + q_2)$$
$$D^{12} = D^{12}(p_1 + q_2 + R,\ p_1 + q_1,\ p_2 + q_2,\ p_2 + q_1 + R)$$
$$D^{21} = D^{21}(p_2 + q_1 + R,\ p_2 + q_2,\ p_1 + q_1,\ p_1 + q_2 + R)$$
$$D^{22} = D^{22}(p_2 + q_2,\ p_2 + q_1 + R,\ p_1 + q_2 + R,\ p_1 + q_1)$$

where the first superscript on the Ds identifies the ATM owner and the second superscript identifies the bank.

Vertically integrated firm i, $i = 1$, 2, sells both A_i and B_i. A_1 is sold as part of A_1B_1 and A_1B_2, since a bank 1 ATM can be used to make a transaction with either bank 1 or bank 2. Thus, sales of A_1 are $D^{11} + D^{12}$. Similarly, since B_1 is sold as part of A_1B_1 and A_2B_1, sales of B_1 are $D^{11} + D^{21}$. Assuming zero costs,[7] the profits of firm 1 are

$$\pi^1 = p_1(D^{11} + D^{12}) + q_1(D^{11} + D^{21})$$

Similarly, profits for firm 2 are

$$\pi^2 = p_2(D^{22} + D^{21}) + q_2(D^{22} + D^{12})$$

SYMMETRIC DEMAND

An increase in the cost of the adapter, R, increases the price of goods A_1B_2 and A_2B_1 that represent transactions across networks owned by different firms. The demand for A_1B_2 and A_2B_1 falls while the demands for the other two composite (nonhybrid) goods A_1B_1 and A_2B_2 increase. What is the balance of the demand and profit changes? It depends on the size, shape, and elasticities of the demand functions of the four composite goods. In practice these can be estimated. Below I provide sufficient conditions for the firms to choose compatibility.

ASSUMPTION 1: *The demands for the four composite goods are symmetric so that all four can be represented by the same function:*

$$D^{11}(X,Y,Z,W) = D^{12}(X,Y,Z,W) = D^{21}(X,Y,Z,W) = D^{22}(X,Y,Z,W)$$

This assumption ensures that the size and the shape of the demand functions are the same for all four composite goods. In particular, the demand for hybrids is of equal size and elasticity as the demand for single-producer goods. This means that the willingness to pay for any of the four composite goods is the same if all four are offered at equal prices. Assumption 1 does *not* restrict the own-elasticity and the cross-elasticities of demand in the substitution of banking or ATM services.

ASSUMPTION 2: *An equal increase in the prices of all four goods decreases the demand for each good.*

This is a very natural assumption. When all goods become more expensive and income is held constant, it is reasonable that demand falls for all products.

ASSUMPTION 3: *The demand functions are linear. The representative demand D^{11} is*

$$D^{11} = a - b(p_1 + q_1) + c(p_1 + q_2 + R) + d(p_2 + q_1 + R) + e(p_2 + q_2)$$

where a, b, c, d, e>0.

The linear structure of demand is not a significant restriction. The results carry through with minor modifications for general demand functions. Note that Assumption 2 implies that $b > c + d + e$. The degree of substitution between composite goods that differ only in the second elementary good is measured by c. In the ATM example, c represents the substitutability between transactions with different banks at the same ATM. Thus c essentially represents substitutability of banking services. Similarly, d represents substitutability between composite goods that differ in the first elementary good only—that is, substitutability between different ATMs. Finally, e represents substitutability between composite goods that differ in both dimensions (ATM and bank).

Consider now a setup where prices and product specifications are chosen simultaneously. Suppose that firm 1 decides to increase the price R of the adapter. The effect on profits is

$$\partial \pi^1 / \partial R = (-b + c + d + e)(p_1 + q_1) < 0$$

THEOREM 1: *Under Assumptions 1–3, firms choose noncooperatively to set adapters' cost to zero—that is, to make their components fully compatible with those of the other firms. Owners of private networks will merge them into a shared network.*

The intuition of the proof follows. Consider first the sales of ATM services by firm 1—that is, sales of product A_1. Sales of A_1 embodied in A_1B_1 increase with the cost of the adapter, R, according to $c+d>0$, and sales of A_1 embodied in A_1B_2 decrease with the cost of the adapter, R, according to $-b+e<0$. The total effect on sales of A_1 when the price of R increases is the sum of the two effects, $-b+c+d+e$, equivalent to the effect of an equal increase in all prices. By Assumption 2, this effect is negative. Therefore an increase in the price of the adapter decreases sales of A_1. Similarly, it decreases sales of B_1 and profits of firm 1. It follows that each firm will choose to minimize the cost of the adapter so that at equilibrium $R=0$. Each firm will try to achieve full compatibility with its competitors. A shared network will be the equilibrium.

Theorem 1 can easily be extended to a world of three or more firms, each producing two components. For example, if there are three component-producing firms, products 11, 22, and 33 need no adapter, while products 12 and 21 require an adapter of cost $x+y$, products 13 and 31 require an adapter of cost $x'+z'$, and products 23 and 32 require an adapter of cost $y'+z$. Firm 1 chooses x and x', firm 2 chooses y and y', and firm 3 chooses z and z'. It is not difficult to extend the arguments made for the two-firms problem and show that at equilibrium all adapters will cost zero—that is, $x=x'=y=y'=z=z'=0$, and there is full compatibility.

COROLLARY 1: *Full compatibility characterizes the equilibrium of $n\geq3$ firms each producing two components.*

The result of full compatibility can also be extended to a world of systems composed of as many components as producers, with each firm producing each type of component. For example, when three components are required for a system there are twenty-seven (i.e., 3^3) systems available, starting with 111, 121, 131, 211, 221, 231, 311, 321, 331, 112, 122, 132, etc. Suppose that each firm controls a part of the adapter's cost through its decisions on the design of its components. Then the problem is very similar to the one discussed above. The proof that full compatibility arises as a noncooperative equilibrium is a straightforward repetition of the previous arguments.

COROLLARY 2: *Full compatibility characterizes the equilibrium of $n\geq3$ firms each producing n components.*

ASYMMETRIC DEMAND

The crucial assumption for Theorem 1 and Corollaries 1 and 2 is that the demand for hybrids is equal to the demand for single-producer composite goods—

that is, Assumption 1. If this is not the case, compatibility may not result. Suppose that the demand for single-producer composite goods is large compared to the demand for hybrids. This may be because consumers lack confidence in composite goods made up of elementary goods of different producers. It may also be that because of historical reasons there are functions of an ATM that are not fully utilized in a transaction that involves a bank that does not own that particular ATM. For example, if a customer has a number of accounts, all accessible through the same magnetic card, an ATM belonging to a different bank may have trouble fully identifying the accounts with the customer. Another reason for low demand for hybrids could be that ATMs are located at the same location as the bank that owns them and consumers rarely travel to other locations.

When the demand for hybrids is small, an increase in the price of the adapter has a small negative effect on profits generated from sales of hybrid systems, but it has a significant positive effect on profits generated from sales of single-producer systems. Thus an increase in the price of the adapter can result in higher profits. Then firms will choose incompatibility.

For concreteness suppose that the demand for hybrids is a scale-down of the demand for single-producer systems. Assumption 1 is replaced by

$$kD^{11}(X,Y,Z,W)=D^{12}(X,Y,Z,W)=D^{21}(X,Y,Z,W)=kD^{22}(X,Y,Z,W), \ 0<k\leq1$$

Then the effects of price increases on the demand for hybrids are smaller than on the demand for single-producer systems. The rate of change in sales of composite good A_1B_1 induced by the increase in R is $c+d>0$, and the rate of change in sales of system A_1B_2 is $k(-b+e)<0$. Thus the total effect on the sales of A_1 is $c+d+k(-b+e)$. Similarly, the total effect on the sales of B_1 is the same, $c+d+k(-b+e)$. For high k including $k=1$—that is, for nearly equal demand for hybrids and single-producer goods—this effect is negative. But there exists a $k_1<1$ such that for $k=k_1$ this effect is zero:

$$\partial\pi^1/\partial R=c+d+k(-b+e)=0 \Leftrightarrow k=(c+d)/(b-e)\equiv k_1$$

When the demand for hybrids is small, $k<k_1$, the increase in sales of A_1B_1 dominates the decrease in sales of A_1B_2, and the total effect is positive,

$$\partial\pi^1/\partial R=[c+d+k(-b+e)](p_1+q_1)>0$$

Then each firm will prefer to introduce incompatibilities. At equilibrium both firms choose the highest degree of incompatibility possible, $x=x_h$, $y=y_h$, and $R=x_h+y_h$.

THEOREM 2: *If the demand for hybrids is sufficiently small compared to the demand for single-producer systems, all firms choose total incompatibility.*

In the above setting, firms have the same incentives on the question of compatibility because none of the private networks has a demand advantage. However, in many markets one private network has a demand advantage. It may be the reflection of good reputation or higher quality for both of its elementary goods. It could also be the result of the fact that both the bank and the ATM of one network are located in an area of high demand for their services.

Suppose that product A_1B_1 has high demand while demand is small both for hybrids A_1B_2 and A_2B_1 and for the single-producer system of firm 2, A_2B_2.

$$D^{11} = (X, Y, Z, W) = D^{12}(X, Y, Z, W)/k = D^{21}(X, Y, Z, W)/k$$
$$= D^{22}(X, Y, Z, W)/L,$$

with $0 < k, L \leq 1$. Demand for hybrids A_1B_2 and A_2B_1 is k times the demand of A_1B_1, and the demand for A_2B_2 is L times the demand for A_1B_1. The relative size of the demand for the small private network and the demand for hybrids is important in the decision of compatibility as seen below.

In this setup, we expect that the large private network (firm 1) will act as in the previous situation when L was one. As before, the effects of an increase in the adapter's price R on sales of products A_1 and B_1 and on profits are

$$\partial(D^{11} + D^{12})/\partial R = \partial(D^{11} + D^{21})/\partial R = c + d + k(-b + e) \qquad (3.1)$$

$$\partial\pi^1/\partial R = (p_1 + q_1)[c + d + k(-b + e)] \qquad (3.2)$$

As in the previous case, for large $k > k_1$ (including $k = 1$), the private network with the demand advantage (firm 1) chooses compatibility because expression (3.2) is negative. However, for $k < k_1$ the large private network will choose incompatibility because the demand reward for compatibility is small (coming from the small demand for hybrids) and does not compensate it for the increase in competition.

The incentive for compatibility for the small private network (firm 2) is stronger because the difference between its single-producer demand and the demands for hybrids is smaller for the small private network (than for the large one). Remember that the demand for each of the hybrids is k times the demand for product A_1B_1, while the demand for product A_2B_2 is L times the demand for product A_1B_1 and both k and L are less than one. Thus there is a strong demand reward for firm 2 for a decision to minimize incompatibilities and it may compensate it for the increased competition even when firm 1 chooses differently.

The effect of an increase in the adapter's price R on the sales of products A_2 (and B_2) is

$$\partial(D^{22}+D^{21})/\partial R = \partial(D^{22}+D^{12})/\partial R = L(c+d)+k(-b+e) \tag{3.3}$$

The effect on profits of firm 2 is

$$\partial\pi^2/\partial R = (p_2+q_2)[L(c+d)+k(-b+e)] \tag{3.4}$$

Firm 2 will choose compatibility as long as $\partial\pi^2/\partial R<0$ or, equivalently,

$$k/L>(c+d)/(b-e)\equiv k_1 \tag{3.5}$$

Clearly, the resulting degree of compatibility depends on the relative size of k and L. Note that, since $L\leq1$, compatibility will be chosen by firm 2 whenever compatibility is chosen by firm 1, as well as in other cases. Figure 3.2 shows the regions of values of k and L that result in full compatibility, partial incompatibility, and total incompatibility. For $k>k_1$ (region A) both firms choose compatibility. For $L>k/k_1$ and $k<k_1$, region B, firm 2 chooses compatibility while firm 1 chooses incompatibility. For $L<k/k_1$, region C, both firms choose incompatibility. If the size of the demand within the small private network is equal to or smaller than the size of the demands for hybrid transactions—that is, if $L\leq k$, at least the small demand network chooses compatibility. In Figure 3.2, note that the line $L=k$ lies in regions A and B and never in region C, where both firms choose incompatibility.

Figure 3.2
Compatibility for Different Relative Demands for Hybrids

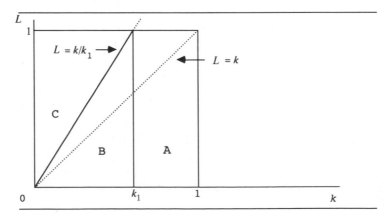

THEOREM 3: *Both firms choose compatibility when the demand for hybrids is large. For smaller demand for hybrids, both firms choose incompatibility provided that the demand for A_2B_2 is sufficiently high. If demand for hybrids is small and demand for A_2B_2 is sufficiently low, firm 2 chooses compatibility while firm 1 chooses incompatibility.*

The important message of Theorem 3 is that the worst case for compatibility is when the demand for hybrids is small. Small demands for hybrids tend to drive the market toward incompatibility. However, this drive is weakened when there is a disparity in the single-producer demand as well. Thus, compatibility tends to arise more often, and incompatibilities when they arise are smaller, when only one single-producer system has large demand. The individual incentives of firms to create a shared network are weak when the demand for services across components of different networks is weak. However, weak demand for services of one of the private networks tends to drive that particular network toward compatibility with the strong network. This desire is, in general, not reciprocated by the network with large demand.

BUNDLING OF SERVICES

Often, complementary services are "bundled" and offered at a discount if purchased together from the same firm. For example, a bank can offer free ATM service at its own ATMs. Bundling is, of course, an imperfect form of price discrimination. The bundled good is offered at a price that does not exceed the sum of the prices of its components when offered separately. Let good A_1B_1, the combined banking and ATM services of firm 1, be offered at price s_1 while separately these services are offered at q_1 and p_1 as before. For consumers to buy the bundled good rather than its individual components, it must be that $s_1 \leq p_1 + q_1$. Similarly, let good A_2B_2 be offered as a bundle at price s_2. Again it is required that $s_2 \leq p_2 + q_2$.[8] The hybrids still require adapters. Thus the cost of A_1B_2 is $p_1 + q_2 + R$ and the cost of A_2B_1 is $q_1 + p_2 + R$. See Table 3.2.

Table 3.2
Composite Goods and Corresponding Prices with "Mixed" Bundling

Composite Good	Price
A_1B_1	s_1
A_1B_2	$p_1 + q_2 + R$
A_2B_1	$q_1 + p_2 + R$
A_2B_2	s_2

The profits of firm 1 are

$$\pi^1 = s_1 D^{11} + p_1 D^{12} + q_1 D^{21}$$

Consider the incentive for compatibility in the case of symmetric demand above under Assumptions 1–3.

$$\partial \pi^1 / \partial R = s_1(c+d) + (p_1+q_1)(-b+e) \leq (p_1+q_1)(-b+c+d+e) < 0$$

The incentive for compatibility is stronger when bundling is allowed. Thus we have

COROLLARY 3: *Provided that the demand for transactions across the two private networks is equal in size to the demand for transactions within each private network, a private network that bundles within-the-private-network transactions (and sells them at a price below the sum of the prices of their components) will choose full compatibility.*

ASYMMETRIC ADAPTERS

So far it has been assumed that the same adapter is required to make systems $A_1 B_2$ and $A_2 B_1$ functional. It is possible, although unlikely, that different adapters are required for systems $A_1 B_2$ and $A_2 B_1$. Let them be of cost R_{12} and R_{21} respectively. The demand functions for the four composite goods are now

$$D^{11} = D^{11}(p_1+q_1, \, p_1+q_2+R_{12}, \, q_1+p_2+R_{21}, \, p_2+q_2)$$
$$D^{12} = D^{12}(p_1+q_2+R_{12}, \, p_1+q_1, \, p_2+q_2, \, p_2+q_1+R_{21})$$
$$D^{21} = D^{21}(p_2+q_1+R_{21}, \, p_2+q_2, \, p_1+q_1, \, p_1+q_2+R_{12})$$
$$D^{22} = D^{22}(p_2+q_2, \, p_2+q_1+R_{21}, \, p_1+q_2+R_{12}, \, p_1+q_1)$$

The effect of an increase in R_{12}, the cost of the adapter required for system $A_1 B_2$ on the profits of firm 1, is

$$\partial \pi^1 / \partial R_{12} = p_1(-b+c) + q_1(c+e)$$

Under conditions of symmetric substitution between ATM services and banking services—that is, $c=d$—and using the symmetry of demand system implied by Assumption 1, $p_1 = q_1$, I can write

$$\partial \pi^1 / \partial R_{12} = p_1(-b+c+d+e) < 0$$

which is negative by Assumption 2. All firms then choose full compatibility for all products (transactions). If the degree of substitutability between ATM services differs from the degree of substitutability between banking services, $c \neq d$, it is possible that a firm will decide to introduce incompatibilities for some transactions, as $d\pi^1/dR_{12}$ can be positive. However, note that it is impossible that a firm will desire to create incompatibilities for *both* products A_1B_2 and A_2B_1. This is because the effect on profits of an increase in both R_{12} and R_{21} is the same as the effect of an increase in R, the cost of the common adapter. It was established above that firms want to minimize R. Therefore, a firm cannot desire to maximize both R_{12} and R_{21}. If it decides to introduce some incompatibilities it will be only in one of the two hybrids.

SEQUENTIAL DECISIONS

Up to this point, the choices of design specifications (that imply the degree of compatibility) and prices were considered simultaneously. This means that the firms had the same degree of flexibility in varying prices and design specifications. This may be the case in some industries. In others, it may well be that design specifications are much less flexible in the short run than prices. Such a situation is best modelled as a game of two stages. In the first stage, firms choose design specifications and the degree of compatibility of their elementary goods is implied by them. In the second stage firms choose prices. The first stage is interpreted as the long run and the second stage as the short run. In choosing design specifications, firms anticipate the effects of their decisions on prices that are chosen later. To be precise, suppose that firms 1 and 2 have chosen x and y as their parts of the cost of the adapter. Then in the second stage, the equilibrium prices depend on x and y (the degree of compatibility) and therefore can be written as $p_1^*(x,y)$, $p_2^*(x,y)$, $q_1^*(x,y)$, $q_2^*(x,y)$. In the first stage, in choosing prices, firms anticipate the effects of their choices (x,y) on the equilibrium prices. Thus, the profit function of the first stage for firm 1 is

$$\pi^{1d}(x,y) = \pi^1(x, y, p_1^*(x,y), p_2^*(x,y), q_1^*(x,y), q_2^*(x,y)),$$

where the superscript "d" denotes the stage of choice of design specifications.

When firm 1 contemplates an increase in the part of the cost of the adapter it controls, x, there are two effects on profits. One is the direct effect, $\partial\pi^1/\partial x < 0$, which is the same as in the games of simultaneous choices that we have seen before in the section on the symmetric case. The second effect of changes in x is through prices. It is

$$\partial\pi^1/\partial p_1 \cdot \partial p_1^*/\partial x + \partial\pi^1/\partial q_1 \cdot \partial q_1^*/\partial x + \partial\pi^1/\partial p_2 \cdot \partial p_2^*/\partial x + \partial\pi^1/\partial q_2 \cdot \partial q_2^*/\partial x$$

The first two terms of this equation are zero from the profit maximization of the last stage. Thus it simplifies to

$$\partial \pi^1/\partial p_2 \cdot \partial p_2^*/\partial x + \partial \pi^1/\partial q_2 \cdot \partial q_2^*/\partial x \tag{3.6}$$

Thus, the difference between the simultaneous and the two-stage games in the individual firm's incentive to reduce the price of the adapter is proportional to the cross-price effect on profits, $\partial \pi^1/\partial p_2$, and to the influence of the price of the adapter on the opponent's price, $\partial p_2^*/\partial x$. For symmetric demand, it is shown in Economides (1989b) that the cross-price effects on profits are positive, $\partial \pi^1/\partial p_2 > 0$, $\partial \pi^1/\partial q_2 > 0$, and that an increase in the price of the adapter decreases the prices of the opponent, $\partial p_2^*/\partial x < 0$, $\partial q_2^*/\partial x < 0$. Therefore the second-stage effect described in equation (3.6) is negative. Firms have greater incentives to reduce the price of the adapter in a two-stage framework than in the simultaneous framework. For asymmetric demand, Economides (1989b) shows for a two-stage framework similar results to the ones in section 5.

CONCLUSION

This chapter has demonstrated that when the demand for transactions across private networks is as large as the demand for transactions within the private networks, each private network has an incentive to establish compatibility with other private networks and facilitate hybrid (across networks) transactions. However, when demand for transactions across networks is low, each private network chooses to be incompatible and to restrict access from outside. The result is maximum possible incompatibility of the two private networks. When the demand for transactions within only one of the two private networks is high, this network chooses to maximize incompatibilities, while the other private network desires compatibility. The result is partial incompatibility of the two private networks.

These results show the significance of the relative scale of the demand for transactions within and across private networks for the decision of compatibility and for the emergence of a shared network. The best scenario for the emergence of a shared network is one of equal demands for all four types of transactions, within each private network and across them. The worse scenario for the emergence of a shared network is when the demand for transactions across the private networks is small. However, the incentive for incompatibility is *weakened* when there is disparity in the demands for transactions within each private network as well. Incompatibilities will occur less often and will be smaller when the demand for transactions within one of the private networks significantly exceeds the demand for transactions within the other network than when the demands within private networks are equal.

NOTES

I thank Paul David for many helpful remarks and extensive discussion and the participants of the Annenberg Conference on Electronic Services Networks and of the Technology and Productivity Workshop at Stanford University for their helpful suggestions. Special thanks to co-editor Steve Wildman for extensive editorial suggestions.

1. In practice, there are more than two elementary goods in each cash withdrawal done through an ATM. Transactions are routed through a network switch that connects ATMs and banks.

2. Of course, the fact that latecomers have individual incentives to attach themselves to old specifications does not necessarily mean that these old specifications are the optimal in the advanced technological environment. For example, nearly all typewriters come with the QWERTY keyboard, so identified by the positioning of the keys in the upper left hand side. The positioning of the keys in the QWERTY keyboard was efficient at the time of its introduction. Since typewriters of the time jammed frequently, it was necessary to force typists to type more slowly. This was accomplished by the awkward positioning of keys in the QWERTY keyboard. Current models of typewriters can easily accommodate even the fastest typist. Although inefficient, the QWERTY keyboard is still virtually ubiquitous because of the large pool of typists that have been trained to use it and because of the keyboard retooling cost. See Paul David (1986, 1987).

3. The crucial assumption relevant to the discussion of this chapter is the assumption of equal demand for hybrids and single-producer goods. As seen in later sections of this chapter, the relaxation of this assumption can lead to equilibria of incompatible components and separate networks inaccessible from the outside.

4. Here it is assumed that firms do not offer discounts for their single-producer goods. The case when such discounts are offered is discussed under "bundling" in the sixth section.

5. There is nothing lost by the assumption of additive and non-negative contributions by each firm to the cost of the adapter. If technology is such that the incompatibility introduced by one firm can be wiped out by the opponent (so that one firm can force full compatibility), any equilibrium of the present model where at least one firm chooses compatibility will be mapped to a full compatibility equilibrium in the model of the new technology. If the technology is such that one firm can force total incompatibility, then any equilibrium of the present model where at least one firm chooses incompatibility will be mapped to a total incompatibility equilibrium.

6. If adapters were produced and sold by the component-producing firms the problem would revert to the standard problem of price discrimination.

7. This setup is equivalent to nonzero marginal costs with p_i and q_i interpreted as the differences of prices above marginal costs.

8. In the terminology of Adams and Yellen (1976), this is "mixed bundling" since the individual components are available as well as the bundle.

4

The Economics of Industry-Sponsored Search Facilitation

Steven S. Wildman

Consumers often find it to their advantage to seek information about the products of competing sellers before making a purchase. Products may vary in price and in quality, and differences in product features may be important too.

From a buyer's perspective, the full cost of a product includes the costs of prepurchase search and negotiation in addition to the price paid to the seller. As almost anyone who has purchased a house or an automobile can testify, the implicit cost of the search that precedes a sale may be substantial. Therefore, it is not surprising that markets have evolved a variety of mechanisms for reducing the costs of buyer search. Examples are industry-wide product standards and professional codes, competency certification exams, brand names, informational advertising, and the Yellow Pages sections of phone books. ("Let your fingers do the walking.") It is also not surprising, given the information-processing capabilities of the technology, that search facilitation is an important feature of many electronic services networks (ESNs). Multiple-listing services (MLSs) used by home-buyers to identify properties for personal inspection, the computer reservation systems (CRSs) most travel agents use to help their clients choose among the flights of different carriers, and the computer networks used in foreign currency markets to compare the bid and ask prices of different traders are examples.

There is an extensive literature on the economics of search (usually job search or consumer search). Very little work has been done, however, on the economics of search facilitation. This chapter builds on some of the fundamental findings of the search literature to develop an economic model of search facilitation appropriate for addressing issues raised by the use of ESNs to reduce buyers' search costs. However, the conclusions apply to industry-sponsored search facilitation generally. While the analyses presented in this chapter are the product of formal economic modelling, the critical insights concerning the nature of search facilitation that drive the argument are fairly straightforward and easily illustrated. Therefore, mindful of the diverse audience for this text, most of what follows is devoted to developing the appropriate intuition concerning search facilitation and the arguments that build on it. The chapter is organized as follows.

The next section examines two types of network search facilitation and their implications for prices in a monopolistically competitive industry when all firms participate in the network. There it is shown that search facilitation may raise or lower the competitive price. The welfare implications of search facilitation under these conditions are developed in the following section. There we show that if sellers sponsor the network, they may either underinvest or overinvest in the search capabilities of the network relative to the welfare optimum. Buyers always benefit from the network when sellers underinvest, but they may be made worse off if sellers have an incentive to overinvest. Buyers always benefit when they sponsor the network; however, both under- and overinvestment are still possible. We then look at the welfare implications of search facilitation when some sellers are excluded from a seller-sponsored network or granted access on discriminatory terms. We show that if search facilitation increases the competitive price, there may be circumstances in which buyers are better off if some sellers are not allowed to use the network, even if exclusion weakens them relative to sellers with access to the network. This suggests an exception to the essential facility argument that firms should be granted access to facilities controlled by other firms when exclusion makes them less competitive with firms that have access.

The chapter concludes with an example and a brief discussion of search facilitation by a monopolist supplier of differentiated products. The example demonstrates that monopolists may also have an incentive to subsidize buyer search because search facilitation increases the profit-maximizing price. Search facilitation may also make possible a profitable increase in product variety.

The formal modelling underlying the competitive market analysis is presented in the appendix to this chapter. Several results developed in the appendix, but not discussed in the main text of the chapter, will be of interest primarily to individuals who follow the economic literature on search. For example, it is demonstrated that Butters' (1977) proof that the competitive price is the monopoly price if consumers have incomplete information and firms supply no price information applies only to homogeneous product markets. Thus, at least for the case examined, product differentiation intensifies, rather than ameliorates, price competition, a finding counter to standard intuition dating back at least to Bain (1956).

SEARCH FACILITATION AND COMPETITIVE PRICES

In this section we examine the implications of two types of search facilitation for the pricing strategies of competitive firms when all firms participate in a search-facilitating network. We follow the bulk of the economic literature on search in assuming that consumers search by inspecting one-by-one the products of different sellers. When consumers search in this manner, an obvious approach to facilitating search, and one of the two we examine, is to develop technologies that make inspecting a product less costly. For example, sellers might file descriptions of their products in a computer database that buyers could access through network terminals. Consumers could then scroll through the listings or call up the names of specific sellers to read their products' descriptions. For products for which relatively complete descriptions can be provided in text, the costs of inspecting products on the network should be less than the costs of inspecting them by, say, phoning sellers for information or inspecting their wares in person.

We also examine the implications of using a network to screen, or sort, products before inspecting them. Most computer database services provide sorting algorithms as aids to search. For example, a real estate broker might use an MLS to search the list of all properties on the market and list only those that meet certain requirements, such as price range, location, and size, specified by her client. The client then personally inspects only the properties on the shorter list. Properties that do not meet the client's minimum specifications are rejected without inspection and the time and energy spent inspecting houses is concentrated on properties for which the odds of satisfying the client's preferences and budget are higher. Screening products before inspecting them improves the odds that products inspected will be satisfactory. We shall see, as we look into the matter, that these two types of search facilitation have very different implications for competitive pricing. We consider inspection cost reduction first.

We assume, as does most of the literature on search, that consumers employ a sequential search rule that maximizes the *expected* value of the utility of the product eventually purchased minus its price and the costs incurred searching. The search rule dictates that a consumer continue to inspect products until she finds one with a net utility (utility minus price) high enough that the expected increase in net utility from inspecting another product is less than the cost of search. The minimum net utility for which the expected payoff to additional search is not positive is called the reservation net utility.

The reservation net utility is an important parameter for characterizing the sequential search rule.[1] An important insight of the literature on search is that if search is costly, the reservation net utility is likely to be less than the net utility of the best option available in the market. Consumers are willing to settle for less than their ideal products because search is costly in terms of time, effort, and other resources, and there comes a point in the search process where the difference between the best product "out there" and the best observed so far is too small to make additional search worthwhile.[2] The reservation net utility rises if the cost of search falls, as intuition would suggest. That is, because consumers can "afford" to be pickier if the cost of inspecting products falls, a higher reservation net utility will have to be observed in a product inspected before the expected payoff to further search falls to zero.

These basic properties of sequential search are easily illustrated with a simple example. Consider a consumer who is searching for one unit of a product that comes in four variants—A, B, C, and D. A large number of nearby retailers carry the product, but each retailer carriers only one of the variants and the consumer must visit a store to determine which it carries. The consumer knows only that each of the variants is carried by one-quarter of the stores and that every store sells the product for $6. The consumer values A at $10, B at $9, C at $8, and D at $7. Net utilities then are $4, $3, $2, and $1, respectively.

Suppose that the consumer values the time and gasoline consumed in going to a store (any store) and inspecting its product at $1. According to the sequential search rule described above, this consumer should be satisfied and stop searching if she finds a store that carries C. Her net utility would improve by a dollar if the next store inspected carried B and would improve by $2 if it carried A, but each of these events has a probability of only 25 percent. Thus the expected gain from inspecting an additional store is $(.25 \times \$1) + (.25 \times \$2) = \$.75$. Since it costs $1 to inspect a store, the expected net gain of continuing to search after having found a store carrying C is $-\$.25$. The consumer would not be willing to buy a D because the expected gain from inspecting another seller's product would be $(.25 \times \$1) + (.25 \times \$2) + (.25 \times \$3) = \$1.50$, which exceeds the $1 search cost. Therefore, if the cost of search is $1, the reservation net utility is $2. This does not mean that the consumer will necessarily come home with product C. She may get lucky and walk into a store carrying B or A before she encounters a C. The rule just states that she will be satisfied buying a C if she observes it before a B or an A.

Similar calculations will show that if the cost of inspection falls to a value between $.25 and $.75 the reservation net utility will rise to $3. In other words, she will settle for nothing less than product B. If the inspection cost is less than $.25, the consumer will continue to search until finding a store selling A. Clearly, since the probability that a store carries A, B, or C is greater than the probability that it will carry A or B, which is greater than the probability that it will carry only A, the average number of inspections required to find an acceptable product will rise as the inspection costs fall. So both the reservation utility and the number of products inspected rise as search costs fall.

Now consider the effect on sellers of reducing the cost of inspecting a product. Searching consumers do not buy from every seller they inspect. Therefore, sellers are able to sell to only a fraction of the consumers that inspect their products. We have just seen that, on average, consumers will search more products before finding one deemed satisfactory if inspection costs fall. To a seller this means that the probability that any given consumer inspecting its product will buy it becomes smaller if search becomes less costly. In other words, the seller will see more consumers inspecting its product for each one that buys.

Consider, for example, a market with twenty firms that sell to 200 consumers entering the market each period. Each consumer buys one unit of the product and the norm has been for consumers to inspect an average of five products before making a purchase. If we assume sales are distributed evenly among sellers,[3] each would expect to sell to one fifth of the consumers that inspect its product. Each firm would sell to ten consumers each period, but would be inspected by fifty. Suppose that in response to a reduction in the cost of inspecting products, consumers become choosier and the average number of inspections required to find an acceptable product rises to ten. Each seller still sells ten units of its product each period because the number of buyers is still 200, but now it must deal with 100 consumers inspecting its product each period—ten searching consumers for every one that buys.

How does this affect a firm's incentive to change price? A consumer interested in net utility will be willing to accept less utility from a product she buys if she is compensated with a lower price. This means that a seller can increase the odds that its product will satisfy the reservation net utility requirement of any given consumer inspecting it by setting a lower price. Therefore, even if market demand is perfectly inelastic (total sales to all consumers are unaffected by changes in price), the demand for the product of any individual seller is somewhat elastic (price sensitive). If consumers learn the prices of different sellers (along with the other characteristics of their products) only through inspection, a product's price will have no effect on the number of consumers inspecting it. In this case, sellers will take the number of consumers inspecting their products as given and consider only the effect on a consumer's probability of purchasing its product in setting price.

If firms set prices in this manner, an increase in the ratio of searching consumers to sales following a reduction in consumer inspection costs creates an incentive for firms to reduce their prices. To see why, suppose that a $1 price reduction increases the probability that a consumer inspecting a seller's product will purchase it by 5 percent, at either the high (presearch facilitation) or the low (postsearch facilitation) inspection cost. That is, the probability of purchase would increase from 20 percent to 25 percent when the cost of inspection is high and from 10 percent to 15 percent after inspection costs have fallen. The 5 percent increase in the purchase probability translates to a 50 percent increase in sales (from 10 to 15) when 100 consumers are inspecting the product compared to a 25 percent increase (from 10 to 12 1/2) when 50 consumers inspect the product. Each seller's perceived payoff to cutting price is therefore much greater when inspection costs are lower and consumers search more. Therefore, under these circumstances, if firms do not collude, we would expect search facilitation to reduce the equilibrium price.

Of course, the assumption that the effect of a price decrease on the probability of purchase is unaffected by changes in the cost of inspecting products is critical to this result. This parameter could change in response to falling inspection costs as well. Both an increase in the price sensitivity of sales and a decrease are possible. If price sensitivity increased when inspection costs fell, it would further increase the incentive for a seller to reduce price; a reduction in price sensitivity would offset to some degree the incentive to reduce price in response to the larger number of consumers inspecting its product.

We have just seen that search facilitation that lowers the cost of inspection creates an incentive for firms to lower price due to the increase in the number of consumers inspecting each product and that this incentive to reduce price may be reinforced or mitigated by changes in consumers' sensitivity to price changes. Search facilitation that makes it easier for consumers to screen products prior to inspection has a very different effect on pricing incentives and the amount of consumer search. Preinspection screening creates a primary incentive for each firm to raise price that may be either reinforced or offset by changes in consumers' sensitivity to price changes. In addition, consumers inspect fewer products when they can screen them first.

The effects of screening on prices and consumer search are much easier to explain. When consumers screen the products in a market to narrow the list of candidates for inspection, they self-select in a way that facilitates interfirm price discrimination. Each consumer naturally screens products to compile a list to be searched composed of those most likely to suit her particular tastes. Screening does not alter per-firm sales; it merely reallocates buyers among products. However, if the screening mechanism is effective, each firm's product is inspected by consumers who value it more than they value most other products. This means they are willing to pay more than the average buyer who would inspect a firm's product without screening. The result, then, is an upward shift in the demand curve for each product. Firms respond by raising prices. This is illustrated in Figure 4.1.

Figure 4.1 depicts a hypothetical firm whose product is searched by two types of consumers, types 1 and 2, when consumers do not screen products prior to inspecting them. The firm sells a type 1 product. Its demand curve for

Figure 4.1
Demand Effects of Product Screening

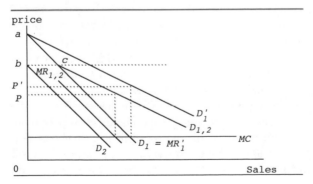

type 1 consumers is D_1, and its demand curve for type 2 consumers is D_2. D_1 lies above D_2 because type 1 consumers value the firm's product more than type 2 consumers. The relative positions of the type 1 and type 2 demand curves are the reverse of those depicted here for sellers of type 2 products. The line $D_{1,2}$ extending to the right and above D_1 from point c is the firm's joint demand curve for type 1 and type 2 consumers, which is the horizontal the sum of the demands of type 1 and type 2 consumers beginning at the price (b) at which type 2 consumers' demand for the firm's product becomes positive. The firm's profit-maximizing price, P, is determined by the intersection of its marginal cost curve (the horizontal line MC) with $MR_{1,2}$, the marginal revenue curve associated with $D_{1,2}$.

Now assume that consumers are able identify the sellers of type 1 and type 2 products by screening descriptions of their products on a network database and the effect for this firm is to replace all of the type 2 consumers that previously inspected its product with an equal number of type 1 consumers. In Figure 4.1, this is reflected in an upward shift of the firm's demand curve to $D_1{}'$. (a is the price intercept for both D_1 and $D_1{}'$ because $D_1{}'$ is created by adding more of the same type of consumers that make up D_1.) The firm responds by raising price to P'.[4]

An increase in price does not mean that consumers do not benefit from screening. Prices are higher, but most consumers find products they value more than those they would have selected without screening. The fact that consumers can avoid the costs of inspecting unacceptable products in the lower range of their net utility distributions also means that on average they have to inspect fewer products before finding one that is satisfactory. Therefore, screening reduces consumer search costs.

EFFECTS OF SEARCH FACILITATION ON EFFICIENCY AND CONSUMERS

In this section we examine the efficiency of investments in search-facilitating networks when consumer search can always be made more effective by increasing the investment in the search-facilitating technology. We want to know to what extent investors' incentives are compatible with maximizing the sum of buyer and seller benefits after the costs of search facilitation are netted out. Search facilitation can be sponsored by either sellers or buyers. We consider both, beginning with sellers. We also want to know the conditions under which consumers (buyers) benefit from seller investments in search facilitation. We begin by itemizing the benefits and costs of search facilitation.

At this point it is helpful to introduce a little notation. Define R to be the number of consumers that purchase the product in the market each period and let μ be the average utility consumers realize on the products they purchase. Let k be a consumer's expected total search cost, which is the number of products she expects to inspect before finding the one she buys times the per unit cost of inspection. Define m to be the per unit cost of producing the product, which we assume to be constant,[5] and let s be a representative firm's cost per sale of servicing all consumers that inspect its brand. Finally, let T be the industry's investment in the search-facilitating technology and define p to be the price of the product (assumed to be the same for all products).

We assume that market demand (but not the demands for individual firms) is perfectly inelastic, so we can ignore the complications of dealing with the effects of changes in aggregate market sales due to changes in price. This simplifies the analysis at the cost of little if any generality. Given this terminology, B, the total economic benefits generated by the industry can be represented as

$$B = R(\mu - k - m - s) - T \qquad (4.1)$$

The inelastic demand assumption means that any change in price merely changes the allocation of the benefits produced by the industry between consumers and firms without altering the total. For this reason, there is no price term in the benefits equation. In an ideal world, the value of T^* would be selected to maximize B.

If sellers sponsor the network, they will set T to maximize industry profits, Π. (We are ignoring complications that would arise if all sellers did not share equally in industry profits.)

$$\Pi = R(p - m - s) - T \qquad (4.2)$$

Equations (4.1) and (4.2) differ in that μ-k, the expected utility minus the expected cost of consumer search in (4.1), is replaced by price in (4.2). The inclusion of p in (4.2)—which is not a benefit or a cost from the social welfare perspective—reflects sellers' concerns with the revenue component of profits. k is not included in (4.2) because consumer search costs do not directly affect sellers' profits.

The difference between equations (4.1) and (4.2) is the key to determining whether sellers will set T at its welfare-maximizing level. A total benefits-maximizing social planner would continue to increase T as long as B also increased. Let T^* be the value of T that maximizes B. If at T^* the effect of increasing T on Π is negative, then profit-maximizing sellers will set T less than T^*. Since all other terms in equations (4.1) and (4.2) are the same, sellers will invest less than the amount required to maximize welfare if increasing T increases p by less than it increases μ-k. That is, T will be less than T^* if price increases by less than the increase in the expected value of utility net of search costs.

We know that both types of search facilitation increase μ. Intuitively, one would also expect both types of search facilitation to reduce k. This is shown to be the case in the appendix to this chapter. Therefore, consumer utility net of search costs always grows if the industry's investment in search facilitation is increased. Therefore, if search facilitation reduces price, profits increase by less than total benefits and sellers will underinvest in search facilitation relative to the welfare optimum. In fact, if search facilitation reduces price, sellers will not invest in search facilitation at all unless there is a commensurate reduction in the cost of servicing consumers. Sellers will under- or overinvest in search facilitation if prices rise, depending on whether prices increase by less or more than the increase in buyers' utility net of search costs, respectively.

If consumers (buyers) fund the network, they will set T to maximize N, the total net surplus realized by all buyers.

$$N = R(\mu - p - k) - T \tag{4.3}$$

The analysis of buyer incentives to invest in search facilitation parallels the seller analysis, so we will not develop it as fully. Equation (4.3) differs from equation (4.1) by the substitution of p for the sum of m and s. In general, m probably is not affected by search facilitation. Therefore, if search facilitation reduces p, buyers will overinvest in search facilitation if p would fall by more than would s (or if s would increase). Buyers will underinvest in search facilitation if p falls by less than s. If search facilitation raises price, sellers will capture some of the benefits of reduced buyer search costs and increased product satisfaction. In this case buyers will underinvest in search facilitation unless s increases by at least as much as p.

The fact that p has a positive sign in equation (4.2) and a negative sign in (4.3) reflects the different incentives of buyers and sellers in designing networks. Sellers naturally will want to facilitate search in such a way as to increase the competitive price while buyers will want to facilitate search in ways that reduce price. This also suggests that buyers may find it profitable to sponsor search facilitating networks when it would not be profitable for sellers and vice versa.

ACCESS DISCRIMINATION

Concerns with access denial and discrimination in the provision of network services are voiced repeatedly in the policy discussions of CRSs and MLSs, both ESNs that facilitate search. Complaints that firms controlling local networks have excluded competitors have predominated in MLSs, while the design of network search procedures to favor the flights of some airlines over others has been the primary concern with CRSs. More recently, there have been complaints that firms controlling networks that assist home-buyers with the tasks of selecting lenders and processing mortgage applications have biased network search procedures to favor the offerings of the networks' owners. In each case, the fear expressed is that firms controlling a network will be able to use their control over the terms of access to create two unequal classes of competitors and that the weakened state of firms unable to fully utilize the capabilities of the network will allow the favored firms to charge prices above the competitive level. In this section we extend the analysis of search facilitation to consider discriminatory terms of access. Since access denial is just the most extreme form of discrimination in the provision of network services to competitors and the qualitative nature of our conclusions would be the same in either case, we do not distinguish between them in the discussion that follows. Therefore, we simplify the discussion by assuming that access discrimination takes the form of access denial. Access discrimination poses a policy problem only if firms discriminated against cannot create an equally effective search-facilitating ESN for themselves. The following discussion assumes that this is the case.

It is easy to show that the pattern described above of firms controlling a search-facilitating network charging higher prices than the competitors they discriminate against is a likely outcome of access discrimination. Assume that firms using the network and firms excluded from the network charge the same price. If the network eases the burdens of search, then buyers will always inspect the products of firms using the network first and examine products not on the network only if none of the network's products prove satisfactory. Left to compete only for buyers who cannot find what they want on the network, the excluded firms will make fewer sales. To offset the advantage buyers see in network search facilitation and increase their sales, firms excluded from the network must lower price. In general, we would expect firms disadvantaged by discriminatory terms of access to be characterized by some combination of lower prices and lower sales than firms using the network.

While access discrimination does place the firms discriminated against at a competitive disadvantage likely to be reflected in some combination of lower prices or lower sales, it is not necessarily the case that mandated equal access will lead to greater economic efficiency or improve the lot of buyers. The model of network search facilitation developed above shows that even if all firms in a competitively structured market have equal access to a network, they may still raise price in response to changes in buyer behavior induced by the network's search-facilitating capabilities. This result also applies to a competitively structured segment of a market with preferential access to a network. In the latter case, the effect of mandatory access would be to increase the prices of formerly excluded firms without reducing the prices of firms already using the network, because all firms would now be responding to the same buyer search behavior when setting price.

We observed above that even if prices rise with search facilitation, buyers may still be better off if they value search assistance by more than the increase in price. However, it is also possible that prices will rise by more than the benefits of search facilitation to buyers. In this case, consumers and general welfare objectives may be better served if some firms are excluded from the network since the prices charged by excluded firms will limit the extent to which firms using the network can raise price. Mandating access in this situation would be harmful to buyers and to economic efficiency.

There are no obvious criteria for distinguishing between situations in which mandating access will promote economic efficiency and situations in which the consequences will be perverse. However, if the segment of an industry with access to a search-facilitating network is structured competitively, requiring that excluded firms be granted access is unlikely to improve the performance of the firms already using the network, while the prices of the excluded firms could rise if access were mandatory. The balance of potential costs and benefits would seem to favor the status quo in this situation.

SEARCH FACILITATION BY A MULTIPRODUCT MONOPOLIST

In this final section, we explore the reasons why a multiproduct monopolist selling products that are imperfect substitutes for each other might invest in a search-facilitating technology. Of course there would be no need to invest in search facilitation if consumers did not have to search to discover important differences among the monopolist's products, and we assume this is the case. More specifically, we assume that information communicated directly to consumers by the monopolist is an imperfect substitute for information consumers gather through search. The information acquired by test driving an automobile is an example.

The fact that consumer utility net of search costs rises with search facilitation provides the incentive for a monopolist to invest in a search-facilitating technology. Because there are no competing sellers, the monopolist can capture all of the consumer benefits of more efficient search by raising prices commensurately. For the same reason, consumers would never find it profitable to invest in search facilitation if all of the products searched were sold by a monopolist.[6]

As an example of a multiproduct monopolist's incentive to facilitate consumer search, consider the situation of the owner of a franchise to sell an exotic imported car. The car comes in two versions built on the same frame. One is a sports coupe and the other is a somewhat more sedate, but roomier, sedan. The dealer pays the same for each. Both potential buyers and the dealer know that most buyers end up valuing one version at $40,000 and the other at $38,000 after they have had a chance to inspect them carefully. However, without inspection, they have no way of knowing which they will like best. If they cannot inspect the cars (the dealer orders them in response to customer requests), risk-neutral buyers would be willing to pay at most $39,000 to pick one of them randomly since the expected value of the random pick is $.5 \times \$38,000 + .5 \times \$40,000 = \$39,000$. If the dealer can find a mechanism for allowing potential buyers to fully inspect both cars prior to purchase, she can raise the price of each to $40,000. Search facilitation is profitable if it can be accomplished for less than $1,000 a car. In this case, the search-facilitating technology might be demonstrator models of each car for customers to test drive.

A slight extension of this example suggests that search facilitation may also make it profitable for a monopolist to increase the number of products offered. Suppose that the car dealer could also import a third, hybrid version of the same car that buyers view as a compromise between the coupe and the sedan. The cost to the dealer is the same as for the other two cars. Suppose further that the hybrid is valued at $39,001 by all buyers. If buyers cannot inspect the cars, the dealer will sell only the hybrid because it is slightly more profitable than the other two. However, if the dealer can make it possible for buyers to inspect the two specialized models at a cost of less than $999 per car sold, the specialized models are more profitable.

APPENDIX: A MODEL OF NETWORK SEARCH FACILITATION

This appendix presents an economic model of industry-sponsored search facilitation that is used to examine the optimality of industry investments in search-facilitating technologies such as ESNs and to compare equilibrium prices and the cost of consumer search with and without industry-sponsored search assistance. The model assumes that the technology employed to facilitate consumer search does not facilitate conscious cooperation among the firms that sponsor it. Firms are assumed to behave as atomistic competitors with and without the network. Nevertheless, the model shows that prices may rise or fall in response to search facilitation. When search facilitation lowers prices, the industry will underinvest in the network's search-facilitating capabilities relative to the welfare-optimizing investment which would maximize the total of consumer and producer benefits. In fact, an industry may fail to develop a search-facilitating ESN because of the effect of falling prices on profits. An industry's investment in search facilitation may exceed or fall short of the welfare optimum when search assistance raises prices. Consumers are net beneficiaries of industry investments in search facilitation in those circumstances in which an industry's private incentives lead to a welfare-inefficient underinvestment. Conversely, consumers are net losers when an industry overinvests in the network.

Access discrimination is treated briefly in the last section of this appendix. There it is shown that in equilibrium firms unable to take full advantage of a network's search-facilitating capabilities will be characterized by lower prices and/or lower sales than firms fully utilizing the network. It is also shown that the argument that discriminatory access limits competition and harms consumers is not valid in all circumstances. Consumers may be worse off if all firms have access to a search-facilitating technology that causes prices to rise.

Competition With Search and Product Differentiation

We begin by modelling competition in a market in which consumers search among different variants, called brands, of a differentiated product. The market is served by n firms, each selling a different brand. Consumers differ in their preferences over the set of available brands. We assume symmetry in the distributions of consumer preferences and brand characteristics such that all consumers perceive the same distribution of utilities in the market, although any given brand is likely to be associated with different values in the utility distribution by different individuals. For example, consumers and brands both may be distributed uniformly around a circle, as in Salop (1979). If the functional relationship between a consumer's utility from a brand and her distance from it is the same for all consumers, and if consumers know that the distribution is uniform but do not know the locations of individual brands until they search for them, all consumers will perceive the same distribution of utilities in the brands available.

Consumers enter the market at rate R per period and each consumer purchases one unit of the product before exiting the market. A consumer inspects brands randomly at the rate of one per period and purchases the first one encountered that satisfies the optimal stopping rule described below. Let p_i be the price of brand i and let b_i be the probability that a consumer inspecting brand i will buy it. We are considering symmetric equilibria only. Therefore, in equilibrium $p_i = p$ and $b_i = b$, all i, where p and b are the market averages for these variables. A probability of b that any given brand inspected will be satisfactory means that on average consumers search $1/b$ brands before buying and leaving the market and that each brand is inspected by r/b consumers per period on average, where $r = R/n$.[7]

We assume that the per-unit variable cost to a firm of producing or procuring each unit it sells is constant at zero. However, each firm incurs a positive cost of s for each consumer that inspects its brand. In other words, all the costs of servicing customers are incurred in the process of displaying and/or pitching the product to the consumer. Any additional costs of closing a sale with a customer that decides to buy are subsumed in the marginal cost, which we have set at zero. Thus, per period profits for firm i are

$$\pi_i = p_i b_i r/b - sr/b$$

The range of utilities associated with brands in the market is bounded from below by zero and bounded from above by u^* and distributed according to c.d.f. $F(\cdot)$. Initially we assume that a consumer enters the market knowing the common equilibrium price and the distribution of utilities, but has no knowledge of how much she will value any specific brand prior to inspecting it. Similarly, firms know the general distribution of consumers' preferences over brands, but a firm has no knowledge of the utility of its brand to a consumer inspecting it until the consumer inspects its brand and makes a buy/no-buy decision. Given symmetry, this means that for any given brand the distribution of its utility over consumers is the same as the distribution of utilities over brands for consumers.

Let $u_{i,h}$ be the utility of brand i to a consumer h who has just inspected brand i. Since all firms charge a common price, for h the expected gain from searching an additional brand over the utility offered by brand i is

$$g = \int_{u_{i,h}}^{u^*} (u - u_{i,h}) dF(u)$$

Consumers incur a search cost of c per brand searched. Lippman and McCall (1976) show that the optimal search strategy in the sense of maximizing the expected difference between the utility of the brand purchased and total search costs is for the consumer to continue inspecting new brands until she finds one offering utility of v or greater, where v is determined implicitly by (4.1.A).

$$c = \int_{v}^{u^*} (u-v) dF(u) \qquad (4.1.A)$$

v constitutes a reservation level of utility in that it is the minimum utility that consumers will accept in a brand priced at p. Since $F(v)$ is the probability that a consumer inspecting a randomly selected brand will reject it and continue to search, $b = 1 - F(v) = b(c)$. dv/dc clearly is negative; therefore $db/dc > 0$. Note that as a consequence of symmetry, the equilibrium value of b is independent of the equilibrium value of p. That is, given F, the equilibrium values of v and b are determined completely by c.

Firms are Nash competitors in price. Since consumers must inspect brands to learn of deviations in individual brands' prices from the value of p they expect to prevail, the demand curve for an individual brand is downward sloping, but more elastic than the perfectly inelastic market demand curve. To see this, let v_i be the reservation utility for brand i. A consumer inspecting brand i will purchase it as long as it offers a utility net of price of at least $v-p$, which is the utility net of price expected from a brand yet to be searched that provides the reservation level of utility. Therefore, $v_i = v - p + p_i$. v_i varies linearly with p_i. Since $b_i = 1 - F(v_i)$ and $F > 0$, $\partial b_i / \partial p_i < 0$. So the number of consumers sampling brand i who buy it is also a decreasing function of price.

Assuming n is large enough such that b is not materially affected by small changes in b_i, the first-order condition for firm i is

$$b_i r / b + p_i r / b \cdot \partial b_i / \partial p_i = 0$$

Since $b_i = b$ in equilibrium, this reduces to

$$r(1 + p_i/b \cdot \partial b_i/\partial p_i) = 0 \qquad\qquad\qquad (4.2A)$$

The second term within the parentheses in (4.2.A) is the elasticity of b_i with respect to p_i, which is equal to the price elasticity of demand for brand i since sales of brand i vary proportionally with b_i given that the rate at which consumers sample the brand is constant. So (4.2.A) is just the usual elasticity form of a firm's first-order condition expressed in terms of purchase probabilities for a market in which consumers search sequentially.

(4.1.A) and (4.2.A) jointly determine the equilibrium values of p and b. Several properties of this equilibrium are worth noting. First, granted that the number of firms is sufficient to warrant the assumption that the distinction between sampling with replacement and sampling without replacement is unimportant for the purposes of this analysis, the number of firms has no effect on the equilibrium values of p and b. In this sense, the market is similar to a perfectly competitive market with constant returns to scale. This is also consistent with Lopatka and Simons' observation in chapter 10 of this book that a 6 percent broker commission is fairly standard across real estate MLSs, which may vary considerably in the number of brokers that belong.

Second, a point already noted, because $p_i = p$ in equilibrium, the equilibrium value of b is unaffected by changes in p. That is, as long as all brands sell for the same price, variation in that price will have no effect on what consumers regard to be a minimally acceptable level of quality or the average number of brands searched before making a purchase.

Finally, from (4.2.A) we know that the equilibrium price is too low to maximize the industry's collective profits. This reflects the sensitivity of b_i (although not b) to p_i. While market demand is inelastic up to the choke price, firms set price according to their own more elastic demand curves. Aside from the policy implications of the fact that sellers do not capture all of the surplus, this finding is noteworthy because it contrasts with the well-known result from the early work on imperfect information and search that the equilibrium price will be the monopoly price (in this case the choke price) when the product is homogeneous and consumers search for the lowest price (Butters, 1977). The logic behind this result is that the firm with the lowest price can always raise its price by an amount less than the cost of search without losing customers. However, the end result of all firms consistently applying this strategy is an escalation in prices until the choke price is reached. Therefore, the argument, dating back at least to Bain (1956), that product differentiation may insulate firms from price competition does not apply in the search environment examined here. Precisely the opposite is true.

Competition and Search Facilitation

We use this model to examine the implications of two ways in which an ESN may be used to facilitate consumer search. One option is for the firms sponsoring the ESN to design it to reduce the per-unit search cost to consumers. In terms of the model, c is lower if search is conducted with the ESN than without it.

The alternative is an ESN that allows consumers to sort available brands on the basis of information in a computer database and eliminate as candidates for further inspection brands that fail to satisfy certain criteria specified by the consumer. This use of the ESN allows consumers to limit search to a subpopulation of brands for which the probabilities of being acceptable are higher than for brands selected randomly from the general population. In other words, a consumer may use the second type of ESN to first screen out brands in the lower portion of her utility distribution and then inspect brands in the upper region. A real estate MLS works this way. Potential home buyers use the MLS to sort through all the entries on a multilist and screen out houses that likely would not be acceptable on the basis of characteristics such as price, location, and size. They then personally inspect houses from a shorter list of prospects more likely to be acceptable. In terms of the model, c is not affected but search is restricted to a range of utilities that excludes some lower portion of the utility distribution. Of course, an ESN may facilitate consumer search in both ways. We will focus primarily on ESNs that either reduce per-unit search costs or restrict the range of utilities searched to highlight the different implications of the two types of search facilitation for the incentives of firms to jointly invest in an ESN and the effects on price and profits.

Consider first the effects of search facilitation on price. From (4.2.A) we have $p/b \cdot \partial b_i/\partial p_i = -1$. p may change in response to changes in b or in response to changes in the partial of b_i with respect to p_i. For the moment we will assume that $\partial b_i/\partial p_i$ is constant to focus on the effects of the two types of search facilitation on b. From (4.1.A) we know $db/dc > 0$. Therefore, if an ESN reduces per unit search costs, equilibrium price will fall in proportion to the reduction in c.

Since market demand is perfectly inelastic, revenues for firms and the industry as a whole will both fall. Therefore, unless the ESN produces a considerably more-than-proportional reduction in s, profits will fall by more than revenues because consumers become pickier when c falls and, on average, will search more brands before making a purchase. This increases the number of searching consumers each firm must service without affecting sales. In addition, each firm will bear its proportionate share of the costs of the ESN.

Search facilitation reduces b and increases the equilibrium price (assuming $\partial b_i/\partial p_i$ constant) if it enables consumers to restrict search to a subsample of higher utility brands. Wildman (1989) shows that v increases when search is restricted to a subsample of brands that excludes brands from the lower range of the utility distribution. This is similar to the effect of reducing c. However, the lower bound of the utility distribution searched by consumers increases faster than v and at some point overtakes it, which means that b increases toward unity as the lower bound on utilities searched rises. At this point, the cost of search equals the expected gain and consumers stop searching. For the present analysis with $\partial b_i/\partial p_i$ constant, this means that p will increase in proportion to the increase in b, but, because the lower bound of the searched utility distribution increases so much faster than v, the average number of searches required to find an acceptable brand falls. Thus firms service fewer searching consumers for each sale generated. Both the increase in b and the reduction in the search to purchase ratio increase the profits of the firms sponsoring the ESN.

Without specific knowledge of the shape of $F(\cdot)$ it is impossible to predict just how $\partial b_i/\partial p_i$ will change in response to changes in the cost of search or changes in the lower bound of utilities searched. For example, if consumers and brands were uniformly distributed in product space, the shape of the utility distribution would be determined by the functional relationship between utility and a consumer's distance from a brand. Given the range of variation possible in this relationship, positive and negative changes in $\partial b_i/\partial p_i$ are plausible, and both are permitted by the second-order condition for profit maximization.

Given the indeterminacy of the effect of search facilitation on $\partial b_i/\partial p_i$, the effect on price must also be considered indeterminate. At best we can say that the effects on b predispose ESNs that reduce per-unit search costs to lowering price and predispose ESNs that screen out brands likely to be in a lower range of the utility distribution to raising price.

Welfare Implications

While the failure of this analysis to provide an unambiguous prediction for the effects on price of the two different types of search facilitation is disappointing, we show below that for purposes of welfare analysis it is much more important to know which direction prices move than why. Thus, price histories may provide useful information to the policymaker.

We consider first the efficiency of investments in search-facilitating technology. Let μ be the equilibrium value of the average utility realized by consumers from the brands they purchase. Since on average consumers search $1/b$ brands before buying one, average search costs per sale are c/b. $\mu - c/b$ is the average consumer's benefits from the product after search costs are netted out. Recall that v is the equilibrium reservation utility. Lippman and McCall (1976) prove that $\mu - c/b = v$. Let T designate an industry's investment in search-facilitating technology and designate the total social benefits produced by the industry by B. Then

$$B = R(v - K) - T$$

where $K = s/b$ is the average cost per sale to firms of servicing consumers that search their brands. Industry profits, Π, are

$$\Pi = R(p - K) - T$$

Assuming that T is variable and larger values of T provide consumers with more search assistance, equations (4.3.A) and (4.4.A) are the first-order condition for maximizing social benefits and industry profits with respect to T, respectively.

$$R(dv/dT - dK/dT) = -1 \qquad\qquad\qquad (4.3.A)$$

$$R(dp/dT - dK/dT) = -1 \qquad\qquad\qquad (4.4.A)$$

We already know that both types of search facilitation increase v. Therefore, $dv/dT > 0$. That is, price effects aside, consumers benefit from both types of search facilitation. This is because on average they select brands better matched to their preferences. The industry will set T at less than its socially optimum value if $dv/dT > dp/dT$ when (4.4.A) is satisfied. This means that the industry will always invest too little in the search-facilitating capabilities of the network if search facilitation reduces or leaves unchanged the equilibrium price. In fact, if price falls, service costs per sale must fall by an even larger amount for the industry to profit directly from an investment in search-facilitating technology. Consumers always benefit from a search-facilitating network in this situation; because utility net of search costs rises faster than price.

The industry will invest more than the socially optimal amount in search facilitation if $dv/dT < dp/dT$ when (4.3.A) is satisfied. Furthermore, if this relationship holds throughout the relevant range of T, the network will effectively transfer surplus from consumers to firms as prices rise by more than consumer benefits net of search costs.

While the industry will set T at its welfare maximizing level if (4.3.A) and (4.4.A) are satisfied simultaneously, this may do consumers no good at all since increases in utility net of search costs are matched exactly by higher prices if $dv/dT = dp/dT$. In this situation all of the benefits of a search-facilitating ESN are captured by the industry. This means that consumers benefit from an industry-sponsored ESN only when conditions are such that the industry's incentive is to invest too little in the technology for social efficiency. Furthermore, if the industry understands how the different types of search assistance affect price, it has an incentive to design ESN services so that price will increase by more than consumer benefits if possible.

To this point we have assumed that a search-facilitating ESN is provided collectively by the firms in an industry. The fact that consumers appear to benefit most when firms in the industry benefit least suggests that it is in these situations that ESNs are more likely to be sponsored by buyers or agents acting on behalf of buyers. Of course, the industry may respond to the threat of a buyer-sponsored ESN with a preemptive ESN of its own which would transfer fewer benefits to consumers, but enough that the incremental benefits of a consumer-sponsored ESN would not justify its cost.

Discrimination and Denial of Access

This section extends the model to consider some of the effects of discrimination against competitors in the provision of network services. Access denial is not examined separately since it is just the most severe form of discrimination. To do this we compare the consumer search rule for two mutually exclusive but jointly all inclusive sub-populations of the brands in the industry. From a consumer's perspective, the distribution of utilities is the same for both subpopulations, but network search facilitation is more effective for subpopulation 1 than for subpopulation 2. (In the extreme subpopulation 2 brands may be excluded from the network.) It is fairly straightforward to prove that if prices are the same for the two subpopulations, subpopulation 1 brands will have greater sales than subpopulation 2 brands. It is also easy to show that if average sales are the same for brands in the two subpopulations, brands in subpopulation 1 will sell at a premium over brands in subpopulation 2.

To prove these propositions it is convenient to restate the consumer search rule in terms of utilities net of price for both subpopulations. Let q_1 and q_2 be the equilibrium prices for subpopulations 1 and 2 respectively, let u_1 and u_2 be a randomly selected consumer's utilities for two brands drawn from these populations, and define $z_1 = u_1 - p_1$ and $z_2 = u_2 - p_2$. z_1 and z_2 are utilities net of price. Finally, let w_1 and w_2 be the equilibrium reservation net utilities and let v_1 and v_2 be the equilibrium values of the reservation utilities (gross of price) for the two subpopulations. $w_1 = v_1 - p_1$ and $w_2 = v_2 - p_2$.

Assume first that $p_1 = p_2$. We showed above that reservation utilities increase with search facilitation and that if all brands sell at the same price, the reservation utility is independent of price. However, search facilitation is more effective for subpopulation 1 brands. Therefore, $v_1 > v_2$. Weitzman (1979) proved that consumers faced with a choice of two or more distributions to search for a single purchase would do best by searching first the distribution characterized by the highest reservation utility, and if failing to find a satisfactory choice, search second the distribution with the second highest reservation utility, and so on. For our two subpopulations of brands, this means that if they are priced the same, consumers will search all subpopulation 1 brands first and only search subpopulation 2 brands if none of the subpopulation 1 brands proves to be satisfactory. Since the distribution of consumer utilities is the same for the two subpopulations, subpopulation 1 brands will have more sales.

Assume instead that subpopulation 2 brands are priced to ensure that they will be searched by as many consumers as brands in subpopulation 1. That is, $w_1 = w_2$. Since $v_1 > v_2$, this implies $p_1 > p_2$. This relationship is consistent with complaints by some users of the PRODIGY network service marketed to consumers by Sears and IBM that consumer goods are priced higher on the network than in the stores. Clearly, if the difference between p_1 and p_2 is positive but less than the difference at which brands from the two subpopulations have equal sales, subpopulation 2 brands will have lower sales and lower prices than subpopulation 1 brands.

How are economic efficiency and consumer welfare affected by discrimination? In this static model with known technologies there appears to be no welfare justification for discrimination when search facilitation lowers price. Firms favored by a discriminatory network policy may increase their profits by capturing customers from firms discriminated against. But this is merely a transfer among firms and does not increase the ability of the industry as a whole to finance the network. Discrimination against competitors when search facilitation lowers price would also seem to exacerbate the tendency to underinvest in the network since the benefits of reduced costs of servicing consumers would apply to a smaller customer base.

If network search facilitation raises price, consumers may benefit if discrimination puts some firms at a disadvantage in terms of search facilitation. Firms favored by discriminatory practices will not be able to raise their prices beyond the point at which their brands' expected utilities net of price and search costs fall below those of the brands discriminated against. In fact, as long as the brands of firms excluded from an ESN are a viable alternative to brands serviced by the network, competition from the excluded firms ensures that network search facilitation will not make consumers worse off. This possibility should temper enthusiasm for granting essential facility status in response to complaints of unfair terms of access to a network. Consumers may be better served by a competitor "weakened" by unfair access restrictions than by one invigorated by admission to the network.

NOTES

This research was funded by a grant from the Ameritech Foundation.

1. If products differed only in price, the search rule would be characterized by a reservation price.

2. See Lippman and McCall (1976) for an extensive treatment of sequential search rules.

3. This symmetry assumption is specified more completely in the appendix. Roughly this means that each seller's product is preferred by an equal number of consumers. We employ this assumption for the convenience of being able to conduct the analysis in terms of a representative seller.

4. This assumes that the sensitivity of consumers to price changes is not affected by screening. An increase in price sensitivity and a decrease in price sensitivity as a result of screening are both possible. The former effect would work in opposition to the effect of the upward shift in the demand curve on price depicted here, while the latter would reinforce the primary effect of the shift in the demand curve on price.

5. We are ignoring fixed production costs because they play no role in this argument.

6. The fact that the monopolist captures all of the consumer benefits of search facilitation means that her incentives should lead to the welfare-appropriate investment in the technology.

7. $1/b$ and r/b must be considered close approximations to the actual average number of searches per consumer and the average number of consumers searching a brand each period. An infinite number of brands would be required for these formulas to hold exactly, since both are derived by summing an infinite series of increasingly small probabilities associated with progressively larger numbers of unsuccessful searches for a single consumer. Since the probability of x consecutive unsuccessful searches is a geometrically diminishing function of x, the weight of very large numbers of searches in the average is not perceptible. Here n is assumed to be large enough that $1/b$ can be used as a reasonable approximation to the true average number of brands searched per consumer.

5

The Economics of Cooperation and Competition in Electronic Services Network Industries

Dennis W. Carlton

Technological improvements in information transmission and processing have led to the emergence and growth of networks in which information can be electronically transmitted among network users at numerous locations. These networks are called electronic services networks (ESNs) and their growth has already had profound effects on the organization of the affected industries. Their growth has created a policy dilemma because networks raise problems that economists traditionally have difficulty grappling with. Unlike many industries, atomistic competition just does not work well in network industries. Some cooperation among competitors may be essential for efficiency in a network but such cooperation is precisely opposite to the way economists usually think about generating efficient behavior. The logical underpinnings of antitrust law are based on the economist's belief in the desirability of competition. Applying traditional antitrust concepts to network industries creates the potential for endless litigation and confusion. I think it no accident that several ESNs such as computer reservation systems (CRSs) used by airlines have already been the subject of complicated litigation.

Some ESNs enable users not only to access data but also to interact and complete transactions. For example, a travel agent can use a CRS to obtain an airline ticket for a passenger or a consumer can use an automated teller machine (ATM) to withdraw cash from a bank account. Such ESNs create "a market" and the economics of such ESNs are therefore related to the economics of "making markets," a subject that economists have begun to understand only recently.

Many of the special economic characteristics associated with ESNs arise in other network and non-network industries. Railroads provide a particularly good example and also provide historical data which can be used as a guide to how ESNs may develop. I will sometimes draw on these non-ESN industries to provide insight into the operation of ESNs.

This paper explains the trade-off between competition and efficiency in ESNs. It draws heavily from my earlier paper (Carlton and Klamer, 1983) and extends that earlier analysis to ESNs. I first discuss why some cooperation may be essential in an ESN and why competition may not lead to efficiency. I next describe the competitive problems that can arise in ESNs. Finally, I discuss the property rights in an ESN and the role of ESNs in facilitating transactions and how that role should affect our understanding of ESNs.

WHY NETWORKS MAY REQUIRE EXPLICIT COOPERATION FOR EFFICIENCY

Compatibility Affects Network Operation

If several firms participate in an ESN, then explicit cooperation is often necessary to assure that equipment and operating procedures are compatible across the different firms. Imagine a simple telecommunications network which is operated by three firms—A, B, and C—each of which controls part of the network. Firms A, B, and C must cooperate in order to make the network work. For example A, B, and C must use equipment that is compatible and must agree on a set of protocols to enable communication to occur. Especially if the equipment and protocols are complicated, it is difficult to imagine how reliance on a decentralized price system could achieve this coordination. Explicit cooperation is needed.

Sometimes the choice of compatible equipment will require the purchase of specialized assets. Because firms A, B, and C must coordinate in order for the network to work, their willingness to invest in specialized equipment will depend on their expectation of the future success of the network. This future success will depend upon the continued cooperation of the network participants. As Williamson (1975) has explained, contractual difficulties are likely to be greatest when firms invest in specialized assets. For example, firm A could demand higher payments from firm B just after firm B purchased a specialized piece of equipment, and firm B may choose to pay rather than face the risk that its equipment would sit idle because of A's refusal to transfer calls to B. In such a setting, Williamson (1975) has shown that there are strong incentives for firms A and B to consolidate into one firm. Whether assets are specialized will, of course, depend upon the particular type of network.

Compatibility Affects Network Development

The close cooperation often required for successful network operation also affects the incentives for network development and R&D. Why should one firm spend money on a service enhancement if the value of that service enhancement depends on the willingness of the other members of the network to accommodate the innovation? The successful innovator could be subject to opportunistic behavior by the other members of the network and be deprived of a profitable return.

When industries are rapidly evolving technologically, the cooperation needed to insure that firm A's latest equipment works with firm B's may be especially difficult to achieve if A and B are separate firms. For example, firm A may have the capability to install a fancy telephone telecommunications switch that allows it to keep track of the address of the caller and display that information to the called party. If firm B doesn't have compatibility with this service enhancement, then calls forwarded from firm B's territory will be unable to take advantage of this enhancement and the value of firm A's machine is reduced. This decrease in the value of A's machine could dissuade firm A from introducing it. Again, these problems of coordination can be solved by consolidation of firm A and B into one firm.

Standard-Setting Can Help Achieve Coordination

Standard-setting is one way to deal with the need to assure compatibility among firms. Indeed, even in an atomistic industry like steel scrap, there are certain types of grades for the product that are uniform nationally. These standards for grades are set by the industry members. Standard-setting is routine for most industries and is facilitated by the American National Standard Institute, an organization composed of trade and consumer groups that develop voluntary industry standards. However, standard-setting among independent firms works best in an industry that is not evolving rapidly technologically. Whether or not an industry is a network, technological change makes standardization difficult to achieve and subject to strategic manipulation. Standardization can retard technological change.

An example from a mature network industry illustrates the difficulty of using voluntary standards to achieve compatibility among independent firms. During the last half of the 1800s, railroads were developing new technologies—both in operating procedures and equipment. There initially were physical incompatibilities among neighboring railroads (one car couldn't ride on another's tracks, necessitating loading and reloading to ship cargo across two rail lines) and operating incompatibilities, such as failure to agree on what time it was (before 1883 there was no time standard) and failure to agree to accept another rail's billing (description of cargo). As rail lines became bigger through consolidations and came under one management, coordination and productivity improved. These larger rail systems were eventually able to achieve coordination amongst themselves. Today, the rail industry has a relatively mature technology and seems able to achieve coordination on physical and operating standards. However, if one looks at one recent area of technological improvement in railroading—development of piggyback shipping platforms—one sees that many of the railroads have not relied upon voluntary cooperation among independent railroads but have instead formed a joint venture, Trailer Train, to bear responsibility for coordinating the development of the new technology. Standard-setting among independent firms and technological change do not go well together.

Many ESNs operate in an environment of rapidly improving computer and telecommunications technology. In such a setting, I am skeptical of several independent firms coordinating voluntarily to introduce efficient standards. However, any attempt to legislate standards in such industries could retard technological change. I should hasten to add that economists cannot say that uncoordinated development of standards and technology will necessarily lead to efficient standard setting. (See, e.g., Farrell and Saloner, 1985; and Katz and Shapiro, 1985, 1986.) Strategic behavior designed to disadvantage rivals could occur. On the other hand, it seems unwise public policy to force cooperation when there is no evidence of its superiority over unregulated behavior.

Why Prices Alone Cannot Achieve Efficiency

Economists are trained to rely on prices as the primary way to achieve coordination among independent firms. Prices work best as a coordination device when there are no unpriced externalities among firms—that is, only when each firm bears the full cost of its actions when it affects another firm's costs. Networks have extensive externalities by their very nature.

The crux of the problem of efficient network operation is that each firm's performance in the network can affect other firms' costs and each firm's performance can affect the performance of the entire network. For example, if the transmission link between firms A and B is operating poorly, transmission can be routed from A to C to B. This could cause congestion on these links and make it more difficult for B and C to communicate.

Suppose that assets are not specialized and that there is no disagreement about standards: Can the price system be relied upon to achieve the requisite amount of cooperation and make firms bear the full costs of their actions? In many cases, the answer is no. Let me explain.

A network can be regarded as a multiproduct industry. For example, a telecommunications network that produces a link between points D and E and between E and F can provide a link between points D and F. If two separate firms own each of the two elements of the network, they must figure out what price to charge for use of their link. This is a complicated problem for several reasons.

First, marginal cost is near zero in many ESNs for much of the time, except for congestion charges. Setting up a pricing system based on congestion charges is often difficult. But if price fails to equal marginal cost, inefficient network operation could result.

Second, many ESN networks provide information as one of their products. It is well known that the pricing system does not necessarily do a good job at allocating resources devoted to information. Information has aspects of a public good whose marginal cost is zero. Moreover, as discussed more fully below, there frequently can be difficulty in ESNs in appropriating property rights in information.

Third, within a network it can be enormously complicated to figure out the correct shadow price for use of one link. Technically, a complicated nonlinear programming problem is involved. It is my understanding that in network industries like telecommunications and airlines, the relevant network problems cannot be completely solved with today's technology. Moreover, there is an important theoretical result, due to Koopmans and Beckmann (1957), that states that use of uniform decentralized pricing by link may not be sufficient to sustain optimal network operation. That is, there may be no system of decentralized prices by link that allows the price system to achieve incentives for optimal network operation. Indeed, in two network industries that I am aware of, optimal network operation is solved by having a single network operator (which may be owned by participating firms). For example, in New England, electric utilities have formed the New England Power Pool, which decides how to run the network. Similarly, in railroading, a joint venture, the previously mentioned Trailer Train, is responsible for the routing of piggy-back cars through much of the U.S. railroad network. In railroading, previous attempts to achieve efficient routing of cars have typically failed unless a single agent has ownership and control of the cars. Apparently, it is too costly to use prices as the sole coordinating device to induce independent firms to provide the optimal routing of cars.

Even if it were theoretically possible to use a decentralized price system to allocate resources efficiently, it may be administratively impractical to do so. If price is not continuously varying so as to equal marginal cost, but is instead set at average cost, then in many ESNs, price will often exceed marginal cost. This creates an incentive for a firm to want business over its link in the network whether or not it is efficient for the network as a whole. In fact, it's easy to see that competing firms that own less-desirable links could also profitably serve a customer. For example, suppose a telephone call can go between points A and B directly, or between A and C and C to B. The indirect route is longer and has higher marginal cost than the direct route. Suppose that the direct route and indirect route are owned by two separate firms. If the price of sending a message from A to B is above marginal cost, it may well be profitable for the firm owning the indirect route to also send the message, even though it is the inefficient route. In short, because it is hard to have marginal cost pricing in a network, any practical pricing scheme will typically differ from marginal cost pricing and thereby create inefficiencies in the operation of the network. Indeed, if the indirect route did not exist, a firm might even find it profitable to build the indirect route. Inefficient incentives to expand the network therefore exist when pricing is not at marginal cost, as seems likely.

An example of network development and expansion in ESNs relates to where "intelligence" is built into networks. Many of the ESNs have intelligence built into them. That is, the networks are capable of performing certain functions with data. This raises two concerns. First, as already discussed, the software used by the firms in the network and their operating procedures must be compatible. For example, if every data transmission from firm A has a particular identifier in the second field, then firm B better know this. There recently was considerable concern over whether IBM would reveal information about the operation of its data transmission (System Network Architecture (SNA)) so that other firms could efficiently function in an IBM network.

Second, the place where the intelligence is built into the network is important. The intelligence could be added by firm A or by firm B or by some third firm that can provide some attachment to either firm A's or B's equipment. Coordination to introduce the service enhancement in the most efficient way is needed to avoid costly duplication, and in light of the Koopmans-Beckmann result, it is not at all clear that price incentives can achieve the efficient result especially if price does not equal marginal cost.

In summary, there are a variety of reasons to expect that network industries are more likely to require a higher degree of explicit coordination than non-network industries to achieve efficiency. Prices are not likely to be able to induce the optimal coordination. Integration of the firms into one or several large units is predicted.

THE COMPETITIVE CONFLICT

Explicit cooperation among firms in a network creates a potential competitive problem because the firms may also compete with each other. For example, in a telecommunications network, direct routes compete with indirect routes and different firms can own the competing routes. Firms may find themselves direct competitors in one part of the network but partners in another in trying to serve customers. Aside from direct competition, there are more subtle ways firms can compete with each other such as through the development of new products. Cooperation among firms raises the possibility that competition will be diminished and consumers will be forced to pay high prices or forgo technological improvements. The policy dilemma is clear and there is no simple way, in general, to resolve the tension between cooperation for efficiency and suppression of competition.[1]

Networks can be thought of as a joint venture, and our antitrust laws have had difficulty figuring out how to square the cooperation that joint ventures require with the preservation of competition. Indeed, the endless litigation regarding sports leagues, a joint venture of independently owned teams, is indicative of the difficulty of knowing where to draw the line between competition and cooperation.

Competitive problems also can occur when firms in the network compete with network and non-network firms at another stage of production. For example, in a telecommunications network, the electronic switches could be manufactured by firms that also own parts of the network. Concerns may arise that firms in the network could manipulate standards and operating procedures of the network to benefit themselves as suppliers of equipment. Examples would be the failure to reveal to other equipment vendors how to design equipment so as to be compatible with the network and the creation of certain requirements that make it more costly for outside firms to compete to supply equipment.

Another example involves an ESN used for marketing purposes like a computer reservation system (CRS). A CRS facilitates the purchase of airline tickets. Each airline does not have its own CRS and instead some airlines sell tickets through ticket agents who use the CRSs of other airlines. The concern has arisen as to whether the airlines that own CRSs used by ticket agents could design the operation of the CRS to disadvantage other airlines. For example, it has been alleged that some CRSs did not display information of certain airline competitors so as to reduce competition.

PROPERTY RIGHTS AND CREATION OF MARKETS

The competitive problems that arise in networks raise many complicated trade-offs that do not have an easy policy resolution. Ex post after the development of an ESN, competitors can self-righteously rail against the unwillingness of the ESN's developer to allow them to use (or supply) the system. But if other firms can use or supply the system, the returns to innovation may fall. The old trade-off between property rights in innovation and market power rears its head.

The problem of protection of property rights in innovations is especially severe in some ESN settings. The reason is that if many firms must coordinate in a network, then an innovation by one firm, as we have already seen, may be valuable only if the other firms know how to interact with the innovator. But revealing how to interact may reveal the innovator's discovery. Indeed, much of the innovation in ESNs is know-how and software. Protection of intellectual property can be difficult in a setting that demands constant interaction with your rivals.

The difficulties of protecting intellectual property arise even in mature network industries like railroads. For example, suppose railroad 1 goes from New York to Chicago to Los Angeles. Railroad 2 goes only from Chicago to Los Angeles. It is possible to ship from New York to Los Angeles by using just railroad 1 or by using railroad 1 from New York to Chicago and by using railroad 2 from Chicago to Los Angeles. Railroad 2 also has a route from New

York to St. Louis to Los Angeles. One's first reaction (if the person is an economist) is that with marginal cost pricing, the most efficient shipping route will be chosen and railroad 1 should not give much thought to whether it interlines with railroad 2. But this conclusion ignores the information that railroad 1 provides railroad 2 when it interlines—namely, the identity of a customer.

Suppose that railroad 1 has a terrific and large marketing department that spends lots of time and money convincing a New York customer to ship by rail rather than by boat. Railroad 1 will not want the existence of that customer made known to its rival, railroad 2. Hence, it will not want to interline with railroad 2 at Chicago for this customer if railroad 2 could learn the customer's identity and then steal away the customer.

Although the specifics are different in ESNs than in railroads, the central point of the previous example also applies to ESNs. Cooperation with rivals necessitates a diminution in property rights in innovation. Information and know-how are the key innovations in many ESNs and protecting such property rights may be difficult if constant interaction with rivals is needed. ESNs whose technologies are rapidly evolving strike me as ones where the property rights problems are most severe. Although ex post, policymakers may complain about the selfishness of the successful innovator to share his ideas, the converse is that the successful innovator may complain that he was the one who took the risks of development and he should be entitled to the rewards from exploiting his property rights.

An example illustrating the unavoidable tension between property rights in information and competition involves the development of a procedure for how data should be encoded in messages (e.g., IBM's SNA).[2] The development of such a procedure which is obviously complicated allows different decentralized devices to read different parts of the message. The specifics of the procedure can influence which peripheral machines will be utilized. Clearly, the developer of the procedure can skew the procedure to favor its own equipment. Although it is conceptually possible to distinguish efficient development of a method for transmitting data from strategic development to benefit the vendors of certain peripheral devices, in many cases, it is empirically impossible to do so. There is simply no clean resolution of the trade-off between promotion of development of data transmission procedures and competition.

The development of certain ESNs can be viewed as the creation of a market—or at least lowering the cost of transacting. I have discussed elsewhere (Carlton, 1991) the close relationship between marketing and the creation of markets. One reason why I predict ESNs will continue to be involved in litigation is because economists really know little about marketing and market creation, neither of which is an activity that fits economists' models of perfect competition. (See Carlton, 1984.)

Suppose a non-ESN firm develops a new marketing method that is unusually successful. Its salesmen are well trained in this new method and as a result of the marketing innovation the firm's sales skyrocket. If a rival approaches the successful firm and asks if the successful firm could also market (though not set the price of) the rival's competing product, most economists would probably applaud if the successful firm voluntarily chose to do so. Most economists would probably not force the successful firm to market its rival's product. For example, I doubt whether anyone would seriously propose that, if I wanted to manufacture cars, GM should be required not only to sell them but to sell them with the same effort as their own cars. Yet the history of the development of CRSs and of their subsequent litigation contains much similarity to the story I have just related. I do not wish to debate the specifics of the CRS case, but merely to point out that it is a mistake to underestimate the costs of creating information useful for marketing and to ignore that even though ex post marginal costs of usage are low, ex ante incentives are what matter for development. Indeed, *after* a successful system is developed, it could *lower* the likely costs of development of a second system because of the likely information spillovers and free riding that the second entrant can take advantage of in an ESN. The fact that no subsequent development of a competing ESN occurs could illustrate the high sunk costs of development—costs that might be highest for the initial developer.

When the Chicago Board of Trade creates a (futures) market, it is only after much research as to how to define a commodity and how to choose delivery points and dates of contract termination. Most times new futures markets fail. There often are elements of natural monopoly once a market is created. The bigger a market, the more liquidity. It is rare to have the identical commodity trading on the different futures exchanges.

ESNs that create the ability to transact have several features similar to the creation of markets. For example, in a data transmission network, the value of the network may be enhanced as the number of participants sharing information grows. If I am a car manufacturer, I would like the same network to connect me to my glass supplier and my windshield wiper supplier. When it is efficient to have only one network, it may be hard to introduce actual competition among vendors who can provide the network.

If there are many potential networks which firms can use to transact, then there can be competition to provide the network, but once in place there may be no further competition. Moreover, the initial network may have an advantage as the technology evolves and adaptations are involved. For example, suppose I supply GM with tires. I develop a terrific information system for GM that allows the scheduling of shipments and deliveries from many warehouses. I develop the system for GM so that it can be used for other products which I also sell. Such a system will undoubtedly be geared to my own supply capabilities. If I now add the ability for my system to be used for other suppliers' parts, it is likely that the system will be automatically geared to favor my own products. Should GM be upset? After all, it could start anew and develop its own system, or could have done the system development itself. Again, the trade-off between static and dynamic efficiency is at issue.

One reason why GM may not develop the network itself is because the tire supplier may have been best suited to the task. The supplier knows certain information that GM does not and so it is best suited to developing the network. This makes it likely that in many cases, development of ESNs will necessitate vertical and horizontal competitive problems later. For example, other suppliers could complain to GM that GM's system is unfairly biased against them. But is this problem really any different than the earlier example where one firm asks its rival to sell its product? Is the concern with competitive problems in ESNs overemphasized because an ESN *could* have been developed that treats everyone equally? Is this concern really any different than the concern that the auto market would be more competitive if the GM sales organization were forced to sell all makes of cars? There is no theoretical distinction between the ESN and GM examples, though for some ESNs there may be a more significant practical effect on competition than occurs among auto manufacturers if firms cannot use a rival to market the product.

CONCLUSIONS

Network efficiency typically requires coordination among firms that compete with each other. The cooperation that efficiency demands plus the possible strategic competitive behavior that is inevitable among independent firms leads me to believe that in many cases a network will eventually be run by a single firm which may compete against other firms that also own their own networks. The massive integrations of rail systems in the late 1800s and of airline and rail systems in the 1980s are good examples of such integration. Many ESN networks have features that make widespread integration likely. As I said in my 1983 article, striking the balance between cooperation for efficiency and suppression of competition is very hard in network industries. The rapid development of ESNs and the subsequent competitive complaints convince me that the trade-offs will get harder to evaluate, not easier. General prescriptions are impossible, except that the more rapidly an industry-specific communications technology is evolving the more likely interference in ESNs could impede efficiency.

The antitrust laws are not well suited to balancing the trade-off between efficiency and competition under a rule of reason. Recognizing the difficulty of measuring efficiency, the Supreme Court's antitrust decisions have frequently emphasized that it wishes to avoid considering the efficiency benefit of a collusive arrangement or merger.

The prospect of easily resolving the trade-off between cooperation and efficiency in ESNs sounds dismal. The details of each ESN must be carefully studied and, even then, the trade-offs may be hard to evaluate. However, it is important to keep the proper perspective. The tremendous development of new communications technologies has facilitated transactions and information sharing that have greatly enhanced consumer welfare. The development of these technologies—some akin to market creation—have simultaneously raised the possibility of competitive harm from the ESNs. We should not let the concerns with competitive harm so occupy us that we overregulate and kill the incentive to continue the pace of technological change. And we should not ignore the fact that policy actions on existing ESNs will affect how future ESNs are developed. For example, if Congress were to pass a law forcing airlines to divest their CRSs so as to eliminate the possibility that one airline could harm a rival that uses its CRS, my prediction is that future developers of ESNs would protect their property rights by preventing vertical competitors from using their ESNs, thereby eliminating the possibility that any competitor could argue that its competitive success is impaired by the control of the ESN by a rival.

In summary, there are no easy answers to resolving the tension between competition and efficient network development. I predict that consumers will continue to benefit from ESNs at the same time that economic research, litigation, and controversy surrounding ESNs grow.

NOTES

Much of what I know about networks has come from my academic and consulting work with them. I have been involved in the following network industries: airlines, telecommunications, railroads, gas pipelines, computer reservation systems, data transmission systems, and banking systems. The views expressed here are my own and do not necessarily reflect the views of the firms for whom I worked.

1. Of course, the appropriate resolution of the tension will vary from case to case and will be simpler in some cases than in others. For example, if product A is an input to product B and cooperation among firms is required to make A but not B, there is no reason to allow firms to cooperate in the making or selling of B, even if they are allowed to cooperate in the production of A.

2. An example illustrating this same tension in non-network industries between property rights in information and competition is *Berkey v. Kodak* (603 F.2d 263), in which the court ruled that Kodak did not have a duty to predisclose its planned innovations so as to assist rivals.

6

Evaluating Network Pricing Self-Regulation

Steven C. Salop

Shared networks benefit consumers by facilitating cooperation among firms selling complementary products that can reduce costs or improve the value of the joint services or products consumers desire. At the same time, shared networks raise potential competitive concerns because they generally involve cooperation among firms selling competing products. Thus, network self-regulation has the potential for either increasing or decreasing consumer welfare.

There has been considerable economic research of issues involved in shared networks. Much of that work—that of Farrell and Saloner (1986) and Katz and Shapiro (1985), for example—has focused on issues of product standards and product compatibility. There has been less research on whether members of shared networks should be permitted to set prices jointly.

This paper focuses on self-regulated joint pricing. It sets out a series of related models to analyze the benefits and potential harms from joint pricing in shared networks. It concludes that while such joint pricing can increase consumer welfare in principle, achieving that goal is very difficult as a practical matter. This is because of the inherent complexity of the pricing problem facing the network. Moreover, the network—or its controlling members—may have no incentive to maximize consumer surplus, preferring instead actions that increase membership profits at the expense of consumers. Indeed, this tension between consumer welfare and member profits can arise even in those cases where the network faces internetwork competition. Thus, self-regulated joint pricing by shared networks should be viewed skeptically by antitrust enforcers and courts.

The seminal contribution to the literature on self-regulated joint pricing by shared networks is Baxter (1983). In particular, this model and Phillip's (1987) extension argued that "per transaction" fees paid by one member to the other member that is party to the particular transaction are necessary for efficiency. Baxter and Phillips then show that this "interchange fee" must be set jointly— that is, it must be the product of network self-regulation. If individualized interchange fees instead were negotiated bilaterally by each pair of network members, transaction costs would be increased and, more important in terms of theoretical development, the potential for opportunistic conduct would arise. This opportunistic conduct then could reduce the value of the network to consumers. See also Carlton and Klamer (1983).

In earlier work (Salop, 1990), I showed that the interchange fee is redundant if both parties to the transaction are able to charge separate component prices to the consumer. Thus, the claim that the interchange fee must be set jointly is equivalent to a belief that independent component price setting by members of a shared network would lead to an inefficient equilibrium. In that paper, I then discussed and answered the typical criticisms made of independent price setting by network members.

This paper takes a more formal approach to these issues in an attempt to refine the policy analysis of network self-regulation. It develops a series of related models of shared networks to analyze the potential benefits and harms of self-regulated joint pricing and derives conditions to evaluate which outcome is more likely. The paper is organized as follows. The next section sets out the basic structure of shared networks as associations of competing firms selling products that are demand complements to the products of some other network members. The following section presents some formal economic models to clarify the potential benefits and harms from cooperation and competition among network members. I then extend the basic model to the case of shared networks and the added complexities this creates for self-regulation. The next section considers the effect of internetwork competition on policy toward network self-regulation. The conclusion summarizes the analysis and reviews some of the practical difficulties involved in self-regulation.

BASIC STRUCTURE OF ELECTRONIC SHARED NETWORKS

There is considerable diversity among shared networks. In this section, I will set out two conceptual models that I think throw light on some of the key issues involved in the regulation and self-regulation of these associations. The first model focuses on demand complements and the second focuses on a transaction complements variant of that model.

Networks as Demand Complements

Many networks can be viewed as associations of products that are demand complements, along with their close substitutes. By this seeming oxymoron, I mean that a particular product that is sold by a member of the network is a substitute for the products sold by some members of the network and a complement for other products sold by other members. The products have this relationship because they can be viewed as components that are combined by consumers into composite products that the consumers value. This type of model recently has been studied by Matutes and Regibeau (1988), Economides (1989a), Baker (1988), Economides and Salop (1991) and others.

Consider the "sandwich vending network." Suppose the producers of different types of sandwich meats (e.g., corned beef, ham, salami, etc.) join with the producers of different types of bread (e.g., rye, white, pumpernickel, etc.) into the joint supply of sandwich vending machines. In this sandwich vending network, the meats and breads are placed separately in the vending machine. The consumer selects a type of meat and a type of bread, pays the posted price, and a sandwich pops out. Breads and meats are complements, of course, in the sense that it takes two slices of bread and a number of slices of meat to make a sandwich. (The analysis obviously would be easier if sandwiches involved the use of bread and meat in fixed proportions.) The different breads each are substitutes for one another—a consumer could choose to have his corned beef sandwich on rye or white or pumpernickel. The different sandwich meats similarly are substitutes.

Many shared networks can be analyzed in the same fashion. Consider a shared automatic teller machine (ATM) network, for example. A shared ATM network is comprised of ATMs and bankcards. These two products are components to an ATM transaction, the composite product. That is, a consumer combines an ATM terminal and a plastic bankcard to carry out an ATM transaction. ATMs and bankcards are complementary products. However, different ATMs in the network are substitutes for one another in the sense that a consumer chooses among the available ATMs to carry out his or her transaction. Similarly, different bankcards are substitutes in the sense that a consumer selects a bankcard from the banks in the network in order to carry out his or her transaction.

In this structure, intranetwork competition involves competition among ATMs for particular transactions and competition among banks to issue bankcards. The structure of internetwork competition varies according to whether banks can be members of multiple networks and, if so, whether there is overlap among the membership of competing networks. Bank credit card networks like VISA or MasterCard have the same basic structure as ATM networks, as do electronic floral networks like FTD or American Floral Services (AFS), or a money transfer network like Western Union Public Money Transfer.

Networks as Transaction Complements

Although the demand complementarity model can be used to formally analyze multiple-listing service (MLS) and computer reservation service (CRS) networks, the model does not capture fully the idea that these networks act as centralized marketplaces in which the actual members (i.e., travel agents and airlines in the case of CRSs, and brokers in the case of MLSs) exchange information and place orders. The focus of the demand complements model is the ultimate consumer, not the broker or agent. This idea of the central marketplace is somewhat better conceptualized by a variant of demand (and supply) complementarity, the concept of transaction complementarity identified by Ayres (1985).

Transaction complementarity refers to the fact that it reduces transaction costs to coordinate shopping for or purchase of certain products. For example, a supermarket (or on a larger scale, a shopping mall) offers a set of diverse products that benefit from coordinated shopping or purchase. In this sense, the supermarket or shopping mall can be viewed as a network offering transaction complements. Transaction complements may not be demand complements. It is efficient to purchase soft drinks and diapers at the same time in the same supermarket because they are commodities used every day, not because they are consumed together. Indeed, substitutes often are transaction complements; it is cheaper to shop if all the substitutes can be examined simultaneously. Transaction complements can be formalized as a type of demand complement. The cost savings from joint sale also share the characteristics of supply complements. However, there also are certain benefits to distinguishing this case.

An MLS thus can be analyzed as a network of transaction complements. There are economies of listing all the houses for sale in a single (electronic) directory according to a standardized form and permitting buying and selling brokers to communicate through the network. In this way, buyer and seller search costs are reduced. A CRS provides the same benefits for travel agents and airlines.

In both these examples, the network membership can be comprised of products that are complements and products that are substitutes. A CRS contains flights that are demand complements (e.g., Washington to Atlanta and Atlanta to Macon, or Atlanta to Washington for that matter) and others that are demand substitutes (e.g., Washington to Atlanta on Delta as well as Eastern). An MLS lists houses that compete with one another on the market. These houses also are transaction complements in the sense that the consumer's search time is reduced (and quality of search is improved) by analyzing the competing houses as a group. In this sense, two houses listed on the MLS are both demand substitutes and transaction complements. This model also fits the case of a hospital supply ordering (HSO) network.

COMPETITION AND COOPERATION IN SHARED ELECTRONIC NETWORKS

Both demand and transaction complement networks have the characteristic that they are comprised of some products that are complements (either demand complements or transaction complements) and some products that are demand substitutes. It is the complementarity relationship that leads to gains from co-operation. It is the substitution relationship that raises competitive concerns. These issues can be formalized in the classic Cournot (1927) model of complementary duopoly and extensions of that model to multiple producers of each component.

The Cournot Model of Demand Complementarity

Cournot's model of two firms selling complementary products provides the clearest introduction to markets of complementary products. We follow Cournot by formalizing the model as follows. Firms A and B produce components A and B at constant marginal cost a and b respectively. Consumers combine these two components in fixed proportions (i.e., one unit of each) to form a composite product AB. Firms A and B sell these components at prices p and q respectively. Demand for the composite product (and thus the components) is denoted by $D(s)$ and depends on the sum s of the two component prices, or $s = p + q$. We follow Cournot by assuming that each firm maximizes profits, taking the price of the complementary product as given. Thus, in modern jargon, we solve for the Bertrand equilibrium (i.e., Nash equilibrium in prices.)

The profits of firms A and B can be written respectively as follows.

$$\pi_a = (p - a)D(s) \tag{6.1}$$

$$\pi_b = (q - b)D(s) \tag{6.2}$$

Noting that $s = p + q$ and differentiating with respect to each firm's own price, we have the first-order conditions

$$(p - a)D'(s) + D(s) = 0 \tag{6.3}$$

$$(q - b)D'(s) + D(s) = 0 \tag{6.4}$$

These two equations define best-response functions $p = R_a(q)$ and $q = R_b(p)$ that can be solved for the Bertrand equilibrium. However, the equilibrium is more easily characterized by summing equations (6.3) and (6.4) to define the Bertrand equilibrium price $\hat{s}$ of the composite good or

$$(\hat{s} - a - b)D'(\hat{s}) + 2D(\hat{s}) = 0 \tag{6.5}$$

The Benefits of Cooperation

It follows immediately that the Bertrand equilibrium price $\hat{s}$ exceeds the price s_m that would be charged by an integrated monopolist selling both components. This is because each Bertrand seller ignores the adverse effect of raising his own price on the demand and profits of the producer of the other complementary component. Formally, the first-order condition of the integrated monopolist would be given by

$$(s_m - a - b)D'(s_m) + D(s_m) = 0 \tag{6.6}$$

Comparing this first-order condition to the equilibrium condition in equation (6.5), it follows that

$$\hat{s} > s_m \tag{6.7}$$

This result states the now-standard intuition that integration by the producers of complementary products is socially beneficial. In the absence of joint pricing, each component producer ignores the negative externality its price rises have on the demand for complementary components, leading to excessively high prices and reduced output and consumer welfare. By allowing the network members to coordinate their prices, the demand externality can be internalized. As a result, prices fall, in contrast to the case of pricing coordination by firms producing competing substitutes.

Application to Transaction Complements

This same basic model applies to networks of transaction complements. Following Ayres (1985), suppose that a shopping mall is comprised of two stores selling products whose demands are independent of one another. Suppose consumers demand one unit of each commodity. Suppose one store's product is priced at p and the other sets its price at q. Thus, if the consumer purchases at this mall, she will pay total cost $s = p + q$ for the two products. At this total price, suppose the number of consumers who patronize the mall is given by $D(s)$, where $D(s)$ is determined by intermall competition and variation among the reservation prices of consumers in the market. Thus, the pricing externality is formally identical to the standard demand complements model of Cournot.

The Benefits of Perfect Competition

For both versions of the model, it is important to emphasize that the claim that pricing coordination of integration raises welfare is only a second-best result. The price charged by the integrated monopolist exceeds the perfectly competitive price s_c. The perfectly competitive price is the sum of the constant marginal costs. Thus, we have

$$s_c = a + b < \hat{s} \tag{6.8}$$

This caveat has important policy implications. If there were perfect competition among multiple producers of each component and all substitute components were fully compatible, then component competition would make pricing coordination among complementary component manufacturers unnecessary. Moreover, if there were competition among multiple producers of each component, pricing coordination among these substitutes would raise its own competitive concerns. If these competitors were permitted to coordinate their pricing, they would have an incentive to eliminate price competition (among substitutes) and raise prices.

This is not the only limitation of the Cournot model for policy analysis. The model not only ignores the potential for multiple brands of each component and resulting intranetwork competition among substitute components; it also ignores the effects of self-regulated joint pricing on the degree of product variety. The model also ignores the possibility that the producers of one component may form a buyer cartel that gains the power to raise the price of its component by forcing down the prices of the complements. Finally, the Cournot model is incomplete in that it does not explicitly model internetwork competition. These four issues are taken up in the following sections.

INTRANETWORK COMPETITION, PRICING COORDINATION, AND OPTIMAL VARIETY

In this section, we analyze intranetwork competition in shared networks. In a shared network, there are multiple brands of each component. In this more general model, the Bertrand equilibrium price may fall short of the fully integrated monopoly price. Shared networks also face the problem of optimal variety. We deal with this by expanding the model to analyze the trade-off between price and variety and its implications for policy on network self-regulation.

Intranetwork Competition and Pricing Coordination

The Cournot complements model can be generalized to the case in which there are multiple producers of each component.[1] The results of the model change significantly in this more general case. Suppose there are m producers of brands of component A (i.e., A_1, A_2, . . . A_m) and n producers of differentiated brands of component B (i.e., B_1, B_2, . . . B_n). We assume all the components are compatible with one another so that each consumer can choose his optimal A_iB_j combination.

In this more general model, the Bertrand oligopoly equilibrium price may not exceed the price that would be charged by an integrated monopolist. Competition among the producers of the substitute components (i.e., competition among the A's and competition among the B's) can prevent this result. For example, suppose that consumers view all the A_i's as nearly perfect substitutes (and similarly for all the B_j's). In that case, competition among the A_i's and competition among the B_j's would drive the prices p and q nearly down to marginal cost and the equilibrium price $\hat{s}$ of the composite product would fall nearly to the perfectly competitive level s_c.

This result is significant. The component prices $p = a$ and $q = b$ and the composite price s_c are the socially optimal (i.e., "first best") prices in this model. Thus, the mere fact that products are complements is not sufficient to ensure that coordinated pricing is necessary to eliminate the negative externalities identified by Cournot. In the context of network self-regulation, the fact that a network is comprised of complements does not by itself provide a sufficient rationale for the network to price as an integrated monopolist.

When the components are differentiated rather than perfectly homogeneous products, Bertrand competition will not drive the prices down to marginal cost, of course. In this case, self-regulation might increase welfare, if it is carried out skillfully with a sufficient database and the intent to maximize welfare.[2] However, that self-regulation is not without dangers. First, as demonstrated by the various models set out below, optimal self-regulation is difficult to carry out in practice.

Second, at least in the absence of perfect internetwork competition, the network taken as a whole has an incentive to set the composite price at the integrated monopoly level s_m. If the number of components (i.e., m and n) is large or if the components of each type are relatively good substitutes for one another (i.e., the cross-elasticity of demand is high), then a network acting as an integrated monopolist will raise price, not lower it, relative to the Bertrand competition equilibrium.

This analysis suggests that network pricing self-regulation should be scrutinized to ensure that it maintains intranetwork price competition among competing component producers. The potential benefit of joint pricing is to internalize the pricing externality. Yet network members have an incentive to use pricing regulation to achieve the integrated monopoly result rather than the perfectly competitive outcome.

Moreover, the fact that network members do not engage in explicit joint activity to set monopoly prices does not mean that market power has not been exercised. Component prices set independently in competition with other network members may be pushed up above the competitive level by network rules that raise marginal costs or otherwise restrict output indirectly. For example, an ATM or CRS network might set a per-transaction switching fee above marginal cost in order to raise the marginal costs of network members, inducing them to raise the prices they charge network users.[3] Alternatively, the network might set an excessive royalty for use of the network logo. Similar cost-raising strategies might be used by MLSs or hospital supply networks. The network then can pass these costs back to its controlling members (in a way so that marginal costs are not reduced, of course), perhaps by lowering membership fees or other fixed costs, or in terms of dividends.[4]

The Optimal Mix of Price and Variety

The analysis is complicated when the number of firms selling each component is endogenous. Monopolistically competitive markets do not, in general, achieve the best mix of price and variety. Thus, in contrast to the results suggested in the previous section, a price ceiling may reduce welfare by reducing variety. A price floor may not be designed to cartelize the market but rather to induce additional variety—variety that benefits consumers more than they are harmed by the higher prices.

Courts must be skeptical of such claims, of course. Variety and product differentiation are ubiquitous in our economy. If firms are permitted to justify joint price setting simply by asserting that pricing coordination is necessary to achieve the optimal variety, then any cartel could immunize itself from serious antitrust scrutiny. If this justification is to be permitted at all, it is important to require the network to demonstrate convincingly that its joint pricing is beneficial. The following analysis sets out sufficient conditions for joint pricing to increase output and consumer welfare.

We can extend the previous formal analysis to the case of an endogenous number of component brands. For example, suppose that there is a fixed (and sunk) cost F_k ($k = a,b$) that must be borne each period for every brand of each component. Suppose that in the absence of any price or entry self-regulation, new brands of each component enter the market until a zero-profit free-entry equilibrium is achieved. For simplicity, we will assume that demand for different components is symmetric and that the equilibrium is symmetric—that is, all brands of component A sell at an identical price p and all brands of component B sell at an identical price q.

In this situation, first-best optimal self-regulation would set component prices at marginal cost and subsidize the entry of the optimal number of brands of each component out of fixed consumer membership fees. The optimal membership fee would be used to ensure the optimal number of brands of each component. The practical derivation of the optimal membership fee is not a trivial matter, of course.

If such subsidies are not possible, then the network faces an even more complicated optimal variety-pricing problem. Little can be said in general. The second-best optimal prices do exceed marginal cost in order to support the entry of components. However, free entry and free price competition may provide either too many or too few brands, corresponding to prices that are too high or too low. That is, optimal self-regulation might involve a price ceiling below the free-entry equilibrium prices or it might have a price floor above the free-entry equilibrium prices.[5]

To simplify the analysis, we focus on the price-variety trade-off for just one of the components, while holding the prices and number of brands of the other component as fixed. In this simplified framework, we can prove three simple, related propositions. These propositions involve the effect of a price floor (or ceiling) on total output and consumer surplus.

The first proposition involves the effect of network regulation on total output or demand. It states a sufficient condition for a price floor on one component to increase total output of that component. This calculation takes into account the fact that the higher price will induce entry of additional brands. The condition is that the elasticity of demand for the component with respect to the number of brands (i.e., the "variety" elasticity) is both less than unity and *exceeds* the elasticity of demand for the component with respect to the price of the component (i.e., the "price" elasticity). This "elasticity condition" must hold in the neighborhood of the initial free entry equilibrium.[6]

The second proposition relates a global version of this "elasticity condition" to consumer surplus. It is well known that, in general, output tests are imperfect proxies for consumer surplus or aggregate welfare. However, the elasticity condition stated above provides a link between output and consumer surplus. Proposition 2 states that if the variety elasticity is less than unity but exceeds the price elasticity for all output levels $Q > 0$, then a price floor will increase consumer surplus. Thus, if the demand for a component satisfies the elasticity condition globally as well as locally, then a network price floor on that component will increase both output and consumer surplus.[7] This analysis also can be applied to the case of price ceilings. An analogous elasticity condition is stated in proposition 3 to define the conditions under which a price ceiling raises output and welfare.

Formally, define by $D(p,m;q,n)$ the "equilibrium" demand for each brand of component A—that is, the demand for each brand when the prices of all brands of component A equal p and the prices of all brands of component B equal q. Consider the symmetric free-entry intranetwork equilibrium for the two components.[8] At that equilibrium, the zero-profit condition for each producer of component A is given by

$$p\, D(p,m) = mF_a \qquad (6.9)$$

where F_a denotes the fixed cost per brand.[9] For simplicity, we assume that marginal costs $a = 0$. We also assume the price q and number of brands n of the second component B are fixed and, for notational simplicity, we suppress the (q,n) pair in the demand function.

To evaluate the price-variety trade-off in concrete terms, suppose the network contemplates instituting a price floor $p' > p$.[10] Of course, this floor will induce an increase in the number of brands to a higher level $m' > m$ that satisfies the zero-profit condition (6.9) at the higher price p'. To evaluate this policy, we need to calculate whether output and consumer surplus at this new (p',m') pair rises or falls relative to (p,m).[11] We first prove the following proposition with respect to output.[12]

PROPOSITION 1: *The price floor policy increases total demand for component A if the variety elasticity E_m is less than unity but exceeds the price elasticity $E_{p'}$ —that is, if*

$$1 > E_m > E_{p'} \tag{6.10}$$

where $E_m = mD_m/D$ and $E_p = -pD_p/D > 0$ and where these elasticities are evaluated in the neighborhood of the free-entry equilibrium (p,m).

We now prove this proposition.

Proof: Let $m = m(p)$ denote the number of brands that are viable at price p—that is, the number of brands satisfying the zero-profit condition in equation (6.9). Totally differentiating (6.9) and rewriting in elasticity terms, we have[13]

$$\frac{pm'(p)}{m(p)} = \frac{1 - E_p}{1 - E_m} \tag{6.11}$$

Assuming that $E_p < 1$ and $E_m < 1$, then $m'(p) > 0$—that is, an increase in price will increase the number of brands that can be supported with the revenues in the market. The values of these elasticities are the key empirical magnitudes in the analysis that follows.

Substituting $m(p)$ into the equilibrium demand curve $D(p,m)$, we have what might be termed the "long-run equilibrium" demand function $Q(p)$, where

$$Q(p) = D(p, m(p)) \tag{6.12}$$

We now calculate the effect of the price floor policy on long-run equilibrium output as follows. Differentiating (6.12) with respect to p, we have

$$Q'(p) = D_p + D_m m'(p) \tag{6.13}$$

Rewriting in elasticity terms, and substituting equation (6.11) into (6.13), we have the long-run demand price elasticity E^ℓ, or [14]

$$E^\ell = \frac{E_m - E_p}{1 - E_m} \tag{6.14}$$

Proposition 1 follows directly.[15] If $1 > E_m > E_p$ at the initial (p,m), then $E^\ell > 0$. Thus, when price rises to p', demand rises to a higher level $Q(p')$.

This is a sufficient condition for output to increase from the price floor policy. The key part of this condition is the relationship between the price and variety elasticity. That the variety elasticity must be less than unity is a stability condition; demand blows up otherwise. We next show that a similar elasticity condition (holding for all $Q>0$, however) also implies that consumer surplus rises, as stated in Proposition 2.

PROPOSITION 2: *If $1>E_m>E_p$ for all $Q>0$, then a price floor above the current price will increase consumer surplus and aggregate welfare.*

Proposition 2 is illustrated by Figure 6.1. A price-induced increase in the number of brands shifts up the demand curve at every point, as long as additional variety is valued by consumers (i.e., if $D_m>0$). Thus, the change in consumer surplus can be divided into two terms, (1) the change in surplus holding output constant at the initial level $Q=D(p,m)$, and (2) the change in surplus arising from the increase in output to $Q'=D(p',m')$ at the new price p'. The first term may be positive or negative, depending on whether the inverse demand curve rises by more or less than the price. The second term is positive as long as output rises. As proved below, if the elasticity condition holds, the first term also is positive. Thus, we now prove Proposition 2.

Proof: Let $p=P(Q,m)$ denote the inverse demand function for component A, where Q is total output and m is the number of brands. The change in consumer surplus S arising from the price floor policy can be written as follows:

$$\frac{dS}{dm}=\int_0^Q \left[P_m-\frac{dp}{dm}\right]dQ+T \tag{6.15}$$

where T denotes the area of the consumer surplus triangle arising from the increase in output $Q'-Q$, if output rises. As demonstrated by Proposition 1, the local elasticity condition implies that output rises; thus, the term T is posi-

Figure 6.1
Welfare Analysis of a Price Floor

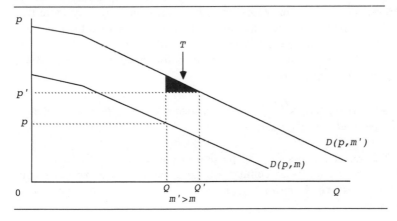

tive. We now show that the first term of (6.15) also is positive if the elasticity condition holds globally.

Differentiating the demand curve $D(p,m)$ to obtain the partial derivative of the inverse demand curve $P(Q,m)$, we have

$$P_m = -\frac{D_m}{D_p} > 0$$

Rewriting equation (6.11) for dp/dm, we have [16]

$$\frac{dp}{dm} = \frac{1}{m'(p)} = \frac{p(1 - E_m)}{m(1 - E_p)} \tag{6.17}$$

Subtracting (6.17) from (6.16) and rewriting, the integrand I of the first term of equation (6.15) is given by

$$I = \frac{p}{m} \frac{(E_m - E_p)}{E_p(1 - E_p)} \tag{6.18}$$

Thus, if $1 > E_m > E_p > 0$ for all $Q > 0$, then the integrand $I > 0$ for all $Q > 0$ and the first term of equation (6.15) is positive. It therefore follows that consumer surplus must rise from the price floor policy. The effect on aggregate welfare follows directly. Because free entry maintains zero profits, aggregate welfare is identical to consumer surplus.

There is a *caveat* that must be noted in this proposition. For Proposition 2 to be technically correct, the demand curve must take on a somewhat altered functional form in the neighborhood of $Q=0$ in order to ensure that consumer surplus is finite. If $E_p < 1$ for all $Q \geq 0$, then consumer surplus is unbounded. To avoid this nonconvergence while ensuring $I > 0$ in the neighborhood of $Q=0$, the demand curve must be bounded from above—that is, reach a finite "choke price." Moreover, when m increases, this choke price must rise by more than dp/dm. If those adjustments are made to the demand curve, then the consumer surplus integral will converge and Proposition 2 will obtain.

A similar sufficient condition can be derived for the case of price ceiling policies, as stated in Proposition 3.

PROPOSITION 3: *If* $E_m < E_p < 1$ *for all* $Q > 0$, *then a price ceiling policy will increase output and consumer surplus.*

Proof: The result follows from inspection of equations (6.14), (6.15), and (6.18). From (6.14), the price ceiling will raise output and make the second term of (6.15) positive. From (6.18), the price ceiling makes the first term of (6.15) positive.

We now discuss the policy implications of these results. The Cournot complements model and its extension to competition among an exogenously fixed number of component producers discussed earlier suggested that price ceilings could increase welfare by neutralizing the pricing incentives of network members and drive prices closer to marginal costs, where output and welfare would be maximized. Those results were flawed in that they ignored the effect of network price ceilings on the variety of components offered. Taking these effects into account changes the results substantially.

This expanded analysis can be summarized as follows. When demand responds more significantly to changes in variety than to changes in price, a price ceiling will not increase total demand. Instead, a price ceiling lowers demand, by reducing the number of brands that can be supported by the marketplace. Moreover, consumer surplus also falls, as the lower price does not compensate consumers for the loss in variety. Instead, in this case, output and consumer welfare are increased by raising price. This permits more brands to be offered—additional variety that benefits consumers more than a lower price.

This analysis can be applied to networks when the demand elasticities can be estimated. The estimates could be used by networks or courts to evaluate proposed price ceilings or floors. In the Pulse ATM network arbitration, for example, econometric and survey estimates of these elasticities were introduced into evidence.[17] The variety elasticity (i.e., the effect of increased ATMs on total volume of network members) was less than unity but considerably larger than the estimated price elasticity. For those elasticities, the proposed price ceiling would not raise output or welfare. If anything, these estimates suggest the network should have proposed a floor, not a ceiling.

However, it is important to recognize the limitations of these results. It is much easier to conclude that a price ceiling would not necessarily increase consumer welfare than to prove definitively that a price floor is called for. This is because the demonstration that consumer surplus must rise requires global information on the relative elasticities. It is difficult, of course, to estimate these elasticities globally.[18] Thus, claims by a network that self-regulated joint pricing is necessary to raise consumer surplus must be viewed skeptically.

At the same time, estimated elasticities can more reliably be used to gauge the effect of pricing self-regulation on network output. Proposition 1 requires only local information that can be estimated more reliably.

Buyer Cartels

This analysis also suggests another potential problem with permitting unrestricted self-regulation by networks. There may be conflicts among the membership of the shared network over the preferred prices to charge consumers. In particular, producers of one component may have an incentive to form a buyer cartel that restricts the price paid for the complementary component. That is, they may join together to place a ceiling on the price received by producers of complementary components. The purpose of this buyer cartel conduct is to permit a higher price for the component sold by the cartel members, for when the price of one component falls, the equilibrium price of the other component may rise. Buyer cartels can be profitable under broad circumstances. This type of opportunistic conduct can be profitable even if it reduces the total output of the network and the welfare generated by the network. This is not surprising. Monopolists generally restrict output and reduce total welfare. Moreover, buyer cartels also can be carried out profitably despite internetwork competition. This more general result may be more surprising and so provides a good focus for the analysis. For that reason, however, a detailed formal analysis of buyer cartels will follow the analysis of internetwork competition in the next section.

INTERNETWORK COMPETITION

It sometimes is argued that network self-regulation should be unconstrained as long as there is competition among networks in providing the composite products the network members produce. This argument flows from a belief that intranetwork competition is unnecessary as long as there is internetwork competition or from a belief that internetwork competition will force the network to maintain vigorous intranetwork competition. It is true, of course, that vigorous internetwork competition can prevent component prices from rising above the competitive level. This is because consumers could buy competing systems from other networks. However, internetwork competition may play only a limited role in substituting for intranetwork competition for three main reasons. First, the number of networks vigorously competing with one another often is limited because of the very economies of cooperation that facilitate the formation of the networks to begin with. Second, potential competition may be weak because of economies of scale, sunk costs, and rules adopted by the networks. These factors can create significant incumbency advantages that imply substantial barriers to entry. As a result, once networks are in place, the market will not be perfectly contestable. Third, even when there is internetwork competition among their composite products, that competition may not be adequate to maintain efficiency and prevent opportunistic conduct by a buyer cartel comprised of the producers of one of the components, at the expense of the producers of the other product. Indeed, the likelihood of such inefficient opportunism is highest in certain circumstances where the networks may appear competitive. We take up these issues in turn.

The Benefits of Network Consolidation

Many networks gain substantial efficiency benefits from consolidation. Such consolidations can lead to a reduction in the degree of internetwork competition. Consolidation is driven by economies of cooperation arising from supply-and-demand factors. On the supply side, networks often are characterized by economies of scale and scope that imply cost savings from consolidation. On the demand side, when consumer value increased variety or locational convenience, consolidation also would increase the value of the network to users.

These demand-side benefits can be illustrated by the "network law of squares." Consider a communications network with n members in which consumers place orders between pairs of members. For example, consumers wire flowers from one FTD member to another or send money from one Western Union outlet to another. In this case, the number of possible communication pairs is $\binom{n}{2}$. Thus, for a large number of members, the number of possible links is proportional to the square of the number of members. Formally, we have

$$\binom{n}{2} = n(n-1)/2 \approx n^2/2, \text{ for } n \text{ large} \tag{6.19}$$

Network consolidation is observed across many different types of networks. There generally is only one MLS in each locale, for example. ATM networks have been consolidating over time into regional networks and now into super-regional networks.

The degree of consolidation varies among networks. For example, Pulse and Cirrus are competing traveler-oriented national ATM networks. Similarly, VISA, MasterCard, and Discover are competing credit card networks. IBM and Apple both continue to be viable. There are multiple shopping malls in many towns. However, this diversity among outcomes does not change the basic point, that in many network contexts, there are benefits from consolidation that imply significant limits on the degree of internetwork competition. Indeed, even where there is internetwork competition, it often is limited to only a handful of providers. Competition is seldom atomistic in network industries.

Barriers to Entry

A similar analysis applies to potential internetwork competition. Economies of scale and scope, the need for critical mass, and sunk costs reduce the competitive influence of potential competitors on the conduct of established networks. Moreover, these barriers to entry sometimes are enhanced by network rules that make entry less likely.

The importance of critical mass can be illustrated with the law of squares. If a new entrant network is able to induce a third of the members of the incumbent network to defect to it, it will achieve only one-fourth the scale of the incumbent that retains two-thirds of the members.[19] In addition, defecting is a risky proposition for members of the incumbent network, unless defections among many members are coordinated. However, such coordinated defection is unlikely in many cases because of the standard difficulties of coordination. First, the defectors must agree on which network to defect to. The agreement may be difficult if the defectors have heterogeneous preferences. Second, they must agree to defect together. This agreement also may be difficult because significant sunk costs must often be incurred in switching networks. These sunk costs create incentives to hold out until the success or failure is apparent, in order to minimize risk.

As a result of these factors, there often will be significant incumbency advantages in networks that reduce the competitive influence of potential entry. Moreover, these advantages sometimes may be enhanced purposefully or coincidentally by network rules and institutions. For example, large one-time membership fees increase the degree of sunk costs. Similarly, exclusive dealing arrangements and technical noncompatibilities increase the role of critical mass and the need for coordinated defections. For all these reasons, in many cases networks are unlikely to be perfectly contestable markets.

Buyer Cartels, Opportunistic Conduct, and Internetwork Competition

Even where internetwork competition is vigorous, its role in constraining inefficient conduct is limited. Actual internetwork competition can prevent the price of the composite product from rising above the competitive level. However, when sunk costs or other factors prevent producers of one of the components from easily defecting to other networks, internetwork competition among composite products cannot prevent opportunistic conduct directed at one of the complementary products.

To illustrate this point most simply, suppose that the component A is a homogeneous product and supplied by perfectly competitive producers according to a rising supply curve $p(x_a)$, $p' > 0$, where x_a is the output of component A. Suppose component B also is a homogeneous product. For simplicity, assume component B is produced with constant marginal cost b and supplied initially by competitive firms. As before, assume the products are used in fixed proportions, so that $x_a = x_b$. Suppose there is intense internetwork competition between the AB composite product (which has a total price of $s = p + q$) and other products, so that network members act as price-takers with respect to a fixed competitive composite price $\bar{s}$.

Initially, when both products are supplied competitively, output $x = x_a = x_b$ is determined at the point where the price of the composite product AB equals the fixed competitive level $\bar{s}$. Formally, we have

$$p(x) + q = \bar{s} \tag{6.20}$$

$$q = b \tag{6.21}$$

These equations determine the market-clearing output x^* that satisfies equations (6.20) and (6.21) and the corresponding price $p^* = p(x^*)$, or

$$p(x^*) = \bar{s} - b \tag{6.22}$$

Assume next that all the producers of component B form a buyer cartel and thereby eliminate competition among themselves. Can they raise the price of component B above the competitive level? It is tempting to answer no. If they raise the price above the competitive level $q = b$ while the price p^* remains constant, the composite price s will rise above $\bar{s}$ and the B producers will lose all their customers to other products. However, this incorrectly assumes that the price of component A will remain fixed at p^*. It will not.

Instead, if the price q of component B rises above b to a new level q', the decrease in demand for the AB composite product will drive down the price of component A below the initial price p^*. It will continue to fall until the equality in equation (6.20) is reachieved. As long as the supply of component A is not perfectly elastic, the component B monopolist will not lose all of its customers from a small price increase. Instead, its price rise will be offset by a price decrease for component A. Rewriting equation (6.20) to derive the component B demand curve, denoted by $D^B(x)$, we have

$$q \equiv D^B(x) = \bar{s} - p(x) \tag{6.23}$$

The intuition of this result can be seen more clearly by viewing the component B cartel as a monopsonist. Suppose the market is organized so that the producers of component B purchase units of component A and package a unit of A with a unit of component B to produce a unit of the composite product that they sell at the competitive price $\bar{s}$. Following the formation of the component B cartel, the cartel can act as a monopsonist with respect to the component A producers, reducing the price it pays for the component below the initial p^* level, while taking into account that fewer units will be supplied at the lower price.

As indicated by equation (6.20), the demand curve facing the component B cartel is what might be termed an *inverse image* of the supply curve of component A, as illustrated in Figure 6.2. The upper panel of Figure 6.2 shows the supply curve $p(x)$ of component A and the competitive equilibrium outcome x^*, where $q^* = b$ and $p(x^*) = \bar{s} - b$. The lower panel illustrates the derived demand curve for component B, as written in equation (6.23). The buyer cartel outcome is illustrated by the output x_b (i.e., where marginal revenue MR equals marginal cost b) and corresponding component prices p_b and q_b.

No matter which interpretation is placed on this analysis, the answer is the same. Despite vigorous internetwork competition, the B producers have an incentive to join together to place a price ceiling on the price received by the producers of component A, allowing the price of component B to rise to a higher level. This opportunistic behavior does not raise the price of the composite product, by definition, but it nonetheless is inefficient. The quantity of the AB composite product supplied is reduced below the competitive level re-

Figure 6.2
Residual Demand of Component B

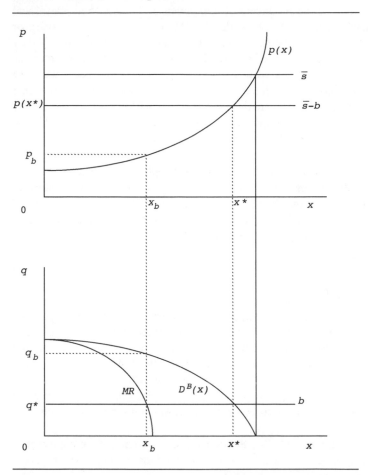

flected by the costs of production. Despite this inefficiency and the internetwork competition, the component B buyer cartel is profitable. Like any cartel, it gains from the transfer of wealth, here from the producers of one component to the producers of the other.[20]

Of course, if internetwork competition is limited, the inefficiency is magnified. In that case, a second inefficiency would be introduced as the price of the composite good rises above the initial level. Moreover, the inefficiency would harm consumers, as prices rise and consumer surplus falls.

This analysis also suggests a reason why unrestricted pricing self-regulation may be a risky policy, even when internetwork competition is vigorous. The profitability of this type of buyer cartel conduct is not deterred by internetwork competition. Thus, even competitive networks that cannot increase the price of the composite product have an incentive to attempt this type of buyer cartel conduct. Of course, once a number of competing networks behave in this way, the "competitive" price of the composite product will rise. This is because each network reduces its output. Then, as the total output of all the competing networks falls, the equilibrium price rises, even if the networks continue to compete with one another. Hence, the initial loss in inefficiency will be magnified and the harm will be passed on to consumers.

It is also interesting, and significant, that this brand of opportunistic conduct does not require that the members of the component B buyer cartel be the only complements for component A. As long as the component A supply curve facing the component B buyer cartel is not perfectly elastic, the opportunism result follows through. Indeed, a smaller buyer cartel has enhanced power to engage in this type of opportunism.

This can be seen in the context of a concrete example of ATM networks. Suppose that component A denotes ATMs and component B denotes bankcards. Suppose that each ATM is a member of a number of different networks. Moreover, suppose these networks are nonoverlapping—that is, each consumer has only one bankcard and each bankcard is only good for a single network. Perhaps the simplest formulation would be the case in which each state had a separate network, so there were fifty non-overlapping networks.[21] However, every ATM will accept cards from each of the fifty networks. Thus, every ATM offers ATM services to the card issuers of all fifty networks. This common service creates a classic public goods problem that leads to an increased risk of opportunistic behavior by a card-issuer buyer cartel in a single network.

In this situation, the supply curve of component A (ATMs) is more complex than in the earlier model. The supply of ATM services depends on the *average* price received by the ATM owner, where this average depends on the prices received in all the networks to which it belongs. As a result, the supply curve for ATM services is less elastic with respect to the price in any one network than if the ATM owner received revenue solely from a single network. For example, suppose the price received by the ATM owner from one of the networks falls by 10 percent. If that network represents only 2 percent of the ATM owner's revenues, its revenue falls by only 0.2 percent. Thus, its supply of ATMs will fall only slightly.

This makes the free-rider problem clear. The card issuers that make up the buyer cartel in one small network have a greater incentive to reduce the price received by the ATM owners, in contrast to the situation where the network is the sole source of revenue for the ATM owner. In the case of multiple networks, the price reduction causes less of a supply contraction. Thus, it is more profitable for the card-issuer buyer cartel to monopsonize the ATM owners.

This analysis implies that the smaller the importance of a network to the ATM owner's overall revenue, the less a given price cut by that network will reduce the ATM services supplied. Thus, smaller networks have a greater incentive to push down the prices they pay ATM owners. This result is different than the standard cartelization theory. Usually, it is large players that have the greatest ability to affect prices while here it is the smallest ones. The difference is that, in this example, the power over price comes from free riding on a common resource, the ATM, not from classical monopoly power.[22]

These free-rider effects create common harm, of course. The monopsonistic price cuts by each network harm every other network by reducing the supply of ATMs they have available for their cardholders. Moreover, like many free-rider problems, the harm is compounded when a number of networks behave similarly. As many networks behave in this way, the supply of ATMs will be reduced substantially. In that case, it is reasonable to relax the assumption of a fixed composite price and note that the overall price, s, will tend to rise, creating consumer injury as well as a loss in efficiency.

The implication of this last model for policy is clear. Market share is not a good proxy for the power to set prices opportunistically. Even where every network represents a small share of the revenue of a single producer of component A (here, a single ATM), the producers of component B who are members of a single network (here, the card issuers in one network) may have the ability and incentive to act opportunistically and monopsonistically by forcing down the price of component A through collective action. Indeed, the smaller the network's share, the greater is its incentive. Only where small network size corresponds to an inability to affect the total revenue of component A producers does a network (more specifically, the component B producers in the network) lack the power to behave opportunistically.

Moreover, it follows that regulators and courts should be skeptical of joint price setting dominated by one side of the network even in situations where the network is small. For even in this case, small size does not imply reduced ability to set nonoptimal prices.

CONCLUSIONS

This paper has set out a series of related models for understanding the potential benefits and harms of network self-regulation vs. intranetwork competition. It generally has taken a skeptical view of network self-regulation, showing how the classical source of benefits identified by Cournot—preventing opportunistic pricing—is weakened when more realistic and complicated networks are analyzed. In these cases, self-regulated joint pricing may raise prices up to the monopoly level instead of reducing them. Networks also may set the wrong degree of variety. Finally, buyer cartels comprised of network members specializing in one component may have an incentive to set inefficient prices in order to monopsonistically exploit the price-variety trade-off of the other component.

Where there is intense internetwork competition, the case for self-regulation generally is strengthened. However, internetwork competition often will be weak for a variety of reasons flowing inherently from the complementarity relationship among components, sunk costs, and critical mass issues. Moreover, as demonstrated by the buyer cartel model, the analysis of internetwork competition is complex in that market share and the power to set opportunistic prices are not equivalent.

Finally, it is important to emphasize the inherent difficulties involved in a network setting efficient prices through a self-regulatory process. Calculating the optimal prices is not trivial, even in simple models. Elasticities must be estimated and compared. Moreover, in more complicated models, the analysis is even more difficult. There is no reason to expect that the optimal prices will be uniform for all the producers of a component where demands are not symmetric. The demand elasticities for particular brands will differ. Brands will also differ in the degree of complementarity—that is, the degree to which they increase the demand for complementary components. Thus, even if a network intended to set the optimal prices, carrying out that program may be difficult. This is another, powerful reason why intranetwork competition is preferred in general to self-regulation.

Governmental regulatory agencies have a poor record in setting efficient prices. They often create rigidities, both across brands and over time. These rigidities are not surprising. Regulators do not get the continuous consumer feedback about demand and costs that is the strength of the free market. These rigidities also lead to inefficiencies, of course. They often are instituted only for the convenience of the regulator, not for consumer welfare. Moreover, the regulatory agencies often become captured by producer subgroups that induce the regulators to set prices in their interest, not the common interest. These flaws in governmental regulation are unlikely to be avoided by self-regulatory bodies. In short, coordination costs are substantial, as Phillips (1987) emphasizes. These coordination costs can be economized by relying instead on intranetwork competition.

NOTES

The author as a special consultant to Charles River Associates has consulted on a number of matters involving shared networks. I have benefitted from helpful conversations with Jonathan Baker, Nicholas Economides, Richard Gilbert, and Garth Saloner. An earlier version of this paper was presented at the Annenberg Conference on Electronic Services Networks, February 1990.

1. This is set out in Economides and Salop (1991).

2. Even this result is oversimplified. This result assumes that the number of producers of each component is given. Thus, it abstracts from the effect of fixed costs on the number of sellers. The more realistic case in which self-regulation affects the number of sellers is taken up in more detail below.

3. This is not to say that switching costs or royalty rates in excess of marginal cost

are sufficient proof, without more, of an intent to monopolize the market. There may be other efficiency-based rationales for such pricing.

4. See, for example, Maloney et al. (1979) or Salop et al. (1984) for the basic analytics of such cost-raising strategies.

5. The optimal variety problem has been studied in the context of monopolistic competition by Spence (1976), Dixit and Stiglitz (1977), and Salop (1979). Optimal variety in particular complementary product networks has been studied by Matutes and Regibeau (1988) and Economides (1989a).

6. That the elasticities must be less than unity is a stability condition, to ensure that the "long-run" demand is downward sloping. If elasticities exceed unity, the inequalities are altered. This case is not considered in the analysis that follows.

7. This analysis ignores the effects on the other component. It holds the price and number of brands of the other component as given. However, my conjecture is that this simplifying assumption is not essential. Under the sufficient condition, it also follows that the demand for the other component rises, due to the fixed proportions assumption.

8. Symmetric denotes the assumption that $p_i = p$ and $q_j = q$.

9. Because demand is symmetric, each producer is able to sell a fraction, $1/m$, of demand, or $D(p,m)/m$.

10. A similar analysis applies to price ceilings, as stated in Proposition 3.

11. Since free entry ensures zero profits, consumer surplus equals aggregate welfare. Note that we ignore the integer issue and assume that free entry implies exactly zero profits.

12. Proposition 1 generalizes the results provided in the examples of Scherer (1983) and Comanor (1985).

13. If marginal cost $a > 0$, then the equation would be more complicated. In particular, the numerator of equation (6.11) would contain an additional positive term $a/(p-a)$. Proposition 1 would still obtain.

14. If $a > 0$, the E_m in the numerator would be multiplied by the expression $(p-a)/p$. Because this expression exceeds unity, the proposition still obtains.

15. Salop (1990) provides a variant of this result. Rewriting equation (6.13), we have

$$E^\ell = E_m E^s - E_{p'} \tag{6.14a}$$

where E^s denotes the elasticity of brand supply—that is, $E^s = pm'(p)/m(p)$.

16. If $a > 0$, the denominator of (6.17) is larger, so that Proposition 2 still obtains.

17. The author was an expert consultant to the plaintiff in that case. See Kauper (1988) for a description of the case.

18. Moreover, because of the second caveat to Proposition 2 discussed above, assuming that the elasticities are constant globally is a bit troublesome in the neighborhood of $Q = 0$ so technical adjustments must be made.

19. The entrant with $n/3$ members will have $n^2/18$ communications links. After the incumbent loses one-third of its members, it still will have $2n/3$ members or $4n^2/18$ links. Thus, the entrant will have only one-quarter as many links—the links that likely translate into market share.

20. It might be noted that this analysis has an obvious application to *Aspen Skiing* (1985). It is sometimes argued that the case was wrongly decided because Aspen is not a relevant market. Instead, it is argued, competition among the many available "destination" ski resorts would prevent any anticompetitive conduct. Under the analysis pre-

sented here, however, elimination of competition among the various slopes in Aspen would permit the price of lift tickets to rise by forcing down the price of hotel rooms and other complementary components with rising supply curves. Of course, this analysis might not save the Court's decision. This competition similarly would be eliminated by permitting (or, indeed by requiring!) the mountains to offer a jointly priced weekly lift ticket.

21. However, to keep things simple and focus on the buyer cartel issue in comparison with the previous model, we continue to assume that each of these 50 networks faces intense competition and so takes the price of its composite product as fixed and unaffected by the buyer cartel.

22. Indeed, in this formulation, where each network is a monopolist in its own state, it would have made more sense to allow s to vary. But the assumption of fixed s was made to allow a focus on this free-rider issue. Where card issuers also are members of multiple networks, the analysis is more complex. In that case, the network may not have the power to set these opportunistic prices. For the ATM owner may be able to avoid accepting the reduced price by switching to a different network that offers just as many incremental transactions.

Part II

Electronic Services Networks
Studies

7

On the Delegation of Pricing Authority in Shared Automatic Teller Machine Networks

Richard J. Gilbert

Networks are typically organized as hierarchies. Management (which I will call the network "executive") is responsible for decisions relating to organization and operation of the network. Consumers access the network at different points, and the conditions of access may be determined by parties other than the network executive. In shared automatic teller machine (ATM) networks, each terminal is owned or leased by a "sponsor" (typically a bank) that may impose conditions on the use of the facility. In airline computerized reservation systems (CRSs), the hierarchy includes travel agents and subscribing air carriers. Points of access for travelers are sponsored by the travel agent (with the terminal equipment typically leased from the CRS vendor), and subscribing air carriers contract with the network executive.

Credit card systems comprise cardholders and card-issuing banks, merchants and their banks, and the card network, which provides data-processing services and may establish fees for settling accounts with participating merchants. Card-issuing banks determine conditions of use, including fees for cardholders, account limits, and interest rates for outstanding balances. An example of a network with a simpler hierarchy is wholesale exchange of electric power. The network executive is the owner of the transmission line. Users (sellers and buyers of wholesale power) access a transmission network and negotiate with the executive for the terms of access.

An important organizational decision for the network executive is the determination of pricing authority within the network. Pricing authority includes the determination of the transaction prices that users must pay to access the network and the prices that the sponsor of a point of access (the ATM owner or the CRS travel agent) must pay for the use of network equipment and services.

The network executive may choose to retain sole authority for the determination of transaction prices and user fees (if not constrained to do otherwise by the antitrust laws). Alternatively, the executive may *delegate* pricing authority for transaction fees to network sponsors. This may be preferable if sponsors have better information about local demand conditions and if delegated pricing allows the sponsor to choose prices that better allocate network services to local demand.

Shared ATM systems differ from proprietary systems which banks develop to serve their own customers. A shared system allows customers of one bank access to the ATMs of another institution, thereby giving customers the benefit of banking services over a larger geographic area. Figure 7.1 shows the organization of a shared ATM network and illustrates a typical fee structure. The network executive provides automated electronic funds transfer services (switching services) between banks or other organizations that sponsor ATMs and also may provide data and accounting services. The network imposes an interchange fee for transactions that occur whenever a customer from one sponsor (the issuing bank) accesses an ATM owned by a different sponsor (the acquiring bank). These fees are paid by the issuing bank to both the acquiring bank and the network for the services they provide. In addition, the network may charge ATM sponsors fixed fees for access to the network and royalties on each ATM card that a sponsor issues to a customer and which can be used to access the network.[1]

The network may permit sponsors of ATMs to set fees for ATM services. A common fee, and one that is often tolerated by shared ATM networks, is a "foreign fee" that a bank charges to its depositor when the depositor accesses

Figure 7.1
Shared ATM Network

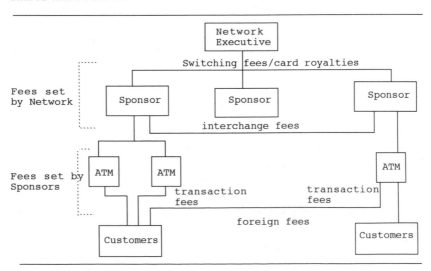

an ATM owned by another bank. In addition, the sponsor may, or may not, have the permission of the network to assess fees that a customer must pay at the ATM terminal. These fees, labelled "transaction fees" in Figure 7.1, may differ for deposits, withdrawals, and other ATM services and are assessed at the point of the transaction.[2] When ATM systems were introduced, the networks were concerned about the lack of demand for ATM services and feared that imposition of user fees would interfere with the acceptance of shared ATM systems and frustrate their development. The networks were particularly uneasy about fees assessed at ATM terminals, fearing that these fees would deter consumers and alienate the depositors of banks that issue ATM cards.[3] Recognizing that ATMs are a potential revenue source for member banks and that such members would be tempted to impose fees, the shared systems prohibited the assessment of fees by member banks for certain types of ATM services or imposed conditions that made it difficult for ATM sponsors to collect fees.

Recent litigation challenged the authority of the ATM network to unilaterally determine transaction fees charged by the sponsors of ATM terminals. In arbitration, First Texas Savings Association claimed that the unilateral establishment of interchange fees by Pulse, the largest shared ATM system in Texas, was anticompetitive and that ATM sponsors should be free to set fees for transactions at their machines (Kauper, 1988). Pulse prohibited sponsors from collecting surcharges by using the Pulse switched network. The practical implication was that sponsors had to use an alternative such as a coin box or cashier, which would have been prohibitively expensive in many cases. First Texas argued that its "free market" approach would better serve consumers because ATM owners possess information about demand and cost at particular locations, individual ATM owners can respond more quickly to changes in economic conditions, and the "free market" approach would not pose the same danger of anticompetitive conduct that is posed by collective setting of interchange fees (Kauper, 1988, p. 352.)[4] Pulse responded that the "free market" approach would cause confusion among cardholders, damaging the bank-depositor relationship, and that "price gouging" by ATM operators would create consumer dissatisfaction with the system and with issuing banks (Kauper, 1988, p. 358). Pulse also noted that collective setting of interchange fees is typical of other ATM systems, and that collective fee setting by the VISA network was held to be legal.[5]

Applying a rule-of-reason approach, the arbitrator in *First Texas v. Pulse* (Kauper, 1988) concluded that Pulse's practice of establishing a uniform interchange fee without provision for ATM surcharges or rebates (transaction fees) was anticompetitive and ordered Pulse to adopt a policy that permitted ATM sponsors to impose or collect fees. In reaching this conclusion, the arbitrator stressed the de facto prohibiton of surcharges and rebates by ATM sponsors using the Pulse network and noted that in the VISA litigation, agents were free to negotiate around the fees established by the network. In the opinion of the arbitrator, "the 'free market' approach is likely to produce a different mix of price/quality/convenience options, and that by doing so consumer welfare would be enhanced'' (Kauper, 1988, p. 364).

Kauper's (1988) endorsement of the benefits of competition fails to recognize the value of cooperation where, as in an ATM network, the actions of members are highly interdependent. Carlton and Klamer (1983) and Carlton (Chapter 5) emphasize that cooperation among competitors is essential in networks, and that the need for cooperation extends beyond the setting of standards and procedures and may include financial dealings as well. While adopting a rule-of-reason approach, Kauper (1988) focused on the collective determination of interchange fees as a vertical restraint of trade, yet one can argue as in *NaBANCO v. VISA* that a shared ATM network is a joint venture and that the members of the network should be free to make agreements that limit their individual conduct according to rules of behavior established by the participants in the venture, provided that such rules are not intended to exclude competition. In this view, restrictions on pricing behavior are no more onerous than the rules of competition established by professional sports leagues or the rules that govern the activities of members in a condominium association.[6]

This paper provides an analysis of the incentives for price determination in a simple model of a shared ATM network and considers the public policy implications of restrictions on the pricing activities of member banks. By delegating the authority for pricing of ATM services to the ATM sponsors, the network can exploit information that is available only privately to the sponsors. Delegated pricing authority would allow sponsors to justify ATMs at locations that would be unprofitable when prices are centrally determined. An example is an ATM location that is "off-site" (not on the premises of the member bank), where few of the customers would be members of the sponsor's bank and hence the sponsor would want to collect fees for ATM services to justify the costs of maintaining the ATM. Another argument in favor of delegated pricing authority is that it would permit intranetwork price competition to the benefit of consumers. Salop (1990) maintains that network "self-regulation" (i.e., restrictions on members' pricing behavior) has resulted in too few ATM terminals (particularly at sites remote from sponsor banks) and that it is unlikely to provide higher consumer welfare than vigorous free market competition among the ATM owners in the network.

ATM services are a potential revenue source for member banks and the sponsors of ATMs are likely to price ATM services at levels that maximize profits from their use. Some shared ATM networks are organized as nonprofit organizations and the pricing of ATM services to maximize net revenues would be inconsistent with the objectives of the network. A nonprofit network may object to the delegation of pricing authority even if centralized pricing policies mean that some ATM locations are unprofitable because the alternative of delegated pricing would result in prices that diverge from the cost of service. Even if shared ATM networks are organized to maximize the profits of the network or its member banks, the network may oppose delegated pricing authority because banks may set prices for ATM services that exceed the levels that maximize joint profits. Unless the network sets a fee for ATM usage-sensitive electronic switching service (i.e., automated funds transfer) that equals the marginal cost of the service, there is a problem of "double-marginalization." The cost of ATM services to member banks will exceed the true marginal cost of the service and the transaction price that maximizes the net revenue of the member banks will exceed the level that maximizes joint profits.

Both sides of the ATM debate call attention to the importance of the network to the viability of the shared ATM service. The proponents of delegated pricing maintain that access fees imposed by member banks will encourage the development of more ATM terminals and that this will increase the demand for ATM services. Salop (1990) also promotes the desirability of intranetwork pricing rivalry, notwithstanding that intranetwork rivalry may result in lower total profits for the network and thus interfere with the objective of universal service. The proponents of centralized network authority emphasize their concerns with the negative effect of transaction prices on ATM demand and argue that individual sponsors will fail to account for the interests of the entire network in their pricing decisions.[7]

I examine the relative performance of centralized and delegated pricing authority in an ATM network under the assumption that individual sponsors have private information about the value of ATM patronage. The analysis assumes a profit-maximizing network and considers alternative restrictions on network pricing instruments. Specifically, the analysis distinguishes linear and two-part pricing. The latter allows the network to set a fixed fee that is charged to each participant in the network. When all ATM sponsors are identical, a uniform fixed fee can eliminate the problem of double-marginalization. The network executive can set a switching fee equal to marginal cost and collect the surplus from participation in the network with a fixed fee. However, as Schmalensee (1981) and Katz (1989) demonstrate, when downstream firms (the ATM sponsors) differ in the value of the service (participation in the network), a uniform fee is an imperfect discriminatory device. In this general case, the network executive would have to balance the exclusionary effect of a fixed fee against the problem of double-marginalization that would result when the switching fee is set above marginal cost.

The results in Schmalensee (1981) and Katz (1989), along with the fact that there is a large variation in fee structures observed among shared ATM networks, provide support for examining the consequences of alternative pricing structures under different assumptions about the use of non-uniform fees. The analysis in the third section assumes that the network may impose only a linear switching fee that is the same for all ATMs. The fourth section considers the use of both a fixed fee and a switching fee. This section also distinguishes fees that are uniform (a fixed fee and switching fee that is the same for all ATM sponsors) from fees that may vary according to the identity of the sponsor.

In each case considered, I conclude that there are many circumstances in which the network is better served by delegating pricing authority to ATM sponsors. However, in each case, the private interest of the network executive is coincident with the public interest. If network profits are higher with delegated pricing, so is total economic surplus. This result offers no support for judicial intervention compelling the delegation of pricing authority in ATM networks.

The structure of the optimal network pricing problem is similar to the manufacturer-retailer problem studied by Blair and Kaserman (1983), Mathewson and Winter (1984, 1986), Rey and Tirole (1986), and others. Rey and Tirole (1986) argue that there are circumstances in which the manufacturer's (the network in this case) choice of vertical restraints is not efficient. In particular, they show that centralized pricing (resale price maintenance in their example) can be worse than unrestrained competition. There are, however, important differences between the model in Rey and Tirole and the case studied here. In Rey and Tirole, the number of retailers is fixed. Hence there is no interaction between the pricing structure in their model and the number of retailers that enter the industry. Moreover, with a fixed number of retailers, there is no interaction between the entry of retailers and demand for the product—there is no network externality. Rey and Tirole focus on the insurance value of vertical restraints in a model where retailers' demands and costs are uncertain. In an ATM network, differences between ATM locations (for example, "on-site" vs. "off-site" ATMs) are likely to dominate variations in demand and cost at a particular location. When the Rey and Tirole model is reinterpreted to reflect variations among ATM locations, their model also shows that if delegated pricing is profit maximizing for the network, it also results in higher total surplus.

EFFICIENT PRICING OF AUTOMATIC TELLER MACHINE NETWORK SERVICES

The ATM network derives revenues from switching fees (fees for the use of data-processing services), from card royalties, and from charges for the use of network equipment and other services. ATMs generate economic value for their sponsors through (1) cost savings achieved by substituting ATMs for traditional teller services and by economizing on administrative costs;[8] (2) revenues from fees imposed on depositors who access the sponsors' ATMs (transaction fees); and (3) revenues from card fees, interchange payments, and foreign fees.[9] Interchange payments are fees that are paid by ATM sponsors if a cardholder accesses the ATM of a different bank. The interchange fee is a payment from the "issuing" ATM to the "acquiring" ATM for the services the latter provides to the issuing ATM's cardholder. Foreign fees are imposed on a cardholder for using an ATM not owned by the cardholder's bank. Sponsors' economic values from potential ATM locations differ according to the volume of transactions at the location, the mix of "on us" and foreign transactions, and other factors such as labor costs.

Consumer demand for ATM services has a network externality: the value that each consumer places on subscribing to the network increases with the number of ATMs in the network. Efficient network pricing encourages the deployment of ATMs when the value of their services exceeds the cost of installation and operation. Moreover, consumers should not be deterred from using the network by prices that exceed the cost of providing the ATM services. In an efficient pricing scheme, prices should equal the incremental costs that the market participants impose on the system, less any benefits that their patronage generates for the network. The parties that derive benefits from the ATM network are:

- Consumers (usually the depositors of the banks who sponsor ATMs), who value the convenience of automated teller services at distributed locations;
- The network owner, who earns profits from switching and other fees;
- The ATM sponsors (usually banks), who value the cost savings from automation and value the patronage of their depositors, and also benefit from any fees they may collect for use of their ATMs.

Several assumptions are made to facilitate the analysis:

A.1 All ATM transactions utilize the shared network switch—they are "foreign" transactions.

A.2 The network may collect revenues only by charging a fixed fee to each ATM sponsor and/or a usage-sensitive fee for switching services. Both the fixed fee and the switching fee may depend on the identity of the ATM sponsor, if the network has this information.

A.3 Each sponsor has a single ATM.

A.4 The marginal value of an ATM transaction differs for each ATM sponsor, but is independent of the number of transactions at each ATM.

A.5 If permitted by the network, each ATM sponsor may impose a fee for ATM transactions. This fee is independent of the number or type of ATM transactions.

A.6 There are no interchange fees (paid by the sponsors of issuing ATMs to the sponsors of acquiring ATMs), or foreign fees imposed on a sponsor's customers for the use of foreign ATMs.

The fifth section considers the value of interchange fees and foreign fees in a shared ATM network. This section also allows for different mixes of "foreign" and "on-us" transactions at ATMs. Interchange fees and foreign fees differ from transaction fees in that the latter do not depend on the identity of the customer that accesses the ATM terminal. The assumption of a two-part fee structure for the entire network is consistent with most shared network practices, although this does exclude fees for services other than network switching and for trademark licenses. The restriction of one ATM for each sponsor is only a mathematical convenience.

Define:

$S(\mathbf{p},m)$ = total consumer surplus from a network of m ATMS, with transaction prices $\mathbf{p}=(p_1, p_2, \ldots , p_m)$.

$X_i(\mathbf{p},m)$ = demand for ATM usage at location $i=1, \ldots , m$ when there are m locations with prices $\mathbf{p}$.

c = marginal cost of network switching.

K = the fixed cost of an ATM (assumed to be paid by the ATM sponsor).

r_i = ATM (usage-sensitive) switch fee charged to ATM sponsor i.

F_i = ATM fixed fee charged to ATM sponsor i.

v_i = the marginal value of an ATM transaction to an ATM sponsor. v_i is a measure of the "goodwill" generated by each ATM transaction for the ATM sponsor, and is ordered such that $v_1 \geq v_2 \geq \ldots \geq v_m$.

B_i = profits earned by the sponsor of ATM i from ATM usage.

         $= (v_i+p_i-r_i)X_i(\mathbf{p},m)-K-F_i$.

N = profits of the ATM network.

         $= \displaystyle\sum_{i=1}^{m}(r_i-c)\, X_i(\mathbf{p},m)+F_i$.

The total surplus from the ATM network is

$$W=S(\mathbf{p},m)+ \sum_{i=1}^{m}(v_i+p_i-c)X_i(\mathbf{p},m)-mK \tag{7.1}$$

Assume $\partial S(\mathbf{p},m)/\partial m \geq 0$, $\partial^2 S(\mathbf{p},m)/\partial m^2 \leq 0$, and $\partial X_i(\mathbf{p},m)/\partial p_i < 0$.

First-Best Network Pricing with Perfect Information about v_i

An increase in the user transaction price at the ith ATM, p_i, has the usual effect on consumer surplus, $-X_i(\mathbf{p},m)$. Varying p_i and m, the first-order conditions for a local maximum of the total surplus function are

$$\sum_{i=1}^{m}(v_i+p_i-c)\partial X_i(\mathbf{p},m)/\partial p_i=0 \tag{7.2}$$

and

$$\partial S(\mathbf{p},m)/\partial m + \sum_{i=1}^{m}(v_i+p_i-c)\partial X_i(\mathbf{p},m)/\partial m+(v_m+p_m-c)X_m(\mathbf{p},m)=K \tag{7.3}$$

PROPOSITION 1: *Total surplus attains a local maximum when the price for user transactions at the* i*th ATM is* $p_i^* = c - v_i$ *and the number of ATMs solves* $\partial S(\mathbf{p}, m)/\partial m = K$.

From (7.2) and (7.3), under the assumed conditions, transaction prices, $p_i = c - v_i$ for $i = 1, \ldots, m$ are locally optimal when the number of ATMs is the solution to $\partial S(\mathbf{p}, m)/\partial m = K$.[10] At the (local) optimum, ATMs should be added to the network until the marginal value to consumers of another ATM location equals the marginal cost. The contribution of an additional ATM to profits is zero when prices are chosen optimally with full information about ATM transaction values. Hence the marginal value of an additional ATM is limited to the marginal network externality. The desired number of ATMs can be supported in a market allocation with the appropriate choice of the fixed fee and/or the switching fee. The number of ATMs is the largest number, m, for which $(v_m + p_m - r_m)X_m(\mathbf{p}, m) \geq K + F_i$.

When the marginal value of transactions to the ATM owner, v_i, is common knowledge, the optimal transaction price should equal the switching cost with a credit for the transaction value. ATM transactions should be subsidized when $v_i > c$, if feasible. Hence:

COROLLARY 1.1: *If subsidies are not feasible, the optimal ATM transaction price is zero if the marginal value of transactions exceeds the marginal switching cost.*

Figure 7.2 illustrates first-best pricing when subsidies are not feasible. ATM transaction values are assumed to be uniformly distributed, so that in order of descending value, $v_i = v(1 - m/M)$ where M is the total number of feasible ATM locations. This is shown in Figure 7.2(a). Figure 7.2(b) shows the optimal price at each ATM with no subsidies. The optimal price at each ATM, p_i, is zero if the transaction value v_i exceeds c and is equal to $c - v_i$ otherwise for $i = 1, \ldots, m$. In Figure 7.2, the optimal transaction price is zero for $m < \bar{m}$. Figure 7.2 shows optimal prices for all M locations, but note that the optional number of ATMs is determined by $\partial S(\mathbf{p}, m)\partial m = K$.

First-Best Network Pricing with Imperfect Information about v_i

The first-best determination of prices described above requires that the network executive have perfect information about the value of transactions at every ATM. This is unlikely to be the case. ATMs will differ according to the mix of foreign and "on-us" transactions, local labor costs, total transaction demand, consumer price sensitivity, and the resistance of consumers to experimenting with automated tellers. Compared to the network executive, ATM sponsors are likely to have much better information about the value of trans-

Figure 7.2
ATM Transaction Values and First-Best Pricing with No Subsidies

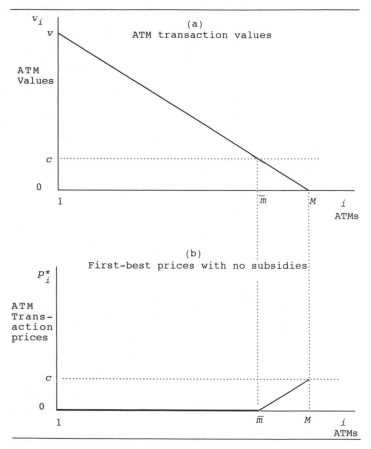

actions at each ATM. The remainder of this analysis assumes that v_i is known privately by the sponsor of the ith ATM. The network executive is assumed to have perfect information about the distribution of values at ATMs, but the executive is uninformed about the value of transactions at any particular ATM.

The derivation is similar when v_i is private information, except that now efficiency may be served by *delegating* pricing authority to the owners of the ATMs because only the owners know the value of the service. If consumer and producer surplus have equal weight in determining social benefits and if there is no penalty associated with transferring revenues between consumers and producers (both of which are implicit in (7.1)), first-best network pricing can be achieved with a Loeb and Magat (1979) compensation scheme. Allow each ATM sponsor a revenue equal to

$$S(\mathbf{p},m) + \sum_{i \neq j}^{m} (v_i + p_i - c) X_i(\mathbf{p},m)$$

This scheme, along with a switch fee $r=c$ and a fixed fee or subsidy to encourage the desired number of ATM sponsors, achieves a first-best outcome when each sponsor chooses transaction prices to maximize ATM profits.

The disadvantages of the Loeb and Magat compensation scheme are well known. It requires full knowledge of demand conditions (and no demand uncertainty). It implies large transfers to firms (in this case the ATM sponsors). The transfers can be mitigated by combining the compensation scheme with a fixed fee for the right to sponsor an ATM. However, the surplus-extracting fee depends on the identity of the ATM sponsor, and an optimal surplus-extracting fee structure would have to respect the incentives of different sponsors to misrepresent their transaction values. This is discussed in more detail below under optimal network pricing.

Suppose that the compensation scheme may allow only a switching fee r and an ATM fee F that is the same for all ATMs. With delegated pricing authority, each ATM owner would choose p_i to maximize

$$B^i = (v_i + p_i - r) X_i(\mathbf{p},m)$$

The disadvantage of delegated pricing is that owners of ATMs would choose user transaction prices to maximize their own profits and not the economic welfare of all the parties. This is the "double marginalization" problem in vertical markets. (See Spengler, 1950; and Telser, 1960.) The ATM owner does not have an incentive to set price at the first-best level ($p_i = c - v_i$), but the owner would at least set prices that reflect the owner's opportunity cost, $r - v_i$.

The network executive can deal with the problem of double marginalization by fixing the transaction price that an ATM sponsor may charge. However, with imperfect information the executive cannot choose prices contingent on the ATM user, and so must establish a single price. When prices are imposed centrally, the efficient price with the information constraint solves (7.2) and (7.3) with $p_i = p$ for all $i = 1, \ldots, m$.

Whether centrally determined prices are preferred by the network to delegated pricing authority and whether centrally determined prices yield higher total surplus will depend on the pricing instruments that are available to the network and on specific parameter values. When prices are delegated, each ATM will add a profit margin to its switching fee to determine a transaction price. The resulting price may be higher than the transaction price that the network would establish, at least for ATMs with low transaction values. While this tends to lower total surplus, delegated pricing has the advantage that prices are related to transaction values. The private and social values of network pricing authority are examined in more detail below, assuming that the rules of network organization are determined by a single, *profit-maximizing* network executive. The next section considers the case of network pricing under the restriction that the network may charge only a uniform switching fee. The third section considers the case of nonlinear fees.

NETWORK PRICING WITH UNIFORM, LINEAR SWITCHING FEES

This section analyzes the problem of optimal pricing under the assumption that the network executive is constrained to choose only a fee for switching services that is the same for all ATMs. The executive cannot choose different fees for different sponsors and cannot assess a fixed fee for participation in the network. Thus $r_i = r$ and $F_i = 0$ for all i. Schmalensee (1981), extending the results in Leland and Myer (1976) and Ng and Weisser (1974), shows that a zero fixed fee can be optimal in a two-part pricing scheme. The reason is that even a small fixed fee would exclude low-value users and it could be more profitable to charge a high variable fee and keep the low-value users.[11] Moreover, the data show a large variation in the use of fixed fees by shared ATM systems, with some systems reporting no fixed fees.[12]

Centralized Pricing Authority

The first case considered is where the network executive chooses prices centrally. The network does not own the ATMs, but can influence their profitability through the determination of a switching fee. The executive cannot choose transaction prices contingent on ATM values, which are private information. The executive's problem is to choose a single switching fee r and transaction price p to maximize network profit.

$$\sum_{i=1}^{m} (r - c)X_i(\mathbf{p},m)$$

subject to

$$(v_i - r + p)X_i(p,m) \geq K, \quad i = 1, \ldots, m$$

For simplicity, assume $K=0$ and $X_i(p,m)=X_j(p,m)=X(p,m)$ for all i,j. Then given a transaction price, p, the switching fee, r, determines the number of ATMs in the network according to $v_m - r + p = 0$. The executive's problem can be simplified to

$$\max_{p,m} \; (p + v_m - c)mX(p,m) \tag{7.4}$$

For a given value of m, the network's optimal transaction price, p^c, is either 0 or p^m, where p^m is the monopoly price corresponding to an effective marginal cost $\tilde{c}_m \equiv c - v_m$. Given the optimal transaction price for any m, (7.4) can be solved to determine the profit-maximizing number of ATMs. This number would be established through the appropriate switching fee, $r = p + v(m)$.

Example 1

Let $\epsilon_{xz} \equiv \partial lnX/\partial lnz$. Suppose $v_m = v(1-m/M)$, $\eta \equiv -\epsilon_{xp}$ and $\gamma \equiv (1+\epsilon_{xm})$ are constants, with η and $\gamma > 1$. If $v > c$ and the limit as $p \to 0$ of $X(p,m)$ is sufficiently large, the profit-maximizing switching and transaction fees and the number of ATMs are

$$p^c = 0$$

$$r^c = \frac{v + \gamma c}{\gamma + 1} \tag{7.5}$$

$$m^c/M = \frac{\gamma(1 - c/v)}{\gamma + 1} < 1$$

Example 2

Same as Example 1, except $X(p,m) = x(m)(A-p)/b$, and for simplicity let $c = 0$. The profit-maximizing switching and transaction fees and the number of ATMs are

$$p^c = \max\left[0, \frac{A - v(m)}{2}\right]$$

$$r^c = p^c + v(m) \tag{7.6}$$

$$m^c/M = \min\left[\frac{\gamma}{\gamma+2}\left(1+\frac{A}{v}\right), 1\right]$$

With linear demand, whether the owner should choose a zero transaction price or the monopoly price depends on parameter values. A zero price is optimal if $A < v/(\gamma+1)$.

Delegated Pricing Authority

If the owner of the network delegates pricing authority to the sponsors of the ATMs, the transaction price p_i at the ith ATM is the profit-maximizing price corresponding to an effective marginal cost $r - v_i$, where r is the network switching fee. The ATM's profit-maximizing transaction price may be zero if $v_i > r$. An advantage of price delegation is that each ATM knows its transaction value and can price accordingly. A disadvantage is that ATMs will double-marginalize. Each ATM will add a profit margin to the network switching fee, which already includes a profit margin for the network owner. In addition, the ATMs cannot coordinate their price choices and they do not internalize the network demand externality.

The disadvantages of delegated pricing depend on a number of factors. Double marginalization may result in higher transaction prices, with lower network profits and lower consumer surplus. But counteracting this is the positive effect of increased ATM profits on the number of ATMs in the network, which benefits consumers through the network externality. Intranetwork price competition among ATMs can mitigate the problem of double marginalization, but when price competition is intense, delegated pricing may result in fewer profitable ATMs. The net consequence of these factors is not obvious because transaction prices and profits depend on network switching fees. Whether the advantages of decentralized pricing outweigh the disadvantages will depend on specific parameter values.

Let $p_i(\bar{c}_i)$ be the profit-maximizing price at the ith ATM when the effective marginal cost is $\bar{c}_i = r - v_i$ and let p^c be the profit-maximizing centralized price for the network executive. Consider two cases corresponding to $p_i(\bar{c}_i) = 0$ and $p_i(\bar{c}_i) > 0$ when $\bar{c}_i \le 0$.

Case 1

$p_i(\bar{c}_i) = 0$ when $\bar{c}_i \le 0$.

PROPOSITION 2: *Suppose that when the network determines prices centrally,* $p^c = 0$. *If* $p_i(\bar{c}_i) = 0$ *for* $\bar{c}_i \le 0$, *delegated pricing authority is more profitable for the network than centralized pricing authority.*

Proof: Suppose the network owner sets the same switching fee with centralized and decentralized pricing. With centralized pricing, the number of ATMs is determined by $\bar{c}_m = r - v_m = 0$. All ATMs with $\bar{c}_i < \bar{c}_m$ are profitable. With decentralized pricing, these ATMs also will be profitable and if $p_i(\bar{c}) = 0$ for $\bar{c} \le 0$, these ATMs will choose a zero transaction price, as with centralized pricing. In addition, other ATMs indexed by $i > m$ will be profitable at a positive transaction price. The contribution to network profits of ATMs $i = 1, \ldots, m$ is the same as with centralized pricing, and ATMs $i > m$ contribute additional profits.

COROLLARY 2.1: *Under the above conditions, if* $X(0,m)$ *is sufficiently large, welfare is strictly higher with decentralized pricing.*

Proof: The network owner is better off with decentralized pricing because demand for switching is increased at the same switching fee. Consumers are better off because they can access more ATMs, facing the same price at the ATMs that would have been operating with centralized pricing and enjoying positive surplus from the additional ATMs. Moreover, in the limit as $X(0,n) \to \infty$, the network's switching fee is unchanged with delegated pricing.[13]

When ATM sponsors would choose a zero transaction price if their effective marginal cost is negative, the network executive need not be concerned about the problem of double-marginalization or the network externality. All of the ATMs that would have operated when prices are centrally determined also operate with delegated pricing and choose a zero price. In addition, other ATMs may be profitable with delegated pricing.

Case 2

$p_i(\bar{c}) > 0$ when $\bar{c} \leq 0$. Consider the linear model of Example 2: $X_i(p,m) = x(m)(A-p)$, $v_m = v(1-m/M)$, and $c=0$. Unlike Example 1, the network manager cannot ensure that the optimal transaction price for each ATM is zero when the effective marginal cost, $r-v_i$ is nonpositive. With linear demand, the profit-maximizing transaction price at each ATM is positive even if the effective marginal cost is zero, and hence double marginalization is a more serious obstacle to efficient network pricing.

The relative performance of centralized and delegated pricing turns on a comparison of the intensity of demand for ATM transactions, as measured by the intercept A of the demand function, and the value of ATM services to the sponsoring bank, as measured by the intercept v of the value function. When A is small relative to v, the profit-maximizing price at each ATM is relatively low. A small value of A reduces the profit-maximizing price for any given cost of switching, while a large v reduces the effective cost of switching, $r-v_i$, at least for some of the ATMs. Hence double marginalization is not too much of a problem in this situation and delegated pricing is preferred by a profit-maximizing network executive to centralized price determination. When A is large relative to v, the profit maximizing price at each ATM is high and the value of ATM services does not succeed in keeping the effective cost $r-v_i$ low enough to overcome the problem of double marginalization. Centralized pricing may be preferred by the network executive in this instance. However, as discussed below, a substantial network externality can reverse this conclusion because higher prices make more ATMs profitable and this has a positive effect on network profits when the demand externality is large.

The results that follow apply to the linear example with $X_i(p,m) = x(m)(A-p)$, $v_m = v(1-m/M)$, and $c=0$ and with M normalized to one.

PROPOSITION 3: *When the network executive acts to maximize profits, the number of profitable ATM locations is always larger with delegated pricing.*

Proof: See Appendix A.

ATM profitability depends on the value of ATM transactions to the sponsor, the transaction price that the sponsor may charge, and the fee for switching services charged by the network. For a given switching fee, delegated pricing must allow at least as many ATMs to operate profitably because each ATM is free to choose its profit-maximizing price.[14] The significant result that leads to

Proposition 3 is that when pricing authority is delegated to ATM sponsors, the network executive would not choose to set a fee for switching services that is so high that it overwhelms the advantage to each ATM of choosing a profit-maximizing price.

PROPOSITION 4: *With uniform pricing, network profits are higher under centralized pricing when* A>v/2. *Network profits are equal under delegated and centralized pricing when* A≤v/2.

Proof: See Appendix B.

As *A* increases, so does the number of profitable locations under either pricing regime. By Proposition 3, the number of profitable locations is greater with delegated pricing. This contributes to the desirability of delegated pricing for a profit-maximizing network. However, the benefits from more ATM locations must be balanced against the higher transaction prices from double-marginalization. When *A* is large relative to *v*, the balance favors centralized pricing.

In the linear example, the benefits to the network from more ATM locations with delegated pricing exactly cancel the costs of double-marginalization when A≤v/2 and network profits are the same under both pricing regimes. Figure 7.3 illustrates why this occurs when A<v/2. This derivation in Appendix A shows that the number of profitable ATMs with delegated pricing exceeds one-half of all potential locations and with centralized pricing fewer than one-half of the locations would be profitable when A<v/2. The additional locations benefit the network, but with delegated pricing, the transaction price is strictly positive (and hence larger than the optimal price of zero with centralized pricing) for all locations between m_1 and m_2 in Figure 7.3. (m_2 is the same as m^d, the total number of ATMs with delegated pricing.) These higher prices lower network

Figure 7.3
ATM Transaction Prices with Delegated and Centralized Pricing

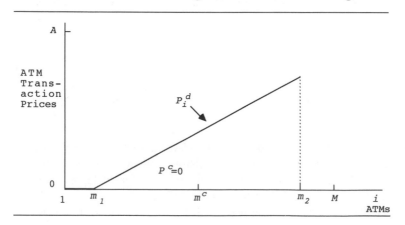

profits by an amount that exactly offsets the benefits of more ATMs. Note, however, that if there were a larger network externality, the greater number of ATMs with delegated pricing could more than offset the adverse effects of higher prices.

At $A=v/2$, all of the ATM locations are profitable when pricing authority is delegated. (See Appendix A.) At larger values of A, delegated pricing cannot increase the number of profitable ATMs because they are all profitable for $A \geq v/2$. But larger values of A contribute to higher prices and more severe problems with double marginalization. Therefore, as A increases beyond $v/2$, centralized pricing is more profitable for the network under the assumption of a uniform switching fee.

PROPOSITION 5: *In the linear example, whenever profits are higher with centralized pricing, so is total surplus.*

Proof: See Appendix C.

Proposition 5 is a key result. Although profits may be higher with centralized pricing, the conclusion is that in these instances total economic welfare is better served with this pricing policy as well. Thus, network profitability is an appropriate guide to welfare-maximizing pricing for the network. There is no evidence from the analysis with uniform pricing that societal interests and network profitability are opposed in the choice of pricing authority. Nonetheless, the two pricing regimes have very different implications for consumer welfare. With delegated pricing, the profit-maximizing price at each ATM is strictly higher than with centralized pricing. For example, when $A=v/2$, the profit-maximizing transaction price under centralized pricing is zero, but under delegated pricing the optimal price is positive at every ATM location, increasing from zero at the ATM with the highest transaction value to A for the ATM with the lowest transaction value. Although total surplus is the same under both pricing regimes when $A=v/2$, consumers are worse off and ATM owners are better off with delegated pricing authority. The benefits of centralized pricing would be reduced, however, if demand were more sensitive to the number of ATMs (a larger network externality). Decentralized pricing results in more ATMs, which would result in a greater increase in surplus if demand is more sensitive to the number of ATMs.[15]

The linear example assumes that there is no price competition among ATMs. Intranetwork price competition would mitigate the problem of double-marginalization. The double marginalization problem would disappear if intranetwork price competition resulted in ATMs pricing at the effective marginal cost $r-v_i$; however, such intense price competition would not be consistent with a consumer preference to access a network of ATMs.[16] Although intense intranetwork price competition eliminates the problem of high ATM margins, it also results in a profit squeeze that can lower the number of viable ATMs relative to centralized pricing. Let $p_i = p(v_i, m)$ be the transaction price for the ith ATM with delegated pricing and intranetwork competition. The number of viable ATMs is determined by $p_m + v_m = r^d$. With centralized pricing, the number of ATMs is determined by $p^c + v_m = r^c$. If the number of ATMs is lower with delegated pricing (because $p(v_m,m) - r^d < (p^c - r^c)$) both network profits and welfare can be lower with delegated pricing.

NETWORK PRICING WITH NONLINEAR SWITCHING FEES

Centralized Pricing Authority

In the most general case the network can set a switching fee r_i, transaction price p_i, and a fixed fee F_i that differ for each ATM, according to the transaction value, v_i, that an ATM "reveals" to the network.[17] The objective of the network is to achieve a "separating equilibrium," in which ATMs with different reported transaction values choose different contracts and no ATM has an incentive to choose a contract designed for an ATM with a transaction value that differs from its actual transaction value. This is a version of the optimal monopoly problem analyzed in Maskin and Riley (1984).

If the network cannot choose discriminatory fees, but is limited to a single usage-sensitive switching fee and a single fixed fee, the use of a two-part pricing structure does not improve network profits or welfare relative to a uniform, linear switching fee when $X_i(p,m) = X_j(p,m)$ and prices are centrally determined. With a two-part pricing structure, the network profits under centralized pricing are

$$N^c = \max_{r,F} (r - c) \sum_{i=1}^{m} X(p,m) + mF$$

and the marginal ATM is determined by

$$(p + v_m - r)X(p,m) = F$$

Substituting for F and rearranging, network profits are

$$N^c = \max_{p,m} (p + v_m - c)mX(p,m)$$

which is the same as network profits with linear prices. When each ATM has the same demand (but different transaction values), control over p and r is equivalent to control over p with any two-part switching fee.

In contrast, a discriminatory two-part pricing structure can, in general, increase network profits under centralized pricing. Consider the following example.

Example 3

Same as Example 2 (the linear model), except that there are only two types of ATMs, with $v_1 > v_2$. Assume that there are equal numbers of both types, normalized to one. With discriminatory two-part prices, the network executive can set prices r_i, F_i, and p_i, with separate values for $i=1,2$. Assuming that the network wants both types of ATM to be profitable, the pricing problem is

$$\max_{r_i, F_i, p_i} \quad (r_1 - c)X(p_1, M) + (r_2 - c)X(p_2, M) + F_1 + F_2$$

subject to

$$(p_1 + v_1 - r_1)X(p_1, M) - F_1 \geq (p_2 + v_1 - r_2)X(p_2, M) - F_2 \tag{IC1}$$

$$(p_2 + v_2 - r_2)X(p_2, M) - F_2 \geq (p_1 + v_2 - r_1)X(p_1, M) - F_1 \tag{IC2}$$

$$(p_1 + v_1 - r_1)X(p_1, M) - F_1 \geq 0 \tag{IR1}$$

$$(p_2 + v_2 - r_2)X(p_2, M) - F_2 \geq 0 \tag{IR2}$$

where ICi stands for the incentive compatibility constraint for type i, $i=1,2$, and IRi stands for the individual rationality constraint.

It is not difficult to see that the network's pricing problem is overdetermined—given the opportunity to regulate transaction prices directly (in a separating equilibrium), the switch fee and the fixed fee are redundant. Arbitrarily, let $r_i = c$. The network pricing problem reduces to collecting the largest amount in fixed fees subject to the incentive compatibility and individual rationality constraints. The solution has the familiar result that the IR constraint is binding only for the type 2 ATMs, and the transaction price for type 1 ATMs is set at the monopoly price. The pricing problem reduces to

$$\max_{p_i, F_i} F_1 + F_2$$

subject to

$$(p_1 + v_1 - c)X(p_1, M) - F_1 \geq (p_2 + v_1 - c)X(p_2, M) - F_2 \tag{IC1}$$

$$(p_2 + v_2 - c)X(p_2, M) - F_2 \geq (p_1 + v_2 - c)X(p_1, M) - F_1 \tag{IC2}$$

$$(p_1 + v_1 - c)X(p_1, M) - F_1 \geq 0 \tag{IR1}$$

$$(p_2 + v_2 - c)X(p_2, M) - F_2 = 0 \tag{IR2}$$

The result is that $p_1 = (A+c-v_1)/2 = p_1^m(v_1,c)$ and $p_2 = (A+c-v_2+(v_1-v_2))/2 > p_2^m$. Network profit with discriminating nonlinear prices is

$$N^c = \frac{1}{2}[(A-c+v_2)^2 + 4\delta^2] \qquad (7.7)$$

where $\delta = (v_1-v_2)/2$. Total surplus is

$$W^c = \frac{3}{4}(A-c+v_2)^2 + \delta(A-c+v_2) + \delta^2 \qquad (7.8)$$

Delegated Pricing Authority

With delegated pricing authority, the network executive cannot control the transaction price, but can only influence the transaction price through the choice of switching fees. The transaction price at the ith ATM is the profit-maximizing price conditional on the switching fee, r_i. There are two cases to consider, corresponding to whether the network can or cannot charge discriminatory fees.

If the network cannot discriminate among ATMs, nonlinear fees can nonetheless improve both network profits and total surplus relative to a uniform switching fee when authority for establishing transaction prices is delegated to the ATM sponsors. For the example with linear demand and two types of ATMs, the network would choose a uniform two-part tariff with r and F chosen to maximize (under the assumption that both types of ATMs operate)

$$(r-c)(X(p_1^d, M) + X(p_2^d, M)) + 2F$$

subject to

$$F \le min[\pi(p_1^d), \pi(p_2^d)]$$
$$p_1^d = (A+r-v_1)/2$$
$$p_2^d = (A+r-v_2)/2$$

The solution is $r=c+\delta$ (where $\delta=(v_1-v_2)/2$), and $F=\pi(p_2^d)$. The fixed fee is set equal to the profit earned by ATMs with the lower transaction value, and the variable switching fee is set above marginal cost. Network profit is

$$\overline{N}^d = \frac{1}{2}[(A-c+v_2)^2 + \delta^2] \qquad (7.9)$$

where the bar denotes nondiscriminatory two-part pricing. Total surplus is

$$\overline{W}^d = \frac{3}{4}(A - c + v_2)^2 + \delta(A - c + v_2) + \frac{3}{4}\delta^2 \qquad (7.10)$$

PROPOSITION 6 (Rey and Tirole): *If the network sets a nondiscriminating two-part tariff, both network profits and total surplus are higher under delegated pricing.*

This result was obtained in Rey and Tirole (1986). The result is easily verified by comparing (7.9) and (7.10) to the corresponding values with a uniform switching fee. The values for network profit and total surplus with centralized pricing appear in Appendix B (recall that nondiscriminating two-part tariffs do not improve profits or total surplus with centralized pricing).

PROPOSITION 7: *Network profits and total surplus are higher with a discriminating, centralized two-part tariff than with a nondiscriminating, delegated two-part tariff.*

If the network executive is unable either to impose transaction prices or to choose prices that discriminate among different ATMs, the best it can do is impose a nondiscriminating nonlinear tariff. Proposition 7 states that both network profits and welfare would be higher if the network could impose final transaction prices and set discriminatory fees. The result is evident by comparing (7.7) and (7.8) to (7.9) and (7.10).

Suppose the network cannot control transaction prices, but can charge a different two-part tariff for different ATMs. One might suppose that this would result in strictly lower profits for the network, because the problem is a constrained version of the centralized pricing model with discriminating two-part tariffs (the constraint being that the network cannot set transaction prices). However, recall that when the network chooses prices centrally and achieves full information revelation with a two-part tariff, the fixed fee and the usage-sensitive fee are redundant because both affect only profit (and not price) when transaction prices are separately determined. This extra degree of freedom implies that pricing delegation need not affect the network's profit with discriminating two-part tariffs. If the network sets $r_1 = c$ and $r_2 = c + 2\delta$, transaction prices and profits are identical to prices and profits when the network sets all prices. Therefore,

PROPOSITION 8: *The delegation of authority for the setting of transaction prices has no effect on prices, profits, or surplus when the network sets discriminating two-part fees. Prices, profits, and total surplus are the same as in the case of centralized pricing with discriminating two-part tariffs.*

The model in Rey and Tirole (1986) is similar to the model in this paper, yet they conclude that there are circumstances in which centralized pricing (resale price maintenance) is profitable, but contrary to societal interests. It is important, therefore, to understand the differences between the model and assumptions in Rey and Tirole and in this paper. Rey and Tirole consider three vertical markets—competition, exclusive territories (ET), and resale price maintenance (RPM)—and permit nondiscriminating two-part tariffs. In the framework of this paper, RPM corresponds to centralized pricing and ET corresponds to delegated pricing. There is no counterpart in this paper to Rey and Tirole's "competition," because the latter assume perfect substitutes, which is a more realistic assumption for retailers than for ATMs.[18] Rey and Tirole conclude that under risk neutrality, ET is more profitable for the manufacturer (the counterpart of the network executive) than RPM; however, social welfare is higher with RPM than with ET. In this paper, ET dominates RPM in both profits and total surplus when the pricing structure allows uniform two-part tariffs.

The models in Rey and Tirole and in this paper differ in important respects. In Rey and Tirole, each retailer has an *uncertain* cost. In this paper, each ATM (retailer) has a *known* effective cost $\bar{c}_i = r_i - v_i$ which is different for every ATM. The ATM sponsor knows the effective marginal cost and the network executive knows only the distribution of costs. Under centralized pricing, the network executive has to set a price high enough so that the desired marginal ATM breaks even. From the point of view of the network executive, the pricing problem (with risk neutrality) is identical to the case of "infinite risk aversion" in Rey and Tirole. In that case they show that both profits and total surplus are higher with ET, as is shown here.[19]

DISPERSION IN AUTOMATIC TELLER MACHINE VALUES AND INTERCHANGE FEES

An interchange fee is a fee paid by bank A to bank B whenever a cardholder who is a depositor at bank A (the "issuing" bank) uses an ATM that is sponsored by bank B (the "acquiring" bank). A main reason for this fee is that the acquiring bank has to provide services to the customer, while the issuing bank derives value from the customer as a depositor of the bank. The differences in transaction values v_i at each ATM can be explained in part by differences in the number of transactions at the ATM that are "on us" (transactions by customers who are depositors at the bank that sponsors the ATM) and the number of transactions that are "foreign" (transactions by customers who are depositors at another bank). If foreign transactions generate no transaction value to the sponsoring bank, but "on us" transactions generate a unit transaction value of v, then $v_i = \alpha_i v$, where α_i is the fraction of transactions at ATM i that are "on us."

The interchange fee is a transfer payment between sponsoring banks. It is not a payment to the network. With centralized pricing authority, the network would establish the interchange fee in order to maximize the profit it can earn from its switching fee. Suppose the network sets an interchange fee $s=v$. Then each ATM would have a transaction value

$$v_i = \alpha_i v + (1 - \alpha_i)s = v$$

There would be no dispersion in transaction values, so the network would maximize profits by setting a monopoly price for transactions and a switching fee $r=p+v$, at which all ATMs are *marginally* profitable. Delegated pricing that is limited to a uniform switching fee could not improve on this allocation, and would equal it only if intranetwork price competition is sufficient to eliminate ATM profit margins. Hence

PROPOSITION 9: *If* $v_i = \alpha_i v$, *where* α_i *is the fraction of transactions that are "on us," the network maximizes profits by centrally determining a transaction price,* p, *and interchange fee,* s, *with* s=v.

Foreign fees are assessed on customers who patronize ATMs not owned by the issuing bank. They differ from interchange fees in that the latter are assessed on issuing banks, while the former are charged directly to customers. Under central price determination, the network would have no reason to impose foreign fees. An interchange fee equal to v, the value of ATM transactions to issuing banks, would equalize differences in transaction values across ATMs resulting from different mixes of "on us" transactions, and a properly chosen switching fee and transaction price would maximize the profit of the network. Neither network profits nor total surplus would be enhanced by foreign fees.

Under delegated pricing authority, interchange and foreign fees are an additional source of income for ATM sponsors. Pursuit of profits may result in interchange fees that exceed substantially the level that would equalize transaction values across ATMs. Interchange fees are an inelastic source of revenue for acquiring ATMs, up to the point where issuing ATMs refuse to honor transactions by cardholders at foreign ATMs where interchange fees are considered excessive.[20] Foreign fees are a source of revenue for issuing ATMs, although the foreign fee competes with the ATM transaction fee as a source of revenue. Let $X_{ij}(\mathbf{p},m)$ be the number of bank i's customers who patronize an ATM sponsored by bank j. Then the profit of bank i, given an interchange fee s_{ji} (imposed by acquiring bank j for transactions by cardholders of bank i) and a foreign fee f_{ij} (imposed by bank i on cardholders for transactions at bank j), is

$$B_i = (p_i + v_i - r)X_{ii}(p_i, m) + \sum_{j \neq i}[(f_{ij} - s_{ji})X_{ij}(p_j + f_{ij}, m) + X_{ji}s_{ij}(p_i + f_{ji}, m)]$$

Bank profits increase with the interchange fee s_{ij} charged for transactions by foreign cardholders, provided the fee is not passed on to customers and provided that the issuing ATM permits its customers to patronize the acquiring bank. The foreign fee f_{ij} also is a revenue source, but the profit-maximizing foreign fee is reduced by the transaction fee of the foreign ATM. For example, with linear demand, the foreign fee that maximizes issuing bank i's profit from transactions at ATM j is

$$f_{ij} = \frac{A - p_j + s_{ji}}{2}$$

The profit-maximizing foreign fee imposed on customers of bank i for transactions at bank j increases with the interchange fee that bank j charges bank i for transactions by the cardholders of bank i. This suggests the possibility that fees could escalate, as higher interchange fees are met with higher foreign fees, with negative consequences for economic welfare. In any case, profit-maximizing interchange and foreign fees are specific to the acquiring and issuing ATMs, and determination of these fees would involve potentially costly bilateral bargaining between banks.

CONCLUSIONS

Many economic systems have the characteristic that, as in ATM networks, consumers benefit from greater participation and that there is a hierarchy of actual or potential decision-making as to the conditions of access and participation in the system. Citing the benefits of delegated pricing authority and intranetwork price competition, Salop (1990) argues that economic welfare would be improved if ATM network executives were compelled to abandon authority for centralized pricing determination in favor of delegated pricing. This analysis does not demonstrate support for the benefits of such a requirement. Although there are instances where delegated pricing authority does increase economic surplus, in those instances it is also a profit-maximizing choice for the network executive.

A requirement to compel delegated pricing authority (or any other pricing rule) should rest on evidence that (1) the suggested rule would have positive implications for economic welfare and (2) in the absence of intervention, agents have no incentive to follow the prescribed rule. While I have offered examples where delegated pricing authority satisfies condition (1), these examples do not satisfy (2). Although the analysis in this paper is not sufficient to show that the private interests of the network executive are always coincident with social objectives with respect to the delegation of pricing authority, it demonstrates parameters under which this correspondence holds. Moreover, shared ATM networks were developed to extend the services that are provided by their member banks to their customers, and may pursue objectives other than maximizing profits of the networks. This is another reason why ATM networks might be reluctant to delegate pricing authority to ATM sponsors, even if the result is higher profits for the network. The complex objectives of ATM networks and the results in this paper which show that even the pursuit of profits need not be inconsistent with economic welfare are at least sufficient to add to the burden of proof for those who argue that intervention is desirable to promote intranetwork price competition in ATM networks.

APPENDIX A: PROOF THAT $m^d \geq m^c$ IN THE LINEAR MODEL WITH UNIFORM FEES

Consider first the case of centralized pricing. Network profits are

$$N^c = rmx(p) \tag{7.1.A}$$

Note that

$$r = p + v_m \tag{7.2.A}$$

By using (1.2), the profit-maximizing price is

$$p^c = max\left[0, \frac{A - v_m}{2}\right] \tag{7.3.A}$$

If one substitutes (7.2.A) and (7.3.A) in (7.1.A) and solves for the profit-maximizing number of ATM locations, then

if $A \geq v/2$

$$p^c = (2A - v)/3$$
$$r^c = (A + v)/3 \tag{7.4a.A}$$
$$m^c = min\left[\frac{1 + A/v}{3}, 1\right]$$

if $A < v/2$,

$$p^c = 0$$
$$r^c = v/2 \tag{7.4b.A}$$
$$m^c = 1/2$$

With delegated pricing, sponsors may choose a different price for each ATM location. Provided p_i^d is between 0 and the choke price A, the profit-maximizing ATM transaction price is

$$p_i^d = \frac{A + r + v_i}{2}$$

Let m_1 be the largest value of i for which $p_i^d \leq 0$. The total number of ATM adopters is determined by the smallest i for which $p_i \geq A$. Let this number be m_2. These numbers are defined by

$$m_1 = 1 - (A + r)/v$$

$$m_2 = 1 + (A - r)/v$$

Note that $m_2 - m_1 < 1$ only if $A < v/2$. Suppose that $A < v/2$. In order to determine m_2 and to compare the result to m^c it is necessary to solve the network's profit-maximization condition and determine the optimal switch fee, r^d. The network's profit is

$$N^d = \int_0^{m_1} rA \, di + \int_{m_1}^{m_2} rx(p_i^d) \, di$$

$$= rA(1 - r/v)$$

and the optimal switching fee is $r^d = v/2$.

Hence the number of adopters with delegated pricing is

$$m^d = 1/2 + A/v > m^c$$

Next consider $A \geq v/2$. Then $m^d = 1$, and from (7.4b.A), $m^d > m^c$ if $A < 2v$. For $A \geq 2v$, $m^c = 1$, but $m^d = 1$ also. Hence $m^d \geq m^c$ always, with strict inequality for $A < 2v$.

APPENDIX B: PROOF THAT WITH UNIFORM FEES, $N^c > (\leq) N^d$ if $A > (\leq) v/2$

From Appendix A, if $A < v/2$, then

$$N^c = rmx(p) = Av/4$$

and

$$N^d = r^d A(1 - r^d/v) = Av/4$$

If $A > v/2$, network profit with centralized pricing is

$$N^c = \frac{1}{v}\left[\frac{A+v}{3}\right]^3$$

Under delegated pricing, one can show that when $A > v/2$, all ATM locations are profitable and each sets a strictly positive price. Then

$$N^d = \int_0^1 rx(p_i^d)di = \frac{r}{4v}[2v(A-r)+v^2]$$

and

$$r^d = (2A+v)/4$$

so that
$$N^d = (2A+v)^2/32$$

It is easy to verify that $N^c > N^d$ if $A > v/2$.

APPENDIX C: PROOF THAT WITH UNIFORM FEES, $W^c \geq W^d$ IF $N^c \geq N^d$

Let $S_i(p_i)$ be the consumer surplus from transactions at the ith ATM. Total surplus is

$$W = \int_0^m [S_i(p_i) + (p_i + v_i)x(p_i)]di$$

Consider first the case where $A < v/2$. Under centralized pricing, $p^c = 0$ and $m^c = 1/2$. Therefore,

$$W^c = \frac{A(A+3v/2)}{4}$$

Under decentralized pricing, using the results in Appendix A, the total profit earned by ATM sponsors is

$$B^d = \int_0^m [v_i - r^d]Adi + \int_{m_1}^{m_2}[p_i^d + v_i - r^d]x(p_i^d)di$$
$$= A(3v^2 + 4A^2)/24v$$

and the total consumer surplus from ATM transactions is

$$S^d = \int_0^m A^2/2 \; di + \int_{m_1}^{m_2} [A - p_i^d]^2/2 \; di$$

$$= A^2(3v - 2A)/12v$$

Hence the total surplus with decentralized pricing when $A < v/2$ is

$$W^d = N^d + B^d + S^d$$

$$= \frac{A(A + 3v/2)}{4}$$

Thus, when $A < v/2$, $N^c = N^d$ and $W^c = W^d$. When $v/2 \leq A < 2v$, $m^c = (1 + A/v)/3 \leq 1$ and

$$W^c = \int_0^{m^c} [S_i(p^c) + (p^c + v_i)x(p^c)] di$$

$$= \frac{2}{v}\left[\frac{A + v}{3}\right]^3$$

If $A > 2v$, $m^c = 1$, in which case

$$W^c = (A + v)(5A + 2v)/18$$

Under decentralized pricing, if $A > v/2$, then $m^d = 1$ and making use of the results in Appendix B,

$$S^d = \int_0^1 [(A - p_i^d)^2/2] di = [(A + 3v/2)^3 - (A - v/2)^3]/196v$$

$$B^d = \int_0^1 [(p_i^d + v_i - r^d)(A - p_i^d) di] = [(A + 3v/2)^3 - (A - v/2)^3]/96v$$

and

$$N^d = (2A + v)^2/32$$

Hence

$$W^d = (2A + v)^2/32 + [(A + 3v/2)^3 - (A - v/2)^3]/64v$$

One can verify that for all values of $A > v/2$, $W^c > W^d$. Also, from Appendix B, $N^c > N^d$ when $A > v/2$.

NOTES

This work was stimulated by discussions with Steve Salop and has benefited greatly from his input. I am also grateful to Paul Allen, Dale Browning, Margaret Guerin-Calvert, Joe Farrell, Tracy Lewis, Stan Paur, Suzanne Scotchmer, and Carl Shapiro for helpful comments and to Nancy Chau and Matt Nagler for research assistance. The views expressed in this paper are solely my own.

1. Technically, the royalty is assessed for the use of the logo of the network that is imprinted on the card.

2. According to Trans Data Corporation (1987a), 62 percent of all banks that participated in shared ATM systems in 1987 charged depositors for foreign transactions, but only 20 percent assessed fees for use of their own ATM terminals.

3. See Kauper (1988).

4. Use of the term "free market" arguably may apply to the freedom of the network to establish restrictions on ATM pricing. This reflects the classic tension over the economic costs and benefits of laws against vertical restraints of trade.

5. See National Bankcard Corporation (NaBanco) v. VISA U.S.A., Inc. (1986)

6. The Supreme Court noted the procompetitive function of pricing agreements in its review of coordinated fees for copyrighted music in American Society of Composers, Authors, and Publishers et al. v. Columbia Broadcasting System et al. (1979).

7. Critics of centralized pricing also argue that foreign fees and transactions fees have similar effects, and that networks typically permit the former. This analysis assumes that under centralized pricing, networks may restrict foreign as well as transactions fees.

8. See Stevens et al. (1987).

9. Retail establishments might sponsor an ATM location to encourage sales. This source of value is not explicitly included in this analysis.

10. If the welfare function is globally concave in p and m, these conditions are the unique optimum.

11. This assumes that the firm cannot impose a different fixed fee for low- and high-value users. Discriminatory two-part tariffs are considered in the fourth section.

12. See Trans Data Corporation (1987b). Start-up and annual fees for membership in shared systems vary substantially for different systems, with some reporting only usage-sensitive fees.

13. The switching fee by itself has no effect on welfare, but it affects the number of ATMs that set a zero price.

14. Note the importance in this result of the assumption that the demand at each ATM is independent of the prices charged by other ATMs. Intranetwork rivalry can reverse the result in Proposition 3.

15. One can show that the benefits of centralized and delegated pricing depend on the shape of the distribution of transaction values. Centralized pricing depends only on the value of the marginal ATM location. Hence, a concave distribution of transaction

values would favor centralized pricing because double marginalization would be more severe for inframarginal ATMs.

16. If all ATMs had the same transaction value, competitive pricing would imply that consumers would frequent only the ATM with the lowest price, which is not consistent with demand for a network of ATMs.

17. The fee structure could be a function of other characteristics not considered here, such as different fixed costs and demand.

18. Moreover, Rey and Tirole assume that the number of retailers is fixed. With a significant demand externality, (perfect) competition would be dominated by centralized pricing to increase ATM profits and encourage development of the network.

19. With only demand uncertainty (a case not considered here), Rey and Tirole show that RPM dominates ET in both profits and total surplus. Thus, in the case of demand uncertainty, the private interests of the network and societal interests coincide.

20. Although issuing ATMs could instruct cardholders that transactions would not be honored at acquiring ATMs whose interchange fees exceed some limit, this would undermine the function of the ATM system. Cardholders would not know when and where they could access ATMs.

8

Computer Reservation Systems and Their Network Linkages to the Airline Industry

Margaret E. Guerin-Calvert and Roger G. Noll

The automation of U.S. travel agencies by means of airline computer reservation systems (CRSs) began in 1976. By 1985, 90 percent of all travel agencies in the United States had terminals or personal computers that were linked via telecommunications lines to sophisticated and massive mainframe computers (U.S. DOJ, 1985, p. 25). CRS mainframes process requests for information and bookings for the millions of flights and fares that are offered by domestic and foreign carriers and then return the information to the travel agent in seconds. The agency uses this information to print tickets, boarding passes, and travel itineraries for its customers. Widespread automation has dramatically improved the efficiency with which travel agents and airlines provide information services, reservations, and tickets to the ultimate consumer—the airline passenger. All but the smallest, most isolated travel agencies now must have some form of automation if they are to survive in the marketplace.

Even before the first CRS was sold to a travel agent, the technology was controversial. Travel agents claimed airlines were too slow in allowing agency automation to proceed, and large airlines with sophisticated internal reservation systems, especially the ones that have been most successful in marketing CRSs to travel agents, have squabbled with other airlines about how the technology ought to be designed and deployed. In recent years, these disputes have led to numerous antitrust and breach of contract lawsuits, and to a seemingly never-ending regulatory controversy in the Civil Aeronautics Board and, later, the Department of Transportation.

The purpose of this paper is to examine the underlying economics of these disputes and to ascertain the policy implications. The second section discusses the basic economic structure of the industry and interprets the policy debate within the context of this structure. The third section provides a historical account of the development of the industry, including the role of public policy in shaping it. The fourth section examines the spate of litigation over CRSs in the late 1980s, and the fifth addresses proposed changes in federal regulation of CRSs. In the last section, we present our main policy conclusions. The essence of our argument is that the underlying economics and technology of the CRS and airline industries do not match well, so that vertical integration of airlines and CRSs reduces the efficiency of both industries.

The paper stresses two major points. First, automation of airline ticketing services has had complicated spillover effects on the airline industry without imposing economic harm on the largest group of consumers of CRSs—the travel agents. The economics of CRSs, owing to scale economies, make its most efficient structure substantially more concentrated than is feasible for an efficient airline industry. In addition, strategic use of a dominant CRS can convey substantial benefits to the airline that owns it. Consequently, the optimal strategy for a vertically integrated airline-CRS company is to use CRS market power to enhance the company position in airline markets. This, in turn, increases concentration and reduces competition in the airline industry. One implication of this strategy is that the controversial practices of CRS vendors—airline access, pricing, and bias—do not tend to raise problems because of their immediate effects on the primary users of a CRS, the travel agents. Hence, travel agents do not have the incentive to complain about or to work to change the most important undesirable effects of CRSs. For airlines and smaller CRS vendors, which have the incentive to complain, their ability to redress the problems either through direct action or in private suits has thus far proven to be very limited. Consequently, our first major policy conclusion is that CRS problems are more likely to be dealt with by regulation or legislation than through private litigation. We illuminate this conclusion by presenting an analysis of the theories and solutions involved in private litigation and by assessing the implications of the outcomes of recent private lawsuits.

The second major point is that quantitative analysis of the consequences of incremental changes in the industry is extraordinarily difficult. Thus, for example, determining which modifications to make in CRS regulations, deciding whether to coordinate U.S. CRS regulation with that of other countries, and computing what the competitive effects will be of a merger of smaller CRSs are all difficult undertakings. Changes or modifications of one aspect of CRS competition can have unintended—or in some cases, no—effects on airline competition or on the competition among CRS vendors. Improvements in CRS competition may have minor effects on airline competition. We consider this point by examining the issues and problems that confronted the Department of Transportation in its review of the CRS rules and in the issues raised by the recently approved Datas II–Pars CRS merger.

TECHNICAL AND ECONOMIC FEATURES OF A COMPUTER RESERVATION SYSTEM

A CRS is a highly efficient means of exchanging information between an airline and a customer, as represented by a travel agent. Internal airline studies have estimated that CRSs have reduced the cost to an airline of making a reservation from approximately $7.50 to $.50 (U.S. DOJ, 1983, p. 119). A survey of travel agents reported that installing a CRS raised their productivity by 42 percent (Harris, 1982, p. 56). As a result, the direct social costs of airline reservation and ticketing have fallen dramatically—as much as 80 per-cent—owing to the development of CRSs. Nevertheless, the profit-maximizing design of a CRS for a vertically integrated airline is probably not the most efficient form of the technology. To understand why this is so requires some details about how the technology works.

Computer Reservation System Technology and Its Links to Travel Agents and Airlines

Although a CRS could be designed in several ways, the existing systems are constructed as follows. Travel agents normally are connected to a large CRS mainframe by a dumb terminal and a private telephone line, both of which are dedicated to exclusive use within a single CRS. In most cases the terminal is owned by the CRS vendor, and the telephone line is also leased by the CRS. The CRS vendor then charges the agent a monthly fee that is normally lower than the cost of the connection. In some cases monthly charges are zero as long as the agent satisfies minimum use provisions in the contract with the CRS vendor.

Typically, agents connect their terminal to various peripheral devices in the agency for printing tickets, boarding passes, and itineraries and for keeping records. When an agent sells a ticket through a CRS, the CRS vendor charges the airline a booking fee—in 1990, $1.85 per flight segment. Booking fees account for most of the revenue of a CRS.

The mechanics of how a ticket agent makes a reservation are quite simple. Typically a passenger requests travel between a particular city pair, with vary-ing degrees of specificity regarding date, time of day, service class, and carrier. The travel agent then sends a message to the CRS mainframe indicating the passenger's basic request. The CRS responds with a list of flights that fulfill the request, indicating the availability of seats in each fare class for each flight, as well as the flight schedule. A passenger expressing the desire to minimize the price of the ticket normally will be presented with a different menu of choices, assuming that the agent requests a list of bargain fares, than will be presented to a passenger requesting a fixed departure time or a specific carrier.

The response to the agent's request is normally a relatively short list of al-ternatives: six to eight flights displayed on the CRT of the agent's terminal. If none of these is suitable or if the passenger requests more options, the agent can ask for more information, and another six or eight alternatives will appear on the screen. For heavily traveled markets over long distances, with numerous feasible connecting flights, literally dozens of separate screens could be made available to the agent. Once the passenger selects a flight, the agent books the reservation; usually the agent obtains a seat assignment and prints tickets and boarding passes for the passenger.

The key to the greater efficiency of a CRS is that it provides a far better means of communication between a travel agent and an airline than the old system of placing a telephone call. A CRS can implement its communication system in three basic ways, each of which has important characteristics in terms of the efficiency of the CRS. An understanding of these methods of designing a CRS is essential to understanding the competitive strategies of CRS vendors and of airlines.

In the 1960s, airlines began developing their own computerized internal reservations systems.[1] Because many passengers seek itineraries over more than a single airline, the airlines needed a means for making reservations in each others' systems before there were CRSs. AR Inc. provided this mechanism. Each airline computer system contains software that communicates through AR Inc. information about the availability of seats on each flight at each price. In the late 1970s, when some internal systems were enhanced and marketed to travel agents, the CRS vendors continued to use the AR Inc. system to obtain information about seat inventories and making reservations.

Two problems arise in this first way of designing CRSs. One is that the information in a CRS (and through AR Inc.) about seat availability is not necessarily current. Indeed, in the postderegulation environment, prices sometimes change daily and airlines use sophisticated computer programs to reallocate seats among fare categories virtually continuously (Levine, 1987). As a result, the information available through AR Inc. may not be up to date. The second problem is that this system involved three separate communications links and three separate computers, and so was more prone to error. As a result, this system led to the "no rec problem," whereby a passenger would arrive at the airport with a properly printed ticket, but the airline would have no record of the passenger in its own reservation system. Even without no rec, however, this CRS design led to situations in which a passenger seemingly had made a reservation, but then was informed by the travel agent several hours or even days later that the reservation could not be honored.

A second way of designing a CRS is called "direct access." This approach enables a travel agent to read fare and availability data in an airline's computer system. Because this information is more up to date, it substantially reduces the chance of encountering the "no rec" problem. Nonetheless, under direct access an agent cannot work in the airline's internal system. The booking must be done through the CRS to which the agent subscribes. Thus, it is sometimes the case that by the time the booking is made, the fare class is sold out.

A third approach is "multi-access" whereby the job of the CRS is to allow the travel agent to work inside the internal computer system of an airline. This approach makes the CRS more of a switch and less of a separate system, although even in multi-access the CRS can, and usually will, maintain some ability to maintain records and display flight schedules and prices. But most of the work by the travel agent is done directly inside the computer system of an airline. This requires that a travel agent know which airline's CRS will provide the best booking most quickly, given the passenger's request. Most likely, this will be the airline on which the agent intends to make a booking. In some cases, however, an agent may pick an airline because it has a well-designed internal computer system and use the airline's direct access capability to sell a ticket on another airline. In this mode, the first airline's terminal computer system is performing as a direct link CRS.

Present CRSs use a combination of the three approaches. The hosts of the system—the owners and perhaps a few other largely noncompeting carriers— use "look and book," a version of multi-access that enables agents to operate in the airline's internal system when they wish to do so. Most other large airlines, and smaller carriers that purchase internal reservation services from large carriers, are connected by direct access. This usually avoids no rec but provides inferior information. Finally, the remaining carriers are served through AR Inc. access, or are not served at all.

One key to understanding the economics of a CRS is that it substantially alters the structure of the costs facing an agent in ticketing a passenger. Without a CRS, an agent would normally search the *Official Airline Guide (OAG)* for suitable flights and then place a telephone call to an airline to make the reservations. For direct flights, the *OAG* is in some ways a superior means for finding schedules, for it lists all direct flights—not just the six or eight selected for display by the CRS. But for connecting flights, the *OAG* lists very few— and only if the airlines so listed pay a fee. Hence, finding a suitable connecting flight can involve a very long search through the *OAG*. In addition, the *OAG* cannot tell the agent which fare classes in each flight are already fully booked. The old system required agents to call the airlines for this information. Hence, booking a flight sometimes could require calls to several airlines.

The effect of all this on agents is as follows. First, a CRS greatly reduces the costs of ticketing for both the travel agent and the airline because is replaces relatively slow, expensive, and error-prone telephone conversations with a quick, inexpensive, and accurate computer link. Second, the part of ticketing costs that is reduced the least is searching for a suitable flight. For direct flights, a page of the *OAG* listing all direct flights is replaced by a small number of candidate flights, so that the time required for comprehensive search actually can be greater on a CRS than in the old system. Connecting flights also can go either way—a few flights in the *OAG*, which are actually advertising, are often replaced by an endless scroll of possibilities in a CRS. The latter can be beneficial if all of the connections paid for in the *OAG* are unsuitable but is costly if the *OAG* listings are usually acceptable or if an experienced agent knows where to look beyond the advertised connections in the *OAG*. Thus, whereas a CRS reduces costs in general, it creates an incentive for the travel agent to do a shorter search for the best possible flight for the customer. As a practical matter, approximately 92 percent of the time travel agents book a passenger on a flight displayed on the first screen that arrives after an inquiry, and over half of the time they book the flight on the first line of the first screen. By comparison, in 1981, an internal American Airlines study reported that SABRE listed an American flight first about 75 percent of the time, even though it was actually the best flight, given the passenger's request, only 46 percent of the time (U.S. DOJ, 1983, pp. 81–83).

If customers were fully informed about flight schedules and fares, comparison shopping among travel agents would force an efficient search for suitable flights and fares and hence force efficient screen displays by competitive CRS vendors. But with imperfectly informed customers—as can be expected with literally millions of flights and fares available in the postderegulation era—the economic theory of efficient consumer search teaches that customer shopping is unlikely to police efficient behavior by agents (Wilde and Schwartz, 1979). In this case, the incentive to search is further diminished by the fact that, in most cities, one or two CRSs dominate the travel-agency market.[2] Hence, comparison shopping among agents does not imply comparison shopping among CRSs. To the extent that CRS architecture influences the behavior of agents, consumers will tend to receive similar service from all agencies using the same CRS, and hence have less to gain from search, if the CRS market is concentrated.

The presence of imperfectly informed consumers creates opportunities for "information rents"—that is, excess profits arising from strategic use of superior knowledge for agents, carriers, and CRS vendors. For example, agents are likely to engage in inefficient conservation of their own time and effort at the expense of their customers. Moreover, agents' incentives are distorted further by the structure of commissions. Agents are paid a percentage of sales by the airlines, and in addition are given bonuses based on sales volume "overrides," so that for each airline an agent's earnings increase more rapidly than in proportion to sales. Hence, agents have an incentive to sell high-price tickets and to concentrate sales on a small number of airlines.

The Problems of Information Bias

The economics of travel-agency behavior lie at the heart of one controversial practice by airline-owned CRSs: display bias. A CRS must have a computer algorithm for deciding which flights to list on the first display in response to an inquiry by a travel agent. Factors that enter into this algorithm are departure and arrival times, whether the flight is nonstop, direct, or connecting, and whether a connecting flight requires a change of carrier. Bias consists of writing an algorithm such that one airline tends to be listed on the first display more frequently than it ought to be according to objective criteria. Given that airlines can rely upon agents to buy nearly all tickets from the first display, a CRS can increase the market share of an affiliated carrier by adopting a display algorithm that elevates that carrier's flights in the display ordering.

In the absence of vertical integration, a CRS, like the *OAG* in selling connection listings, might simply sell display positions to the highest bidder. This would enable the CRS to capture information rents; however, it would not necessarily lead to greater concentration of airline markets because each airline would be likely to buy some display preference for some of its flights. Vertical integration, however, can confer display preferences on the carriers owning the CRS. Indeed, it may increase the potential profits of CRS in two ways. First, it may retard entry and facilitate collusion in the airline industry if, as is the case, the number of CRS firms is substantially fewer than the number of airlines. Second, vertical integration permits a CRS to prevent inefficient substitution of other airline ticketing methods for CRS sales through travel agents. Airlines without a CRS have an incentive to bypass CRSs if booking fees are high and if the display bias works against them in each CRS; however, now that nearly all major airlines are CRS partners, this circumstance does not arise.[3] For small, regional carriers, substitution away from a CRS is less likely because they are especially dependent on large carriers for the sale of tickets on connecting flights (i.e., interlining). By 1990, the only significant carrier that did not sell tickets through a CRS was Southwest Airlines.

The Computer Reservation System as a Network Technology

Another key to understanding the economics of a CRS lies in the relationships among its users. A CRS is a network technology in all of the technical and economic senses of the term, with all that this implies economically.

First, a CRS is an extremely large telecommunications network in which thousands of terminals simultaneously can access a central processor to engage in the exchange of information. Most intelligence in the network is centralized in large mainframe computers, which store and process vast quantities of data that are constantly being changed. Not only are airlines frequently altering routes, fares, and schedules, but seat availability changes with every sale. The core data management problem implied by CRS technology, therefore, has a substantial element of scale economies in software and data storage.

Second, a CRS is a network technology in the sense that airline customers create an important "subscription externality" with respect to travel agencies.[4] The value of a CRS to agents depends on the number of airlines that allow reservations, ticket sales, and seat assignments to be made on the system. Normally, travel agents subscribe to only one CRS. To agents, by far the most important characteristic of a CRS is whether the agent can use it for automated ticket sales on all of the airlines that the agent's customers want to fly. Hence, a CRS is unlikely to succeed in a particular geographic area if it does not do at least as well as its competitors in providing booking services for the airlines serving the area.

Third, even among airlines there can be a "subscription externality." For airlines with connecting but noncompeting routes, a CRS reduces the cost of interlining—that is, routing a passenger over more than one airline. Hence, when one airline becomes a CRS customer, its interlining partners benefit.

Fourth, travel agents create a corresponding "subscription externality" for airlines. The number of tickets an airline can sell through a CRS depends on how many agencies use it. From the perspective of an airline, dealing with a CRS is not a decision that is usefully regarded as the result of conventional marginal analysis. Just as a CRS cannot succeed without including information and booking capabilities for all the major airlines, an airline cannot expect to operate profitably in a market if it does not sell its tickets through all of the CRSs that are active in that market. In most large cities all CRSs have significant market shares, so a national air carrier must use the booking services of all CRSs. In the late 1980s, Delta Airlines's Datas II was by far the smallest CRS, but its national market share exceeded 5 percent, and its share in several large cities served by Delta exceeded 20 percent. Typically, airline companies have operating profits of less than 5 percent of sales and have a "lumpy" cost structure. That is, not only do fixed costs account for a large fraction of total costs, but even variable costs depend in large measure on the number of flights, rather than the number of passengers flown. In most markets, the number of flights is also lumpy—a small integer—which prevents adjustment of flights in response to a small change in total passengers. Hence, the loss of a few passengers per flight, such as would occur if an airline withdrew from even a small CRS, can eliminate a large fraction—if not all—of an airline's profits. Thus, the subscription externality from travel agents to airlines produces a large discontinuity in the net revenue effect for an airline from subscribing to a CRS. As a result, an airline normally has no choice but to sell tickets through all available CRSs.

The combination of scale economies and subscription externalities confers market power on a CRS. Specifically, it can extract subscription externalities from subscribers without fearing competitive entry as long as entry requires substantial sunk costs—as is obviously the case in the CRS business. However, with several CRS vendors in the market, rent extraction from travel agents is impractical without collusion. If travel-agent subscribers are of value to airlines, a CRS can increase the discontinuity in an airline's revenues arising from CRS participation by adding more agents. The latter increases the airline's willingness to pay for participation; hence CRS vendors will bid down the price of agency subscriptions to reflect their externality value to airlines. But no such mechanism exists to bid down airline participation fees. One CRS is not a substitute for another as long as each agency uses only one CRS. Thus, nothing prevents a CRS from extracting excess profits from airline customers. In fact, because CRS participation by an airline involves payments of booking fees, airline participation can be used to cartelize airline markets and to pass the gains from cartelization through to the CRS. Booking fees enter into the marginal cost of a passenger; hence, they can be used to enforce a monopoly price in airline markets. As long as the cartelizing booking fee is low enough not to cause airlines to drop out of a CRS, all airlines will continue to use all CRS vendors, and CRS vendors will succeed in collecting both efficiency gains arising from CRS technology and monopoly profits created in the airline industry. The extent to which CRSs are being used for these purposes is the heart of the policy controversy.

THE COMPUTER RESERVATION SYSTEM CONTROVERSY IN HISTORICAL PERSPECTIVE

The automation of travel agencies developed concurrently with, and was spurred by, the deregulation of the domestic airline industry in 1978. Deregulation removed restrictions on entry and exit into city-pair markets and on the types and numbers of fares. Generally, the new regime allowed airlines to change prices quickly in response to market conditions. The result was an immediate proliferation in the number of flights and fares. Moreover, the elimination of entry and exit restrictions permitted carriers to rationalize their route structures into the more efficient hub and spoke system. New carriers were established, and both new and old carriers began to enter new city-pair markets that had been served only by one, two, or three firms.[5]

The growing number of carriers and the increased number of new options for consumers increased the importance to an airline of getting information about new services to consumers. Nearly all carriers found that listing their flights and fares in a CRS, and having reservations made through a CRS, was the easiest and most efficient way to reach the maximum number of consumers. They also found that the information in a CRS about sales patterns across flights and fare categories could be extremely useful in informing pricing and scheduling decisions.

The Nature of the Computer Reservation System Controversy

All analysts agree that CRSs came to play an essential role in the distribution of air transportation services in the United States. Automation provided substantial efficiencies in providing information to consumers about flights and fares and in facilitating bookings, ticket sales, seat reservations, and other aspects of airline services. Nevertheless, even though the development of CRSs created an opportunity for dramatic improvements in the efficiency of the distribution system for air transportation, the last decade has been marked by continual debate, litigation, regulatory intervention, and threats of congressionally imposed divestiture of CRSs. While the nature of the controversy surrounding CRSs is complex, the issue behind these events can be stated simply: the ownership of CRSs by airlines, as suppliers of CRS services and competitors with CRS consumers (other airlines), creates the potential for dramatic gains from market power in CRSs for reasons described in the second section. These gains have traditionally not been found primarily in selling CRS services to travel agents. Rather, most of the benefits of market power in CRSs accrue in the form of booking fees from airlines, deterred or reduced entry and competition in airline markets, higher prices for airline services, and additional revenues from diversion of passengers to the airline that owns the CRS.

The primary reason for the intense litigation and federal and state intervention into the CRS industry is that it is directly linked with the performance of the so-recently deregulated airline industry. One manifestation of the controversy over CRSs is found in two groups of antitrust suits. The first were filed in 1984 by a large number of carriers against United and American, then the sole owners of the two leading CRSs, APOLLO and SABRE, with market shares at that time of about 30 and 50 percent, respectively. These suits alleged that United and American had exercised market power and dramatically reduced competition in CRS and airline markets by imposing excessive booking fees and by using CRS ownership to disadvantage competing airlines. Eventually, these suits were consolidated into two separate cases, one involving the various Texas Air Corporation airlines (*Continental Airlines et al. v. American Airlines and United Airlines*, 1986), henceforth referred to as the Texas Air case, and the other involving several other carriers, including U.S. Air, Northwest, Midway, and Alaska, henceforth referred to as the Northwest case. All but Northwest, Midway, Alaska, and Muse (Southwest) eventually settled and the latter case was decided in favor of United and American but is on appeal.

The second group of suits is the so-called travel-agency litigation.[6] Although many of these lawsuits pit a travel agency against United, American, or TWA, the travel agents were actually represented in most cases by Texas Air Corporation. The central allegation in these lawsuits is that the CRS vendors imposed liquidated damages in the event of conversion to another CRS that substantially exceeded the actual damages caused by conversion. The plaintiffs further alleged that these clauses deter entry and competition in CRS markets. In these cases, United and American claimed that the liquidated damages clauses were reasonable under contract law. In all but one case, the U.S. District Court has ruled in favor of the defendants; however, while these were on appeal, and before many others were litigated, all the cases involving Texas Air were settled as part of the settlement of Texas Air's antitrust claim. In the only travel-agent case lost by a CRS vendor, TWA lost after claiming that it was following industry practice and, in any case, lacked market power to impose onerous terms.

Essentially everyone involved in the debate about CRSs, except for the two largest vendors, believes that the problems engendered by these vertical linkages between CRSs and airlines have reduced substantially the potential gains from deregulation. At the same time, deregulation would not have been able to proceed as swiftly without the widespread automation of travel agencies. In any case, the airline industry became substantially more concentrated during the 1980s due to mergers and bankruptcies. This consolidation, combined with several joint ventures in the CRS industry, has led to a situation in which few "have-not" carriers remain.[7]

If almost everyone now has a stake in a CRS, why is there continuing debate and controversy? The battleground has switched in part to the terms and conditions of CRS competition. With the automation of travel agencies in the United States virtually complete, vendors are battling over market share. Conversions of agencies from one vendor to another have become the main focus of competition. In addition, concerns remain over airline booking fees and the effects of market power in CRSs on airline competition.

The Structural Background of the Computer Reservation System Controversy

There is widespread agreement that if there is ease of supply-side substitution, the relevant markets at issue here are the national markets for computer reservation services and for airline transportation. In a perfectly competitive world, with easy entry and exit, both CRSs and airline companies would easily by able to substitute service in one locality for service in another. Nonetheless, the departure from the competitive norm appears to vary substantially among localities.

With respect to airlines, although each major national carrier tends to concentrate service in few long-distance routes and out of a handful of hubs, several airlines are firmly established as national carriers, with at least some presence in all or most regions and major cities. In principle, each can respond to major changes in supply or demand in a particular area by altering its route structure and pattern of daily flights to take advantage of emerging market opportunities. In addition, large regional carriers are positioned to expand their networks rapidly when competitive opportunities arise. For example, a relatively small, regional carrier—Midway—for awhile displaced Eastern in Philadelphia by taking advantage of the sale of Eastern's gates in Eastern's bankruptcy and reorganization.

Likewise, CRS vendors face few technological barriers to entering a new market anywhere in the nation, although varying perceptions among travel agents concerning the quality and functionality of some systems may affect the likelihood of successful entry. The basic technology of a CRS is essentially fungible among agencies. Terminal hardware and support can be provided to any travel agent wishing to acquire the services of any CRS, and can be moved easily and quickly from one agency to another. Telecommunications links are acquired on short-term rental from common carriers, and can be connected or disconnected in days, if not hours. Hence, even though the travel-agent market (and hence one aspect of the demand side of the CRS market) is local, the possibility for supply substitution throughout the nation makes the CRS market national in scope.

Nevertheless, the current reality for both airlines and CRSs is that the extent of meaningful CRS competition (and, likewise, the degree to which specific local markets are monopolized) varies considerably. To understand why this is so requires an understanding of the historical development of both the airline and CRS industries. The postderegulation airline industry is widely studied and understood and so requires only brief summary here.[8] In essence, the story turns on the development of the hub-spoke route structure. During the Civil Aeronautics Board (CAB) era, route structures were allocated through a regulatory process and not on the basis of the optimal structure from the perspective of cost and demand considerations. The major national carriers tended to be awarded a crosshatched structure, usually with some concentration in particular regions. In addition, regional carriers were awarded a dense pattern of shorter routes involving large numbers of smaller cities.[9]

Owing to the underlying economics of the airline business, the old route patterns only made sense among a relatively few of the nation's largest cities. For most service, it made sense to develop hubs: cities which served as a primary home for service and management of the airline, and the home base of in-flight personnel. The route structure would then be a large number of spokes from the hub—flights to cities of all sizes originating from the home location. Long-distanced travel between two medium-size cities, or even between a large city and a medium-sized or small one, would then normally involve travel through one of these hubs and a change of planes. Whereas some hubs had developed before deregulation, the regulated route structures had prevented as much hubbing as was economically warranted. After deregulation, most of the nation's airlines restructured their routes around several hubs; TWA was an important exception, hubbing only in St. Louis.

The structure of the airline business that emerged from hubbing was one in which the effectiveness and extent of competition differed substantially from region to region and locality to locality. Smaller hub cities did not have sufficient demand to support more than one hubbing carrier, so except for routes connecting hubs of different carriers, passengers in these cities often experienced less than full competition on many routes. In some large cities, one carrier, sometimes through merger, acquired nearly all of the capacity of an airport, and so achieved market power in serving that city. Examples are USAir in Pittsburgh, Northwest in Detroit, and TWA in St. Louis. Meanwhile, in most large cities (especially cities serving as a hub for more than one airline), airline competition was vigorous. The upshot is that hubbing and airport capacity constraints have caused the degree of competition to vary substantially from region to region and route to route because the deregulated structure of the industry involves an uneven pattern of entry barriers—relatively high in some places, quite low in others. Hence, the extent to which airlines compete differs dramatically among the airlines, depending on the details of their hub structure and their rights to scarce airport capacity.[10]

The Historical Roots of the Controversy: Three Eras of Computer Reservation Systems

The development of the CRS industry parallels the evolution of the postderegulation airline industry. Its history can usefully be separated into three "eras": (1) from the early 1970s to the early 1980s—the origin and development of CRSs amidst allegations that the largest CRS vendors engaged in bias and other anticompetitive practices; (2) from the early 1980s to the mid 1980s—the first public investigations into CRS practices and the development and implementation of the CABs CRS rules in November 1984; and (3) 1985 to 1991, the postregulation period of intensive litigation.[11] Most expected the last period to have fewer problems and substantial improvement in the technological achievement of CRSs. Instead the last period has been marked by private litigation and a renewed look at regulation. Indeed, some have concluded that divestiture or some other dramatic structural change is the only effective solution to the problems that have arisen in the industry during the past decade.

Before examining these three eras in detail, some overall background information about trends in the industry is useful. To begin, the explosive growth in the importance of CRSs to travel agencies took place from approximately 1979 to 1982. In 1979, about 14 percent of agencies were automated, but by late 1981 and early 1982, nearly 70 percent were automated (ASTA, 1983, p. 45; Harris, 1988, p. 15). During roughly the same period, the fraction of airline tickets sold by travel agents also grew, from 38 percent in 1977 to 60 percent in 1983 (CAB, 1982, p. 19; U.S. DOJ, 1983, p. 1). Thus, taking into consideration that the largest travel agencies were automated first, by 1981 or 1982— at the transition from the first to the second era automated travel agencies first accounted for more than half of airline ticket sales.

Throughout the history of the CRS industry, APOLLO and SABRE have been the most successful systems, and as a result have been almost continuously monitored by government. Hence, for these systems we can obtain data on their historical patterns of revenues and expenditures, which are shown in Table 8.1. An important feature of this table is that it does not include estimates of either the enhanced profits of the owner-airline owing to CRS synergies or the savings in lower ticket-selling costs of the sponsoring airline obtained by using computers, rather than airline personnel, to communicate with travel agents. It also does not include imputations for the booking fees that the CRS would charge to its owner-airline if the two were not affiliated. Thus, the table substantially understates the value of the CRS to its owner, as is born out by the fact that references made to documents from both American and United show that they regarded their CRS ventures as profitable from the beginning despite the cash losses shown in the table.[12]

Table 8.1
Historical Cash Flows Generated by Airline Computer Reservation Systems
(in $ million)

APOLLO	1975	1976	1977	1978	1979	1980	1981	1982	1983	1984	1985	1986
Cash Revenues												
Participant Fees[1]	0.0	0.0	0.0	0.0	0.0	3.9	9.3	21.2	51.9	60.1	152.6	174.4
Subscriber Fees	0.0	0.2	1.6	4.7	10.3	20.0	33.3	43.8	52.0	73.0	78.8	97.5
Total Cash Rev.	0.0	0.2	1.6	4.7	10.3	24.0	42.6	64.9	103.9	141.1	231.4	271.9
Cash Expenditures												
Op. Expenses	0.2	0.4	1.1	4.8	6.4	15.7	23.8	34.4	39.9	43.0	53.6	68.6
Equip. Investments	0.4	0.4	2.5	7.0	4.2	23.8	21.4	11.9	34.9	44.0	64.0	45.7
Develop. Expenses[2]	1.0	1.0	1.2	1.8	2.8	4.0	6.2	9.5	8.6	17.3	13.1	17.4
Sub. Network[3]	0.2	0.7	3.0	5.9	12.2	29.4	33.1	46.1	50.1	60.9	79.0	95.2
Total Cash Expend.	1.7	3.4	7.9	19.4	25.7	72.9	84.5	101.9	142.6	105.2	209.8	227.0
Net Cash Flow	(1.7)	(3.2)	(6.3)	(14.8)	(15.4)	(48.9)	(41.9)	(37.0)	(38.7)	(24.1)	21.6	44.9

SABRE

Cash Revenues

Participant Fees[1]	0.0	0.0	0.0	0.0	15.4	23.5	21.7	46.7	86.6	199.1	230.9	—
Subscriber Fees	0.3	2.4	5.9	13.9	16.6	30.2	59.7	71.6	83.5	93.4	105.7	—
Total Cash Revenues	0.3	2.4	5.9	13.9	32.0	53.7	81.4	118.3	170.1	292.5	336.6	—

Cash Expenditures

Operating Expenses	1.1	3.4	6.3	10.8	14.1	22.9	32.8	41.5	45.2	65.5	87.2	—
Equipment Investments	2.9	8.6	22.4	24.6	28.4	19.5	22.9	18.6	21.0	64.4	55.7	—
Development Expenses[2]	0.9	1.6	1.9	3.5	4.5	4.2	6.6	8.0	11.3	16.7	17.1	—
Subscriber Network[3]	1.7	4.7	8.2	15.2	21.3	25.8	33.8	44.7	53.6	78.7	92.6	—
Total Cash Expenditures	6.6	18.3	38.8	54.1	68.3	72.4	96.1	112.8	131.1	225.5	252.6	—
Net Cash Flow	(6.3)	(15.9)	(32.9)	(40.2)	(36.3)	(18.7)	(14.6)	5.5	39.0	67.0	84.0	—

1. Includes back log fees and charges for sales of marketing data and other CRS-generated products to participants.
2. Includes computer programming, software acquisition, and other expenses for developing the capacity to generate and store computerized reservation records.
3. Includes expenditures for marketing CRS services to current and prospective subscribers, installing and servicing equipment at subscriber locations, and training and supporting subscriber personnel.
Source: U.S. Department of Transportation (1989, pp. 51, 53).

The first major lesson from Table 8.1 is that both APOLLO and SABRE faced very low initial costs of entry. Each managed to begin operations and to serve its first few hundred travel agencies for an investment of less than $20 million. Thus, very little investment was risked by either entrant to resolve the earlier disagreement within the industry about whether a CRS for travel agents was a viable business. For both SABRE and APOLLO, significant investments in their systems did not begin until after two to four years of experience had been gained, when the massive growth in automated agencies took place. Moreover, nearly all of this investment was in hardware, not software. The hardware requirements of a CRS are mainly determined by the number of agencies subscribing to the system and their volume of ticket sales. This hardware can be acquired in small units of capacity as demand requires. The software does involve significant fixed costs; however, software has never been a substantial cost to either CRS.

The third major lesson from Table 8.1 is that neither APOLLO nor SABRE derived any revenue from airlines until 1980, when about half of all travel agencies were subscribers. Moreover, immediately after the CAB rules were promulgated in late 1984, revenues from airlines approximately tripled, thereafter accounting for approximately two-thirds of CRS revenues. Neither APOLLO nor SABRE showed a positive cash flow until airline booking fees became a significant part of revenue. This, in turn, did not occur until nearly all of the agencies were automated and were signed to long-term contracts with stiff liquidated damages and minimum use provisions, as described in the third section.

The fourth lesson is that CRS pricing to travel agencies probably has *never* been designed to recover the marginal cost of providing service to a subscriber. Three entries in Table 8.1 record costs of automating an agency. "Subscriber network" refers to training and servicing agencies, promoting CRS capabilities to them, and installing and maintaining hardware. When the capital components of these costs are appropriately amortized, these costs are essentially strictly proportional to the number of terminals connected to a CRS, so average and marginal subscriber network costs are approximately equal. "Operating expenses" include some important costs of serving travel agencies, notably communications costs, which also are essentially proportional to terminals in use. Finally, "equipment investments" include terminals and other devices owned by the CRS which are installed in an agency. These, too, when properly amortized, are essentially proportional to terminals in use. But note that in most years revenues from subscribers are less than subscriber network costs, and never are very much larger. If subscriber prices were set equal to long-run marginal cost, subscriber revenues would have to exceed subscriber network costs in every year. Thus, it appears likely that subscriber prices have always been below the marginal cost of service.

To understand these broad trends in the industry requires understanding how the industry developed and what business strategies were selected by its participants. Hence, we turn to a detailed discussion of events and practices during each of the three eras.

The First Computer Reservation System Era: 1970–1980

In the early 1970s, travel agents wanted desperately to obtain computerization of their operations. At this time, airline ticket sellers in airports and airline offices in cities used the internal computer systems of the airlines. The major domestic carriers had automated their internal systems by the early 1960s, and had made great strides in improving these systems since then. Of course, the use of computers greatly enhanced the efficiency of booking and ticketing, giving the airlines' direct sales offices a significant advantage over travel agents. Until the deployment of CRS, travel agencies did most of their business booking package tours and charters, while airlines sold most of the standard fare tickets.

In 1974, the American Society of Travel Agents (ASTA) was on the verge of reaching an agreement with Control Data Corporation to create a CRS for travel agents that was independent of the airlines. Fearing a loss of control should a third party enter this business, the airlines formed an industry consortium to explore the feasibility of a Joint Industry CRS (JICRS) making computerization available to agents. The idea was that the JICRS would be an industry-wide joint venture, producing a single CRS that would be used by all travel agencies that desired automation. This succeeded in forestalling the ASTA/ Control Data venture. But then in early 1976, the three most important national domestic carriers—United (APOLLO), American (SABRE), and TWA (Pars)— each launched its own CRS for sale to travel agents, and the JICRS collapsed. These airlines were soon followed by smaller carriers (Frontier and Allegheny). Each new CRS venture was based on the sponsoring airline's internal reservation system. Each airline included the flights of other airlines—albeit on a limited basis—in its own system to facilitate ease of interlining. Hence, the new CRS offerings, despite their affiliation with a single airline, could offer information on a variety of flights beyond those of the sponsor.

At the time that these systems were initially marketed, there was considerable disagreement over the potential market for travel-agent computerization. The travel-agent trade association, ASTA, took the position that the potential market was large; however, most airlines regarded it as limited to the largest agencies. The early entrants apparently expected to automate only a few hundred locations. But ASTA was correct; American and United, in particular, soon discovered that the demand for their CRS was far greater than they had expected. They automated more agents in the first few months of their operations than they had expected would be automated in two years, and, until the early 1980s, had long waiting lists of agencies seeking automation.

During the first five years of CRSs, from 1976 to 1981, the vendors learned several lessons about the business. One lesson was that a CRS was more likely to succeed in a given locality if its sponsoring carrier was a major airline player in that area (or in the nearest large city). For the most part, the success of each CRS venture followed the route structure of the affiliated airline. One reason for this was synergy in marketing—if a carrier already had extensive dealings with an agency, it faced an easier time (lower costs) in selling the agency its CRS. Another was that an airline could reduce its reservation costs the most by automating the agencies that sold the most tickets on the airline.

The second lesson, derivative from the first, was that an airline-sponsored CRS could be successful only if the sponsor was a major national carrier. And, because the first CRSs were launched in 1976 before deregulation, only three carriers—American, TWA, and United—flew to a nationwide network of cities and so could effectively market their services everywhere. The marketing of the larger airlines' CRSs was also enhanced by the fact that the internal reservation systems of large airlines included a larger number of flights, in part because the airline itself had more flights and in part because it connected to more flights of other airlines that were used for interline operations. Hence, the capabilities of these systems were greater and more attractive to travel agents. Finally, in the early years, the fixed costs of even the largest CRSs loomed large in total costs. These fixed costs included the large central computer for handling services to travel agents and the software for sending and receiving messages between agents and the central system. Thus, the small systems based on regional carriers (Frontier, Western, and Allegheny) were not viable and disappeared.[13]

Toward the end of the first era, the airlines learned still another lesson of great economic importance. If an airline succeeded in getting a travel agent to subscribe to its CRS, the airline would experience an increase in its ticket sales through that agent. Indeed, the internal financial studies of CRS operations by American and United from the late 1970s claim that nearly all of the profit of APOLLO and SABRE was derived from increased ticket sales on the sponsoring airline. Even though on the basis of direct revenues and costs APOLLO and SABRE were barely breaking even, financial studies, including those conducted by the companies themselves, that take incremental revenues into account show that these companies were earning very substantial rates of return— by some estimates in the hundreds of percents. Hence, for the successful CRS entrants—American, United, and TWA—the CRS came to be perceived primarily as an extremely effective means for selling their tickets.

The reasons for the airline marketing orientation of CRSs are complicated and controversial, but three effects of CRSs on ticket sales are generally agreed to have influenced this development. One is bias, as described above. Another is economies of scope. An airline can combine marketing and customer service to travel agents for its ticket sales and its CRS. As a result, marketing a CRS can have spillover effects on marketing tickets and vice versa. The last effect is the industry concept of halo: the reputational value of the best airlines spills over into their marketing of CRSs, and then the great benefits of a CRS to a travel agent spill over to increase the likelihood that the travel agent will sell tickets on the airline. One source of halo, of course, is that in the original CRS architecture, an agent had an incentive to buy more tickets on the airline owning a CRS in order to avoid the "no rec problem," because a CRS would have direct access only to its sponsoring airline.

The last lesson from the early period was that because a CRS was an effective tool for selling tickets, it was also an effective tool for imposing competitive disadvantages on airlines that had no CRS affiliate. Because CRSs developed out of proprietary internal reservation systems, they were not initially designed to permit bookings on all flights of all carriers. As the focus of ticket sales switched from airline ticket offices to travel agents, the pressure mounted from both agents and airlines to make the capabilities of the CRS more comprehensive—indeed, to include essentially all flights of all airlines. But CRS vendors faced distinctly mixed incentives in responding to this pressure. Specifically, providing a means for booking flights on their competitors benefited CRS sales but hurt airline sales. The two largest carriers, American and United, had the most to lose from the greater competition arising from airline deregulation. Hence, they moved slowly in incorporating bookings on competing airlines—especially expanding small carriers or de novo entrants—into their CRS.[14]

An important fact about the CRS business in the early period is that airlines were not charged a booking fee when a CRS was used to sell a ticket. Until about 1980, airline CRS vendors sought profits from three sources: fees to travel agents for connecting an agency to the CRS (which were not related to ticket sales), enhanced ticket sales (and profits) for the airline affiliated with the CRS, and lower costs of handling reservation requests by substituting computers for telephone sales agents.

The Second Computer Reservation System Era: 1981–1984

The second era began in 1981, but had roots a year or two earlier in the practices of American and United in dealing with bookings on competitive airlines. This period lasted until the new regulatory rules for CRS promulgated by the CAB became effective in November 1984. The second era had several characteristics. First, as discussed in the beginning of the second section, by 1981 most travel agencies were automated, and most airline tickets were sold through automated agencies. A CRS was clearly the dominant method of selling tickets, and when airline spillover effects were taken into account, had high and growing profits. Second, CRSs began to charge booking fees, which soon became still another major source of CRS revenues and profits. Third, other airlines and an independent nonairline party which had tried to enter the CRS business in the first period faltered and withdrew. Fourth, the leading CRS vendors made special efforts to increase the degree of emphasis on the use of CRSs as a marketing tool for tickets. To do so, the vendors increased display bias in schedules, prices, and seat availability and adopted discriminatory practices toward airlines regarding CRS participation, booking fees, and other airline-related matters. Fifth, because the airline marketing advantage of a CRS was seen as its main business purpose, airline CRS vendors began to place CRS systems in larger travel agencies at a price substantially below the marginal cost of service.[15] Below-cost pricing was profitable because agency placements produced additional revenues from booking fees paid by airlines and incremental revenues from additional ticket sales on the owner-airline. In some cases, the agents were given the hardware in their offices that enabled them to connect to the CRS.

Because of airline deregulation, some large regional carriers were able to expand their route structures to become true national carriers in the late 1970s and early 1980s. Among these were Delta and Eastern, which, despite being very large carriers, were primarily regional during the regulated era. Noting that a national presence apparently was essential for success in the CRS business, and fearing the effects of a proliferation of biased systems sold by their rivals, these airlines launched System One (Eastern—originally SODA) and Datas II (Delta). Meanwhile, ITT began experimenting with an independent CRS, MARS (for multi-access airline reservation system). MARS, the first multi-access CRS, enabled travel agents to select which biased display to use, depending upon the trip plans and carrier preferences of the customer.

During the second era, much effort was devoted to building and using bias. Moreover, CRSs also began to sell bias, or freedom from bias, to other airlines. For example, according to internal company documents, United began its "Parametric Marketing Study" to bias displays in a manner that travel agents would not be likely to detect. American and United started the practice of selling "co-host" and "participating carrier" status to airlines with which they had little route overlap. In return for paying a booking fee, an airline would have its flights given preferential treatment in schedule displays. Figures 8.1 and 8.2 illustrate the effects of bias at its height, just before the CAB investigation leading to the 1984 rules. Figure 8.1 depicts the first display in APOLLO after a request for a 6 P.M. flight from Washington, D.C., to Seattle, Washington, on April 20, 1983. The screen first lists a nonstop United flight within two hours of the requested departure time—in this case, two hours later. Were there nonstop flights on other carriers between 6 P.M. and 8 P.M., they would be listed next; however, no such flights existed. The screen then shows some connecting flights through Chicago involving one leg on American and one leg on United, beginning in a window two hours before the requested time. But the screen does not show a nonstop Northwest flight from Dulles to Seattle leaving at 5:40. Likewise, Figure 8.2 shows an APOLLO screen listing flights from San Diego to Denver on July 18, 1983, at 3 P.M. The screen does not list a nonstop Frontier flight leaving at 2:53 P.M.

The use of a CRS as a marketing device (combined with the practice of supplying CRSs to travel agents at a price below cost) doomed the prospects for an independent CRS vendor. Independents like MARS had no airline revenue benefits, and so no other business on which to make up the revenue short-

Figure 8.1
Display Bias I

April 20, 1983
APOLLO
WASHINGTON, D.C. TO SEATTLE, WA
6:00 P.M.

1		UA	149	DCA	SEA	800P	1155P
2		AA	529	DCA	ORD	415P	520P
3		UA	157		SEA	640P	855P
4		AA	529	IAD	ORD	415P	520P
5		UA	157		SEA	640P	855P
6		UA	609	DCA	ORD	415P	519P
7		AA	689		SEA	700P	900P

OOPS		NW	79	IAD	SEA	540P	808P

Source: Association of Retail Travel Agents (1983, pp. 372-373).

fall from prices to travel agents set below costs.[16] Travel agents had no desire to pay more for an unbiased system. In fact, airlines introduced commission rates which increased with total monthly sales so that travel agents had reason to concentrate their sales on one or a few airlines, and so, in some cases, the agents would have *preferred* biased displays. As a result, MARS could not charge agents more than the other CRSs to effect its absence of bias and incremental revenues.

Likewise, the relationship between airline and CRS sales created an entry barrier for Eastern and Delta in the CRS business and the airline industry. Although extending their routes nationwide, these carriers did not have the total sales in most of the country of especially United and American, and so they were not very successful in selling CRSs outside of their former regional bases. Likewise, TWA, although possessing national routes, lacked large presence in most of the nation, and so it succeeded in marketing its CRS only in a few areas in the Midwest and Southwest plus in major international connecting points for its routes to Europe. Thus, in the first instance, national carrier status gave American and United a distinct early advantage; then bias and other linkages between CRS and airline sales kept their airline shares high despite competitive entry in the airline business after deregulation.

Toward the end of the second era, United and American discovered another use of CRSs: differential booking fees and other forms of discrimination to

Figure 8.2
Display Bias II

July 18, 1983

APOLLO

SAN DIEGO TO DENVER

3:00 P.M.

1	UA	178	SAN	DEN	100P	359P
2	UA	572	SAN	DEN	355P	655P
3	II	707	SAN	LAX	130P	210P
4	UA	310		DEN	350P	655P
5	PS	857	SAN	LAX	200P	240P
6	UA	310		DEN	350P	655P
7	II	551	SAN	LAX	200P	240P
8	UA	310		DEN	350P	655P
OOPS	FL	696	SAN	DEN	253P	555P

Source: Association of Retail Travel Agents (1983, p. 634).

punish price competitors in the airline business. Initially, booking fees were charged only to foreign carriers or to largely noncompeting airlines that would then receive benefits from bias.[17] Major domestic carriers paid either nothing or quite modest booking fees—approximately $.25 per flight segment—in return for receiving display preferences. But in late 1981, the booking fees charged to carriers other than co-hosts and to competing carriers actually began to surpass the fees charged to noncompeting carriers who received the benefits of bias. The pricing scheme based booking fees on (1) whether a carrier had route overlap with the sponsoring airline, (2) whether the carrier was an interline feeder for the sponsoring carrier, and (3) whether the carrier was an aggressive price competitor. For example, some new carriers, such as Midway and Jet America, often faced booking fees more than ten times the fee charged to co-hosts (generally noncompeting established carriers). Moreover, to obtain inclusion on APOLLO, Air Florida and Jet America promised not to compete with United on routes and fares. Finally, numerous carriers were required, as a condition of CRS participation, to use various other airline services and to pay extremely high interline fees.[18] Regional and commuter airlines sell a large number of interline tickets, for their passengers often fly a short (often monopolized) route to a nearby city, and then use a major trunk to complete the journey or to connect to another small airline elsewhere. High interline fees enabled the trunk carrier to capture monopoly profits from the feeder routes.

The effect of these practices was to diminish competition in both airline and CRS markets. In the airline market, United and American used booking fees and CRS access to raise costs (and hence prices) of aggressive competitors. Hence, the operation of the dominant CRSs, SABRE and APOLLO, undermined the competitive vision of the industry that motivated deregulation. In addition, by making co-host arrangements with major noncompeting carriers, SABRE and APOLLO reduced the likelihood that the smaller, more regional carriers would combine to create an effective new airline-sponsored CRS. And, of course, by selling CRS services below cost and basing the profits of CRS ventures in part on spillover effects on airlines, the two leaders assured themselves that no third party would successfully market an unbiased system. Nailing down the certainty of no entry, they also elected not to participate in MARS, so a MARS agent had to book United and American flights through another airline's CRS (usually Eastern's SODA).

Finally, to assure the early advantages from the synergies between CRS and airline combinations, at the close of the second era SABRE and APOLLO began to insist upon long-term contracts with minimum-use provisions and roll-over clauses.[19] Adopting a system in which agent hardware and telephone connections were dedicated to a single CRS was already a barrier to the use of multiple CRSs by an agency. Unlike other database services, CRS vendors did not allow a customer to use a single terminal and telephone lines to access multiple CRSs. Hence, to become a subscriber to more than one CRS required installing duplicative hardware in an agency. Nonetheless, some large agencies began to use more than one CRS. The purpose of the new restrictions was to provide further protection against switching to another CRS or using another CRS as a secondary system. Only very large agencies could satisfy the minimum-use criteria and still have enough business to make a second CRS worthwhile; even these typically could use the second system only to a very small extent. Obviously, an entrant could not impose minimum use, for it had to be content to be a second system in an agency having a long-term contract that committed the agency to use another CRS for most of its bookings. The outcome, shown in Table 8.2, was that almost all agencies came to use only one system.

The Third Computer Reservation System Era: 1985–1991

Because of complaints from other airlines and travel agents about developments during the second era, the CAB undertook an investigation of CRS practices, and issued final rules in August 1984, which went into effect the following November (CAB, 1984, pp. 32540–32564). These rules banned certain types of display bias, limited the term of CRS contracts with travel agents to

Table 8.2
Distribution of Travel Agencies by Number of CRSs in Use, 1986

NUMBER OF CRS VENDORS	AGENCY LOCATIONS	PERCENT DISTRIBUTION
1	23,090	93.50%
2	1,410	5.70%
3	147	0.60%
4	34	0.10%
5	12	0.05%
TOTAL	24,693	1.00%

Source: U.S. Department of Transportation (1988, p. 32).

five years, and prohibited price discrimination in airline booking fees or other forms of discriminatory access of airlines to CRSs. This ushered in the third era of the CRS industry as the new rules were implemented.

An important fact about the CAB rules is that they had relatively little effect on the CRS industry.[20] Even though the smaller CRSs initiated a two-year "conversion war" in which they agreed to pay the liquidated damages for agents if they would replace APOLLO or SABRE with another CRS, the market shares of the leading CRS vendors, APOLLO and SABRE, suffered very little after the rules were adopted. The spillover effect of CRS affiliation on airline business was reduced only slightly, and the profits of the leading CRSs, if anything, increased after the rules were adopted. The current competitive conditions in the industry certainly appear to be roughly as they were before the rules, except that one firm, MARS, has exited, and two more, Pars and Datas II, have merged.

To search for reasons, we need look first at what the rules did not change. Five-year contracts are still long term; most other nations limit contracts to a much shorter term. Because few contracts expire at any time, few agents are available for competition.

The rules probably reduced display bias, but they did not eliminate it—as United executives promised when the rules were promulgated. Carriers still have wide latitude in many areas of display design.[21] For example, for listing connecting service between two cities, the number of connecting cities that are considered need not be every feasible connection, so carriers can bias the selection of connecting flights by choosing connect points that are their own hubs. Likewise, "penalties" can be assigned to interline connections. This makes sense in very large, multiterminal airports such as Dallas or Chicago O'Hare, where airline gates can be widely separated, but little sense at smaller airports.

Of course, a penalty for interlining benefits larger carriers, for they have more flights to more cities, and hence a greater likelihood of providing both ends of a connecting trip.

In any event, the rules did not alter the synergies between CRSs and airline share in a given locality. Hence, large CRS shares and large airline lift shares in a city continue mutually to support each other. In most areas, post-rules shares have not changed substantially. Only when one airline-sponsor of a CRS abandons a city and another takes its place, or when new airlines join with a CRS in a joint venture, does a major switch occur in CRS market shares.

After the rules CRS vendors substantially strengthened the "liquidated damages" contracts on agents seeking to switch CRS vendors. According to the terms of the contract, any agent who fails to satisfy the minimum-use provision can be subject to cancellation and liquidated damages liability; however, the terms of the contract are only enforced when the failure to comply is the result of using another CRS. The liquidated damages are based on the subscription fees and the booking fees that would be collected during the contract.

To understand why the liquidated damages contracts are onerous requires examination of one additional feature of the post-rules environment. The rules required that CRS vendors end price discrimination in booking fees. The result was that booking fees were raised for the large domestic carriers that had previously been co-hosts. The reigning fee is $1.85 per flight segment, which turns out to be slightly less than 2 percent of airline revenues, in contrast to airline profits, which are typically below 5 percent of revenues.

Immediately after the CAB rules were promulgated, some CRS vendors charged lower booking fees; however, this had absolutely no beneficial competitive effect. It put no pressure on APOLLO and SABRE because it induced absolutely no change in CRS market shares. With travel agents receiving systems well below cost, and with airlines requiring access to all CRS systems to sell tickets nationally, a lower booking fee provided only lower revenues—and no improvement in CRS market share—to the low-priced vendor.

In turn, the higher booking fees (at $1.85) were enormously profitable. They are now by far a more important source of CRS revenues than agency subscription fees, and they cause the profits of the two largest CRS vendors to produce a substantially supracompetitive return on investment. As shown in Table 8.3, the 1988 Department of Transportation study has a best estimate of 50 to 90 percent annual rates of return, without taking into account synergy effects on airline revenues. In litigation over CRS contracts, American's expert witness estimated that the after-tax return on investment in SABRE was about 30 percent, also not including the spillover benefits to the airline. References during these proceedings, however, were made to documents from American Airlines that estimated the annual rate of return to exceed 500 percent, and from United that stated that APOLLO should not be installed in any agency unless it will immediately produce a return exceeding 33 percent.

The liquidated damages provisions of CRS contracts require that travel agents

Table 8.3
Adjusted Accounting Profitability of SABRE and APOLLO (in $ million)

(In $ Million)	SABRE		APOLLO	
	1985	1986	1985	1986
INCOME				
Participant Revenue	199.1	230.9	152.6	174.4
Subscriber Revenue	93.4	105.7	78.8	97.5
Imputed Income from Host	31.0	35.2	36.3	46.4
Total Income	323.5	371.8	267.7	318.4
Operating Costs	110.7	134.6	95.0	117.7
Total Depreciation & Amortization	42.7	59.2	48.2	64.1
Total Costs	153.4	193.7	143.2	181.9
Net Income	170.1	178.1	124.5	136.5
Total Invested Capital*	187.7	234.1	224.7	260.4
Net Income as a Percentage of Investments	90.6%	76.1%	55.4%	52.4%

* Estimated year-end total value of outlays for facility, equipment, product development, marketing & subscriber conversion that remain to be depreciated or amortized.
Source: U.S. Department of Transportation (1988, p. 86).

reimburse the CRS vendor some of the booking fees that the agent would have produced had the contract been fulfilled.[22] They also require full payment of the subscription fees (the monthly lease arrangements) for the full term of the contract, even if the CRS vendor places the terminal in another agency or sells it on the used equipment market and cancels immediately its telephone links to the agent. Moreover, in some cases an agency does not actually have to pay all or part of the subscription fees unless it fails to fulfill the other terms of the contract. If the contract is not fulfilled, it must then pay the full subscription fee for the entire five-year term. The effect of these provisions is to impose liquidation damages that sometimes are several times the cost of providing CRS service to an agency.

Because of the high profits in the CRS business, smaller CRS vendors launched a ''conversion war'' in about 1986. The nature of the battle was for the vendor to assume the liability for liquidated damages if the agent would switch. System One, by this time a larger entity because of the acquisition of several airlines by its new parent, Texas Air Corporation, was especially active in converting agents. It had relied in part on the possibility that the courts would reduce the damages for contract cancellation; however, this expectation was dashed by subsequent decisions, all but one of which have ruled that the provisions are enforceable. In 1988, soon after these cases were lost, the conversion war abruptly ended as the smaller vendors concluded that the price of converting an agency (the liquidated damages plus subscription fees below management cost) was simply too high.

The public policy implications of the liquidated damages provisions were a central concern in the 1990 review of the CRS rules at the Department of Transportation. A wide range of participants, including airlines, CRS vendors, and travel agents, appealed to the department to eliminate the liquidated damages provisions despite—or perhaps, because of—the outcome of these lawsuits. Interestingly, the Canadian Competition Tribunal, in the context of evaluating the merger of the two large Canadian CRSs, prohibited all liquidated damages based on booking fees in Canada. (This case is addressed in detail in Chapter 9 of this book.) Despite these rules, Canadian CRSs and U.S. CRSs that operate in Canada continue to market CRS services to travel agents, unhindered by their inability to recover damages in the event of agency conversions.

The lesson from the conversion war was that, for the most part, it was not a sound business strategy. To induce the travel agent to switch, a competing vendor must compete—offer a better deal than SABRE or APOLLO. It must also pay the old CRS vendor most of the monopoly profits remaining to be extracted from the contract, plus some unpaid subscription fees. Obviously, buying out a monopoly to increase competition is generally an unattractive economic prospect. The only case in which it makes sense is when the purchasing vendor has the potential to take advantage of the CRS-airline synergy to get a much larger share of ticket sales by a travel agency. Thus, if the airline sponsors of one CRS have a local share of airline capacity that is comparable to or greater than an entrenched CRS vendor, converting agents may make sense; otherwise, it does not. This phenomenon explains why the few examples of large changes in CRS market share in a given city are associated with changes in airline service.

Likewise, established CRS positions in large cities discourage an airline from substantially increasing its presence in an area served primarily by a CRS-sponsoring carrier. Because CRS presence protects some of the market share of the established carrier, a new entrant without a CRS expects lower sales from a given effort on entry. Moreover, if it sells through its competitor's CRS, it must pay nearly 2 percent of the sales it wins from its rival back to the rival's CRS. Or, the entrant can try to convert agents to its own CRS, to save booking fees and capture synergies. But even then, it must reimburse the established airline-CRS combination for its loss of a monopoly through the liquidated damages provision.

Soon after declaring a truce in the conversion war, financially troubled, cash-poor Texas Air Corporation began to explore possibilities for selling all or part of System One. In February 1990, Texas Air and Electronic Data Services (EDS), a major computer services firm, reached an agreement. For $250 million plus the assumption of undisclosed liabilities, EDS acquired nearly all of the assets of System One and established an equal partnership with System One to operate and market the CRS business. Texas Air, in turn, committed Continental and Eastern to buy data-processing services from EDS, including operation of the airlines' internal reservation systems. The most salient aspect of this agreement was that, once again, an independent has a major investment in a CRS. The question raised by this agreement is whether it signals a sufficiently great reduction in bias and halo such that these sources of entry barriers have been eliminated for independent vendors. For two reasons, we believe that this conclusion is unwarranted. First, because of Texas Air's precarious financial position, its sale to EDS plausibly was under duress. Second, although the terms of the agreement were not made public, it is also plausible that the prices EDS expected to charge to Continental and the now defunct Eastern for data processing, and to System One to use the hardware and software formerly belonging to System One, would have produced a reasonable return on the EDS investment. In any case, Texas Air does not appear to expect its airline synergies with System One to change. Thus, the most likely interpretation of the joint venture is that Texas Air would have acquired needed cash now from EDS in return for a commitment to pass back to EDS some of System One's halo benefits in the future.

The final issue to emerge in the third era arises from the value of the information stored in a CRS and the airline computers that are linked to it.[23] A CRS contains two types of valuable information: data about the travel patterns of every customer of every agency that subscribes to the service, and data about airline prices and seat availability. Customer information is a valuable marketing tool for an airline. It tells the airline which agencies to target to increase airline market share, and in some cases even which customers. One plausible source of a growing synergy between CRS and airline integration is greater use of the information in a CRS for marketing purposes.

The 1984 CRS rules require that CRS vendors make sales data available to airlines at a reasonable cost, but they do not require that the data be provided in a usable format for marketing purposes. Hence, to make use of CRS data, an airline must write or acquire extensive software to interpret the raw data from the CRS. Of course, having each airline acquire separate, duplicative software is socially wasteful. Moreover, it is a fixed cost that is not worth paying for small airlines. Hence, the practice of providing CRS data is still another aspect of CRSs that seems to cause more concentration in the airline industry.

The performance problems created by the third era of CRSs show no signs of abating without regulatory intervention. The strategies promulgated by the leading vendors, APOLLO and SABRE, have succeeded in blockading CRS entry and have retarded airline competition. Third parties cannot successfully enter because they have no airline synergy (or halo) to offset the fact that prices to travel agents are below cost and to use as a basis for converting agents. The profitable prospect of booking fees is offset by the liquidated damages clauses of the contracts. New airline entry is foreclosed in part because the most important national carriers all are now partners in one or another CRS. A new entrant, therefore, faces the prospect of giving its competitors $1.85 for every passenger it wins from them. The remaining carriers that are not CRS partners are Pan Am, a financially weak national and international carrier, and several regional carriers. None of these airlines has enough airline business in most markets to justify entry: the synergy effect is too low to attract travel agents, and inadequate to justify paying the liquidated damages. Indeed, the smaller CRS systems—Pars-Datas II and System One—abandoned the conversion war in 1988 other than in a few cities where they already had a major airline presence but a low CRS share. Once CRS shares approach airline shares in these cities, the conversion war will end there as well, so that in the future there is little prospect of much competition of this form.

The Structural Implications of the Three Eras

Many analysts as well as the CAB predicted that the outcome of the 1984 CRS rules would be to equalize market shares among CRS vendors. As agents' contracts expired and restrictions on entry were eliminated, it was thought that the smaller systems would expand well beyond the regions of the country that they occupied prior to the rules. Some expansion has occurred, but the key to understanding this expansion and the present structure of the industry is the relationship among airline ownership, airline presence, and CRS market share.

The only major changes in shares in the last five years have been driven by airline market presence, nearly all of which has been driven by mergers and bankruptcies. Thus, Texas Air's acquisition of Eastern (and its SODA system) created an airline-owner for System One that had a large presence in markets where Continental was a hubbing carrier, such as Houston and Denver. System One has undertaken substantial conversions only where its airline-owners have a substantial presence. Similarly, Delta's acquisition of Western Airlines created the incentive and opportunity for Delta to expand the marketing and conversion efforts of Datas II in cities where Western was a hubbing carrier, such as Salt Lake City. The joint-venture partnership of Northwest and TWA in Pars added new Pars locations in Northwest's hub cities of Detroit, Minneapolis, and Memphis. Finally, the bankruptcy of Braniff provided the opportunity for Eastern to capture airline share and then CRS share in Kansas City, at least until the subsequent bankruptcy of Eastern.

Examination of the pattern of local market shares highlights the regionality of the smaller CRSs. Regional concentration is a direct reflection of the underlying airline network of the affiliated airlines. TWA, with its St. Louis hub and European routes, is a major player out of the largest international ports of entry, in cross-country routes between the largest population centers, and out of St. Louis. Northwest is primarily an east-west carrier focusing on northern cities, plus an important international carrier over the Pacific. This gives it a strong presence in large cities where it offers flights to the Orient and in its hubs in Detroit, Memphis, and Minneapolis. Thus, Pars has most of its locations in the Midwest and in other cities where its airline-owners have substantial presence. It has few or no locations in the Southeast, where its owners have traditionally had modest or no service.

Delta is primarily a domestic carrier along north-south routes from the East to the Southeast, and east-west routes along the southern tier of states. It also has the old Western Airlines routes in the West. Thus, the Datas II network tends to be concentrated in the Southeast, with a few additional cities where it has a high market share due to the acquisition of Western. Because the three carriers involved in the Pars and Datas II merger serve largely nonoverlapping areas, operate out of different hubs, and compete only in very large markets between major cities and in hub-hub routes, there was relatively little geographic overlap between their CRSs. Hence, only in a few markets did the merger significantly increase local concentration, which probably explains why the merger was not challenged by antitrust authorities.

The System One network follows a pattern similar to that of Datas II. It has relatively few CRS locations in areas where its airline-owners do not have a major presence. Like Datas II, System One has many locations in the Southeast due to the historic presence of Eastern in Atlanta and Miami. Other than in these areas, System One does not overlap to a significant extent with either Pars or Datas II.

In marked contrast, APOLLO and SABRE have a very substantial presence in almost all large cities, reflecting the size and extensive route structure of United and American. Among the 57 largest markets in the country, in 1986 SABRE's market share exceeded 35 percent in 33, whereas APOLLO's exceeded 35 percent in 24. The corresponding figures are four for System One, four for Pars, and none for Datas II. Datas II and Pars each had less than 5 percent of the market in more than half of these areas, and System One captured less than 5 percent in one-third of the top 57 markets. Table 8.4 shows the distribution of market shares in the 57 largest markets. In 39 of these markets, the share of the largest CRS exceeded 50 percent. Of these, 23 were SABRE, 14 were APOLLO, and 2 were Pars. In most of the remaining markets, the share of the largest CRS was greater than 40 percent, and usually it was SABRE or APOLLO. At the other end of the scale, Datas II enjoyed little or no presence (less than 5 percent) in over half of these markets; System One and Pars were also small or absent in nearly half. The 1990 data are similar.

For the most part, these market patterns were established prior to the 1984 CRS rules. Only limited erosion of SABRE or APOLLO CRS market shares has taken place since then, with the exception of changes in specific markets due to the new affiliations between airlines and CRSs. Table 8.5 shows market share data before and after the rules. The combined market shares of APOLLO and SABRE range from about 80 to about 70 percent. This is due primarily to

Table 8.4
Presence in Largest MSA Markets for All Five CRS Vendors

	DATAS II	PARS	APOLLO	SABRE	SYSTEM ONE
No Presence	7	9	0	0	3
0.0 - 5.0%	34	25	7	1	24
5.1 - 10%	8	5	4	2	9
10.1% - 20%	4	7	13	8	13
20.1% - 35%	4	7	9	13	4
35.1% - 50%	0	2	10	10	4
50.1%	0	2	14	23	0
TOTAL	**57**	**57**	**57**	**57**	**57**

Source: U.S. Department of Transportation (1988, pp. 159-167).

Table 8.5
Nationwide CRS Market Shares

	Nov. 1983	Nov. 1984	Nov. 1985	Year 1986	Year 1988
Apollo	31	29	28	32	22
Datas II	2	5	6	5	5
Mars Plus	2	1	1	0	0
Pars	12	11	10	10	15
Sabre	49	45	46	43	45
System One	5	9	10	9	13

Source: 1983-1985, U.S. Department of Justice (1985, p. 17); 1986, U.S. Department of Transportation (1988, p. 21); 1988, U.S. Department of Justice (1989, p. 23).

shifts in a few large cities owing to targeted conversion wars after mergers and after Northwest joined Pars. Examples are System One in Continental's Denver hub, Pars in Detroit and Minneapolis, after Northwest acquired partial ownership of Pars, and Datas II in Salt Lake City after Delta acquired Western. The shares of all other metropolitan areas, including such major centers as New

York, Chicago, Los Angeles, and Washington, have been virtually unchanged since 1983. These cities account for a sizable percentage of all airline travel booked in the United States.

The stability of the market shares of the dominant vendors raises tough public policy issues. Are these shares stable primarily because APOLLO and SABRE are offering the best products, or are they primarily due to liquidated damages, minimum-use provisions, and other practices that make CRS competition difficult, if not impossible? These are precisely the issues raised in the private lawsuits filed against American and United and at the Department of Transportation in its review of the CRS rules. The economic issues in these two areas are addressed in the next two sections.

THE PRIVATE LAWSUITS

Thus far, American and United have a perfect record in defending their CRS practices against antitrust plaintiffs, although they have settled some cases rather than litigate to conclusion. This section presents the core arguments by the parties in these lawsuits, and the opinions expressed by the judges in the two most important cases. As of the time we are writing this chapter, the CRS litigation can hardly be construed as over, because appeals have not been exhausted on all decisions rendered thus far. Thus, our inferences about the role of private litigation in this arena must be regarded as provisional. Nonetheless, almost all the cases have been decided or settled; and we believe that these cases illustrate four especially important difficulties with using private antitrust to attack the kinds of problems that have arisen in the CRS industry.

First, if there are serious anticompetitive problems, as we believe, they arise from informational imperfections in the market. Informational imperfections are not only a relatively new issue in antitrust, but they are not easily conveyed to judges and juries. The economic theory of market power arising from informational imperfections is complex. Moreover, information-based monopolization is hard to distinguish from the valid antitrust defense of superior efficiency and foresight, which can result from better knowledge that is obtained and used perfectly innocently.

Second, the CRS industry is an oligopoly, and no firm has even 50 percent of the market. Although economic theory and empirical research provide reasons to believe that a five-firm industry with two dominant firms and blockaded entry might be something less than perfectly competitive, antitrust actions against oligopolies—in the absence of direct evidence of conspiracy—have rarely been successful. The difference in the market structure policies embodied in the Department of Justice's *Merger Guidelines* and the actual results of attempts to apply antitrust remedies to existing oligopolies bears testimony to the gap between the domain in which market imperfections might arise and the domain where antitrust laws can effectively remedy them after the fact.

Third, at the core of the antitrust issues in the CRS cases is the form of the contracts between CRS vendors and travel agents. Although economics provides good reasons to believe that contract forms can be an effective precommitment and coordination device for creating market imperfections, obtaining favorable antitrust verdicts on the basis of contract forms has proved to be virtually impossible. Witness, for example, the outcome of the litigation against the manufacturers of tetraethyl lead regarding the "most favored nations" clause in their contracts with petroleum refiners for the sale of gasoline additives. The difficulty encountered in such cases may arise in part from the explicit protection of contract rights in the Constitution. In legal curricula, constitutional law is required, but antitrust usually is not. Moreover, most judges hear very few antitrust cases and have tried few or none before ascending to the bench. Hence, judges may be prone to hang valid antitrust claims on the hook of the contract provision of the Constitution.

Fourth, the injured parties in these cases (other than airline consumers) are not, for the most part, the people who actually buy CRS services—the travel agents. Although individual travel agents have participated in some lawsuits, in fact, the damages they have had to pay for breaching CRS contracts have been covered by the CRS that caused them to breach. Standard industry practice has been to give travel agents CRS service at prices far below cost— indeed, sometimes for free. To the extent that there are injured parties, they are airlines, potential CRS entrants, and passengers. Potential entrants face a serious problem of standing unless they can prove that they have the intention and the ability to enter (*Grip-Pak, Inc. v. Illinois Tool Works, Inc.,* 1982). Passengers do not have standing because they do not buy CRS services directly (*Illinois Brick Co. v. Illinois* 1977). Airlines face the difficult task of convincing judge and jury that in a competitive CRS business the travel agents would pay more for CRS services (while airlines would pay next to nothing). This makes the case appear to be about cost-shifting rather than competition, and even about big guys (airlines) beating up on little guys (travel agents).

Both the travel agency and airline cases have focused on the contract provisions between CRS vendors and travel agents. The essence of the arguments by plaintiffs is that the contracts cannot be justified on the basis of any legitimate business interests. A CRS vendor does not make a significant investment in adding an agency to the CRS. All that is required is an inexpensive dumb terminal, some other peripheral devices, a telephone line on a monthly lease, and some software in the CRS mainframe to keep records concerning the activities of the new agency/customer. Only the last is a sunk cost, and it is trivial. The equipment can be reused in another agency, or can be sold on the equipment market. In any case, the revenues collected from liquidated damages include the profits of the CRS arising from market power. Hence, the de facto effect of the contract form is to require a competitor to reimburse a monopolist for lost monopoly profits should competition emerge.

The airline case raised several additional issues, three of which were especially important. Plaintiffs first accused defendants of predatory pricing. Recall from the history of the industry that CRSs did not charge booking fees until, around 1980, they began to charge some trunks a very small fee for buying out of the carrier bias in CRS displays. Then, in the early 1980s, once all of the large travel agencies (and 70 percent of all agencies) were automated according to contracts with subscription fees below costs and other barriers to switching, CRSs began to charge significant fees even to carriers against whom displays were biased. In the beginning, the booking fees varied widely, raising the issue of price discrimination. But for all large domestic carriers, fees began to increase dramatically even before the 1984 rules, and after the rules rose to $1.85. Thus, the predatory pricing charge is that until the market was saturated both booking fees and agency subscription fees were set too low to recover costs, and then when saturation occurred, one price—the booking fee to large domestic airlines—was increased so much that monopoly profits ensued. By then, because of CRS entry barriers, the large domestic carriers could not effectively respond by entering; hence, the sequence of booking fees is interpreted as predatory.

Defendants also were accused initially of leveraging airline presence into a greater market share in CRSs. This charge was one vehicle through which plaintiffs introduced the issue of bias. Plaintiffs did not argue that biased displays violated the antitrust laws. To do so would have implied a possible antitrust violation by the *OAG*. Instead, plaintiffs argued that CRS vendors violated the antitrust laws by giving themselves the bias preference, rather than selling it to the highest bidder, as the *OAG* had done. But because of rulings in the case discussed below, the plaintiffs did not argue that this was illegal leveraging of CRS into airline markets; instead, they argued that this was an illegal, discriminatory practice and de facto cross-subsidy from airline markets to CRSs.[24] In other words, prices too low to recover costs in the CRS business were being subsidized from excess profits in the airline business arising from bias. In essence, plaintiffs argued that to avoid antitrust problems, airlines had to operate a CRS as a stand-alone entity, dealing with all airlines on an equal footing. Finally, plaintiffs recited the list of discriminatory practices toward particular airlines: failing to provide accurate, up-to-date fares, schedules, and seat availabilities for competitors; engaging in price discrimination; refusing to provide service to some competing carriers.

In both cases, the arguments of the plaintiffs were constrained by court rulings that were favorable to the defense. In the first travel-agent case, Judge Harold Pollack ruled that the relevant market was sales to travel agents located on Long Island. Hence, no evidence could be introduced regarding relationships between travel agents and CRS vendors that did not take place in Long Island. Moreover, because the defendant, United, had a relatively small share of Long Island agencies, the plaintiffs faced an impossible task in arguing that the contract terms in Long Island arose out of market power there. United won the early travel-agency cases on summary judgement, a result that is hardly surprising given the rulings about relevant market and admissible evidence.

In the airlines cases, Judge Edward Rafeedie defined the market as the national market for CRS services to travel agents, quite contrary to the travel-agency case. This required that the airline plaintiffs show that anticompetitive actions affecting airlines arose from market power over agents. Moreover, the court also ruled that a CRS was not an essential facility to an airline (prior to hearing evidence on the issue) and that the plaintiffs were precluded from arguing that CRS market power was used to leverage the airline market. That is, all of the issues discussed here about how a CRS spills over into reducing competition in the airline industry were ruled outside the bounds of the airlines cases. In the Northwest case, plaintiffs interpreted this ruling as precluding the most natural use of the evidence regarding bias (to increase market shares in the airline business) and as precluding arguments about how CRS vendors use booking fees and access to facilitate collusion in airline markets. It also precluded introduction of any evidence pertaining to tying CRS participation to interline arrangements, baggage handling, airline route structure, or anything else related to the airline business. By this interpretation, the rulings in the airline cases reduced the dispute to two major issues: contract provisions and CRS pricing (in particular, whether more than de minimis booking fees were illegal and subject to recovery by the plaintiffs). As a result, the travel-agent and Northwest cases were far more overlapping in content than plaintiffs had anticipated. But in the Texas Air case, plaintiffs essentially ignored the rulings and based their case on bias effects in airline markets. This strategy succeeded in achieving settlement before the case went to jury.

The defendants' arguments in all cases were simply that neither the CRS nor the airline industry was monopolized, and that the contract provisions were standard business practices to assure that they would recover their enormous investment in CRSs. Defendants emphasized that, in the mid-1970s, CRSs appeared to be a highly risky business. Very large computer networks were in their infancy and might not work, and in any case few travel agents might actually buy the service. The airlines that entered the business were risking millions of dollars on an unproven market. Moreover, as time progressed, the two leaders, American and United, invested hundreds of millions more in constantly upgrading their systems. They succeeded in maintaining their early dominance because their systems were superior to the competition and saved both travel agents and airlines costs by substituting for a less efficient system of ticketing. The facts that many agents were converted by System One, and that travel-agent subscription fees are so low, were said to demonstrate that the CRS market is competitive. Thus, the market shares and profits of the two leaders were justly earned from taking a business risk and producing a superior product in the face of robust actual and potential competition. With respect to the contract forms, defendants argued that long-term contracts are common in the economy (and, indeed, beneficial because both sides can rely upon an enduring relationship), and that lost profits are a perfectly reasonable basis for assessing damages from early termination in this instance because the profits were deserved and legal.

Thus, the essence of the defense was that to the extent there were excess profits, they derived not from market power, but from superior efficiency and a reward to risk-taking. If CRS vendors lacked market power, they could not be guilty of monopolization through predatory pricing or illegal price discrimination, nor could the contracts be construed as anticompetitive barriers to entry.

In the course of the Northwest litigation, the arguments of both sides made it clear that a core issue was whether CRS vendors should charge a booking fee, and that should plaintiffs prevail, prices to travel agents would be likely to increase. An apparently insurmountable problem for plaintiffs was to explain why the antitrust laws should care whether airlines or travel agents paid for CRS services. The argument at trial also made clear that a significant factor in determining the nature and scope of competition in the CRS industry was the fact that travel agents typically use only one CRS. Numerous explanations were offered for why this is so: system incompatibilities and training costs, lack of space for multiple systems, contract provisions, the choice of system architecture by the vendors. Plaintiffs faced another problem in explaining why multiple system use by a travel agent could help overcome the information problems faced by consumers, how switching among CRSs by travel agents might lower airline booking fees, and how this was possible technically and economically through a different organization of the industry or from the presence of a MARS-like multi-access, or an unbiased, no-host system.

The defendants' story would doubtless have been much the same regardless of the court's limitations on the boundaries of the airline cases. Neither CRS nor air service is dominated by a single firm, and no evidence was adduced to show that the leading firms actively collude.[24] In general, neither airline nor CRS profits are particularly high, except for APOLLO and SABRE, which arguably are the best CRSs in terms of capabilities. The claim that CRSs nonetheless have market power arises from information problems among consumers and the absence of a mechanism for inducing travel agents to switch among CRS vendors. Both prevent airlines and passengers from forming a competitive marketplace. One simply cannot understand how anticompetitive problems could arise in this industry without understanding both of these issues. And the argument about why they might arise is extraordinarily complex for adequate resolution in litigation. In fact, the defendants in these cases essentially ignored both issues.

Although the Texas Air strategy was successful financially, it would not have had any significant policy effect even if litigated successfully to conclusion. The forms of bias in the Texas Air complaint are largely history. The core current practices have to do with booking fees, access to CRS data, and agent contract forms. By winning the Northwest and travel-agent cases, American and United have obtained, at least for the present, legal approval for these practices.

REVISING, REVAMPING, OR REJECTING THE
COMPUTER RESERVATION SYSTEM RULES

The substantial private litigation and public controversy over CRS market structure and performance have occurred despite the presence of substantial federal regulation of the industry. While the CRS rules established by the CAB in 1984 do not directly regulate price, they include numerous provisions that were designed to control bias, to guarantee access to services, and to promote competition among vendors and airlines.

The rules have been essentially unchanged since their 1984 implementation. Moreover, there has been no substantial enforcement activity by the Department of Transportation, despite numerous complaints by other CRS vendors, travel agents, and airlines alleging violations of the rules on bias, contract provisions, treatment of airlines, and use of sales data. The major hearings that have occurred have involved controversies that have arisen as U.S. CRS vendors have expanded overseas and encountered either conflicting CRS regulations or the actions of unregulated CRS vendors with market power. For example, the department reviewed and finally approved a settlement of the dispute between American's SABRE and British Airways concerning British Air's denial of ticketing authority to SABRE in England. The prohibition had effectively limited American's ability to expand into England, but the settlement required American to develop a display that complied with the European Civil Aviation Conference (ECAC) CRS rules. As U.S. vendors continue to expand their marketing efforts overseas, such as APOLLO's arrangements with Gemini in Canada and Galileo in Europe, and as foreign vendors consider operations in the United States, there are likely to be more controversies of this sort. Surprisingly, however, future controversy is likely to be over how to reconcile different regulatory regimes—all vendors operating in Europe and Canada are subject to CRS regulation that is substantially more restrictive than the rules in the United States.

The regulations governing the Canadian and European CRS industries, detailed in Chapter 9 of this book, have developed since the implementation of the 1984 rules and in many facets parallel those rules. In certain important areas, such as price, contract terms, requirements for direct access links, and treatment of nonowners, there are substantial differences. These differences are at the heart of the controversy concerning the U.S. CRS rules. The Department of Transportation is required to review the performance of the 1984 rules and to determine whether the rules should be kept in place, modified, or eliminated. All of this was supposed to be accomplished before the rules expired at the end of 1990. However, a final ruling had not been made by the spring of 1991. In response to a proposed rulemaking issued by the department in September of 1989, every major player in the CRS industry—vendors, airlines, travel agents, car rental companies, ECAC, and the Department of Justice—filed comments with proposed changes to the CRS rules. The purpose of this section is to assess the proposed changes and their implications for future performance in the CRS industry. A very large number of parties filed comments; we will focus here only on the major proposals and the department's reply.

The comments filed at the department parallel exactly the positions and problems described above in private litigation and in the three "eras" of CRS. The key issues are the level of booking fees, the nature and implication of long-term subscriber contracts that contain liquidated damages based on booking fees, and the treatment of nonhost carriers (often referred to as functional parity) in loading data, accessing data, and providing direct computer links. Roughly, the positions split such that American and United stand on one side, with comments that recommend that the rules should remain essentially unchanged or be eliminated, while all other parties are arrayed on the other side, seeking varying degrees of action from substantially more restrictive regulation of pricing, access, and performance to outright divestiture.

As always, the differences in opinion come down to one's view of the implications of airline ownership of CRSs. Proponents of divestiture or improved regulation believe that airline ownership creates the incentive and ability to use the CRSs to earn supracompetitive returns—in monopoly booking fees and in incremental revenues from bias or the lack of functional parity. These commenters point to estimates of costs in the DOT's May 1988 report to demonstrate that current booking fees are well above costs, and to numerous cases where host airline services were favored over other airlines.

In contrast, both American and United believe that additional regulation is unnecessary (with the exception of possible changes in the enforcement of tying provisions). Indeed, United argues that the industry is sufficiently competitive that the CRS rules could be allowed to expire. The two largest CRS vendors argue that neither has market power and that any returns earned by the vendors are a reasonable result of their marketing efforts and the quality of their CRS product. While the two vendors present data and expert analyses to support their views, the fundamental basis for their arguments is the private court findings discussed in the preceding section. Thus, the claim that booking fees are reasonable is predicated on the outcome of the Northwest case, and the claim that liquidated damages clauses and other subscriber contract provisions are reasonable and justified as legitimate business practices is based on the decisions reached in the travel-agent cases. American and United argue that the Department of Transportation should rely on these decisions in formulating any changes to the rules.

Of necessity, the private court decisions focused on narrower issues than those considered by the CAB when they implemented CRS regulation in 1984. Antitrust litigation deals in part with whether market power was lawfully obtained, whereas regulation can seek to constrain market power regardless of its cause. The majority of commenters are urging the department to reverse a substantial lessening of competition in CRSs or airlines. In general, this is a broader policy scope than any considered in private litigation, where the standards include demonstrating a dangerous probability of monopoly, specific harm to specific companies, and illegal monopolizing actions.

While many different solutions have been proposed, the basic thrust of all of the other commenters' filings is similar. First and foremost, all argue that market power by at least the two dominant vendors and possibly the others is pervasive and nondiminishing. All argue that this market power has led to booking fees that are well above competitive prices and to continued bias in the display or access to information that favors the host carrier. While some commenters state that liquidated damages provisions may be justified under contract law as reflecting actual damages, most commenters express the view that the liquidated damages provisions based on booking fees yield damages far in excess of actual damages. Vendors, airlines, and travel-agent associations argue that the liquidated damages and other contracting provisions inhibit conversions and reduce intersystem competition.

The proposed solutions parallel the perceived problems. The Department of Justice, among others, calls for partial or complete divestiture of CRSs as a remedy to the persistent problem of incremental revenues and reduced airline competition caused by various forms of bias. Bias includes display bias, which most admit is well regulated, and bias in the quality and timeliness of information on nonhost carriers. The DOJ recommends a mandatory move ahead to look and book links—that is, equal real-time information on all as in a complete multi-access structure—or a move back to direct access links for all, including the host. For host carriers, this is essentially a partial divestiture of the system. This solution was adopted in Canada, where look and book links have been made mandatory.

Commenters who recommend changes in the contract terms look to Canada and Europe to support the notion that CRS markets can perform efficiently under different contract terms. U.S. vendors are performing under these alternative regulatory regimes with little apparent difficulty. The major changes recommended are for shorter contract terms (between one and three years), elimination of liquidated damages based on booking fees, and prohibition of other practices that prevent or deter conversions. These provisions are comparable to those in force in Canada and Europe.

Several proposals deal with alleged abuse of market power in booking fees. The DOJ proposes to permit booking fees only if they are charged to travel agents. Another proposal is to require that booking fee revenues not exceed subscriber revenues in any one year; all excess fees would have to be proportionately rebated to airlines. Still another proposal is to adopt the European policy of regulating fees on the basis of costs. The primary differences among the proposals are in the nature of continuing enforcement. The zero-price option—booking fees paid by travel agents—would require an immediate and radical change in the mode of operation, but then little regulatory oversight. Any of the other proposals, even if based on nondiscriminatory pricing rules, would require active oversight by the department. In general, the department has shown itself to be reluctant to pursue enforcement proceedings against vendors in the past five years.

Among the simplest but potentially the most dramatic recommendations is to require vendors to permit the connection of any compatible hardware or software to any CRS, and even to permit the resale of CRS services. In essence, this proposal would free the aftermarket for hardware and software. It would permit agents to access different CRSs through the same terminal and encourage the entry of intermediaries into competition with CRS vendors. If coupled with nonexclusive contracts without minimum use provisions, this proposal would dramatically alter the configuration of the CRS industry. Other network industries, even services with serious security concerns such as automatic teller machines (ATMs), have long had multiple interfaces, whereby the same terminal can be used to access different networks and switches. The development of such an industry structure in CRS would substantially undermine the market power of the individual vendors.

In response to the vast array of filings, the Department of Transportation, in March, 1991, issued proposed new CRS rules that have many of the features of the Canadian and ECAC rules—that is, subscriber contract terms of three years, elimination of minimum-use provisions, improved ability to attach other equipment to the CRS at the agency level, and modification of rules governing access to inventory. Many comments on these rules, which will be under consideration by the Department of Transportation for final promulgation in late 1991, continue to encourage the department to adopt some of the more substantive and structural changes, such as the zero-price option and the ability of agents to access all CRSs through one terminal and a common switch. Whether the department will adopt these changes in the final rules and whether, absent such changes, any new rules are sufficient to constrain market power will be central questions that determine whether the ultimate resolution lies with Congress in the more dramatic form of relief—divestiture.

CONCLUSIONS

The airline and CRS industries are not as robustly competitive as they otherwise might be. The CRS industry, in particular, is hampered by business practices that erect serious barriers not only to entry but also to competition for existing travel agents among the established vendors. Despite nearly two decades of controversy over how the CRS industry could be structured so as to be competitive and/or so as to have minimal anticompetitive spillover into the airline business, the basic structural problems in the industry remain pretty much as they were from the beginning. The 1984 CRS rules and recent court decisions have failed to produce any significant changes. The nation is now at about the long-run equilibrium structure and performance in both airlines and CRSs that it can expect—unless there are major public policy changes. Essentially, all major carriers are now partners in one or another CRS; the remaining carriers are too small and cover too little of the country to offer any serious prospect for airline-sponsored entry; because of existing practices, third-party vendors have no incentive to enter, despite the high profits of the leading vendors.

The newly merged Pars and Datas II have announced plans to create an unbiased, no-host system, which is an attractive prospect for solving part of the CRS problem. Likewise, troubled Texas Air has sold a major interest in System One to Electronic Data Services, which has no airline interests, with the same purpose in mind. We are skeptical that either venture will cause fundamental changes. In the present CRS environment, the likelihood that large numbers of agents will prefer a neutral, unbiased system does not appear very great. Hence, the new System One and Pars–Datas II systems will not put much pressure on APOLLO and SABRE to follow suit. In any case, neither will erode the anticompetitive aspects of booking fees, nor induce a change in the design of systems to encourage agents to subscribe to and use more than one system.

While this is a somewhat dismal assessment after two decades, there is, nonetheless, some hope for solutions to these complex and seemingly intractable problems. The hope lies primarily in the arena of federal action—by regulation or legislation—that would impose striking and substantial changes in the structure and operating practices of CRSs. More elaborate regulations, and perhaps vertical divestiture, are required to solve these problems. We suspect that the realistic choice is either to tighten rules regarding CRS practices relatively soon (such as by eliminating airline booking fees and/or requiring "equal access" by travel agents to all CRSs from a single terminal), or, as airline performance becomes more cartelized by CRS practices, to suffer the return of economic regulation of airlines and CRSs in the not-too-distant future.

NOTES

Professor Noll gratefully acknowledges financial support from the John and Mary Markle Foundation. This paper was drafted while Ms. Guerin-Calvert was at Economists Incorporated and she would like to express appreciation for the support and advice of her colleagues there. The authors would like to thank Ann I. Jones, Michael E. Levine, and Clifford Winston for generous comments on an earlier draft. The reader is entitled to know that while both authors are expressing their own views, neither is a novice in the policy disputes over CRSs. Both have consulted for airlines that have advocated eliminating some of the business practices of the leading CRS vendors— American (SABRE) and United Airlines (APOLLO). In addition, Ms. Guerin-Calvert, while at the Antitrust Division from 1985 to 1987, was involved in the drafting of a Department of Justice study that concluded that some of the practices of CRS vendors in the early 1980s were anticompetitive, and Professor Noll testified on behalf of plaintiffs against American and United in one of the antitrust cases cited herein.

1. Internal reservation systems are also called CRSs; however, to avoid confusion, we will use the term CRS only to denote a system marketed to travel agents.

2. The market structure of the industry is discussed more fully in the third section.

3. By 1990, Pan Am was the only national trunk carrier which was not a partner in a CRS. In addition, a few large regional carriers—Alaska, Midway, Southwest—also had no ownership shares in a CRS.

4. A subscription externality arises when the addition of one customer to a service enhances or diminishes the value of the service to another customer.

5. The benefits of these developments after deregulation are well documented in a number of studies, See, for example, Morrison and Winston (1989) and references therein.

6. Although there are many travel-agent cases, the key one is *United Airlines v. Austin Travel* (1987).

7. In 1990, the lineup of CRS ownership connections with airlines is as follows: SABRE—American Airlines; APOLLO (Covia)—United Airlines and U.S. Air; Pars–Datas II (Worldspan)—Delta, Northwest, TWA; and System One—Texas Air Corporation (Continental).

8. For a good summary, see Levine (1987).

9. See George Eads (1970).

10. For recent analyses of the deregulated airline industry, see Borenstein (1989) and Morrison and Winston (1989).

11. Because nearly all litigation was settled or decided, and new CRSs were being developed during 1990, a fourth era is almost certainly beginning as we write this chapter.

12. Some of these documents are cited in U.S. Department of Justice (1983, p. 51ff).

13. For an excellent history of CRS developments from the initial idea in 1953 to the systems of the early 1980s, see Copeland and McKenney (1988).

14. Several examples are discussed in U.S. DOJ (1983) and (1985).

15. Information has been presented in the regulatory and court proceedings involving CRS practices concerning instances of contracts in which agencies had subscriber fees completely waived as long as they satisfied other contract terms, such as minimum use and duration. CRS vendors do not dispute the claim that standard practice is to sell service below cost to many agencies, especially the larger ones and, indeed, cite this practice as evidence that the industry is highly competitive. For example, see *United Airlines v. Austin Travel* (1987) and filings by System One Direct Access concerning a travel-agent case in comments to the U.S. Department of Transportation on the CRS rules (System One, 1989, Volume II, Appendix K).

16. The entry of MARS was also greatly hindered by the refusal of American and United to participate in a multi-access system. Hence, MARS could not offer the principal technical advantage of the system for ticketing on the two largest carriers.

17. For example, APOLLO contacted Allegheny (USAir) to become a co-host with a booking fee of $.22 on July 21, 1981. But on December 15, 1981, it contracted with Jet America to charge a booking fee of $3.00 without co-host status. The latter was competing with United on the Los Angeles–Chicago run, and was viewed as an aggressive new competitor. (*USAir et al., v. American and United Airlines*, 1984, Ex. 25267).

18. For several examples of these practices, including the ones cited here, see U.S. DOJ (1983, pp. 110–115 (SABRE) and pp. 124–130 (APOLLO)).

19. The rollover clause provided that if an agency added another CRS terminal, its CRS contract for all CRS services was renewed. Hence, a growing agency would never have its long-term contract actually expire.

20. The CRS rules have had other effects, notably on the airline industry by reducing display bias and ending price discrimination in booking fees.

21. For further discussion of postdisplay bias, see U.S. DOJ (1985, pp. 33–38), U.S. DOT (1988, p. 56ff.), and Delta (1986). In the second study, DOT estimates that the rules eliminated only 10 percent of the effect of bias, halo, and other forms of airline synergy for APOLLO, but about one-third for SABRE.

22. The details of liquidated damages provisions differ among carriers: APOLLO charges half of the agent's average monthly fees from booking for the remainder of the contract; SABRE charges the average bookings per cathode ray tube display terminal (CRT) from all its agents, multiplied by the number of CRTs in the agency and the number of months left on the contract. See U.S. DOJ (1985, p. 24).

23. For a more complete discussion of these issues, see Levine (1987).

24. The main difference in the two airline cases was in the plaintiff's emphasis on bias. Bias was not a part of the complaint in the Northwest case, being used instead as evidence of market power. In the Texas Air case, it was the most important part of the complaint and the basis of the damage claim.

9

Comparative Regulatory Regimes for Computer Reservation Systems

Richard Annan

Computer reservation systems (CRSs) have become powerful and necessary tools in the distribution of airline services. These systems have created new opportunities for airlines to market their products and have greatly enhanced the efficiency of the travel agent channel of distribution. They have also demonstrated a significant ability to distort airline competition. In addition to the concern about the impact of these systems on airline competition, the rapid consolidation of CRS vendors through global alliances, joint ventures, and mergers had raised concerns about increased market power within the CRS industry itself.

In order to address these concerns, a number of regulatory regimes have been instituted. The United States was the first country to develop a set of competitive rules in 1984. The Europeans developed two similar codes in 1989—one by the Council of the European Communities (EC), the other by the European Civil Aviation Conference (ECAC). Although both codes have been adopted by the member states of these respective organizations, only the EC code is legally enforceable at this time. In Canada, a CRS code was developed as a solution to an antitrust case, with rules incorporated into a Consent Order, issued July 7, 1989, by the Canadian Competition Tribunal. In addition, the International Civil Aviation Organization is continuing to study the feasibility of some form of worldwide or coordinated regional approach to CRS regulation, the objective being to prevent major conflicts arising between the CRS rules of different jurisdictions (Lyle, 1987).

In the many years that have passed since the United States first introduced the CRS rules, some important lessons have been learned about the effectiveness of the rules. European and Canadian rulemakers have certainly benefited from the U.S. experience, and each code reflects the learning that has taken place, although differences in markets and in the viewpoint of the regulators have led to different provisions or modified versions of the U.S. precepts. The U.S. experience is well documented elsewhere.[1] The purpose of this chapter is to outline the Canadian experience with the CRS industry, how it came to be regulated, the differences between the Canadian CRS rules and those of other jurisdictions, and the prospects for future regulation.

COMPUTER RESERVATION SYSTEM OVERVIEW

CRSs provide travel agent subscribers with the ability to electronically view the schedules, fares, fare rules, and seat availability of airlines that are hosted or participating in the CRSs and allow these agents to make reservations on, and print tickets for, those carriers. The level of quality of these services is referred to as the "functionality" of the system. These systems also often allow subscribers to reserve hotels, rent cars, and access a variety of other travel-related services, although the primary service remains the distribution of airline services. In most cases, the CRS vendor maintains a single database which is electronically linked to cathode ray tube (CRT) terminals or personal computers located at the travel agency. The travel agency enters into a contract for provision of the CRS service and pays various charges and fees for terminals, ticket printers, telecommunication lines, and computer access. In addition to price, CRS vendors compete for travel agents by increasing the functionality of their systems. By developing extensive software, many CRSs are able to offer a wide variety of additional capabilities that allow the travel agent to quickly and efficiently make reservations and to respond to particular client demands, such as ensuring the lowest cost fare or providing detailed reporting for corporate accounts. Two measures which are commonly used to assess the penetration of CRS vendors in the travel agent market are the number of travel agent locations that the vendor has established and the number of CRT terminals in place in those locations.

CRS vendors also provide a distribution service to airlines that choose to participate or host in their system. The "participating carrier" enters into a contract whereby the CRS vendor agrees to list the schedules, fares, fare rules, and seat availability that the participating carrier chooses to provide to the CRS vendor, either directly or through carrier-supported central agencies.[2] In exchange, the participating carrier pays a booking fee for each flight segment booked on the CRS.[3] In the case of a "hosted carrier," the CRS vendor agrees to store the complete airline inventory of that airline in the database and in fact provides the carrier with both an internal reservation and management system to manage its inventory and an external reservation system to distribute its product to travel agents. As a practical matter, an airline can only be hosted in one CRS, although it will usually participate in all CRSs that have more than a modest number of travel agents in the airline markets it serves. One measure of the penetration of a CRS vendor in the provision of airline distribution services is the number of airline booking segments its system has generated.

In order to generate the display of flight options, the CRS will use a set of decision rules in order to edit and rank order flights. Each CRS algorithm employs a different set of criteria or different weighting to criteria to arrive at a screen display. The criteria usually include the total elapsed journey time, number of connections or stops, and time of departure from requested time, among others.

The importance of CRSs in airline distribution is demonstrated by the fact that 95 percent of U.S. travel agents and 90 percent of Canadian travel agents use a CRS to book travel (U.S. DOJ, 1989a, p. 10; Director of Investigation and Research, 1989, p. 7). About 97 percent of the tickets issued by Canadian travel agencies are booked through a CRS (Director of Investigation and Research, 1989, p. 7). In both Canada and the United States, over 70 percent of airline seats are sold through travel agencies (U.S. DOJ, 1989, p. 10; Director of Investigation and Research, 1989, p. 7).

It is precisely this importance of CRSs to airline distribution, coupled with the fact all major CRSs are airline-owned, that has caused U.S., Canadian, and foreign regulators to closely examine the impact on airline markets of the growth and conduct of CRS vendors. CRS vendors have a significant incentive and ability to distort airline competition and raise their airline rivals' costs. (See U.S. DOJ, 1983, 1985, 1989a,b.)

Subtle and not so subtle biases in the display of travel options can cause competitors' flights not to appear or to appear on subsequent screens, dramatically reducing the chances that the travel agent will recommend these services. One study indicates that 80 percent of the bookings will be made from the first screen displayed, and as much as 50 percent of the bookings will be made from the first line of the first screen (*The Avmark Aviation Economist*, 1987, p. 21). The additional airline revenue that biases in these systems can generate for their airline parents can, in the absence of regulation, be significant. Indeed, before the U.S. Civil Aeronautics Board (CAB) prohibited the most blatant forms of bias in 1984, the major source of revenues for U.S. CRS vendors was incremental airline revenues generated for the airline parents (U.S. DOT, 1988, p. 130)

Segment booking fees can also significantly erode competitors' profitability and deter new entry. For example, in 1984 the CAB was concerned that CRS vendors had charged some competitors booking fees exceeding $3, when the average airline profit per segment in 1978 was $2.50 (Civil Aeronautics Board, 1984a, p. 28). The effect of these fee levels seemed to have deterred a number of carriers from entering markets dominated by the airline parents of the major CRS vendors (Civil Aeronautics Board, 1984a, p. 28).

It is not surprising, therefore, that all of the codes of conduct developed so far have focused on the impact of CRSs on airline markets. The Canadian Consent Order and accompanying rules, however, are somewhat unique in that they also contain a number of additional provisions designed to protect and promote competition among CRS vendors.

CANADIAN COMPUTER RESERVATION SYSTEMS INDUSTRY

Before June 1, 1987, there were three CRS vendors that had a meaningful presence in Canada. The largest system, called Reservec, was owned and operated by Air Canada. It held a dominant position, holding 73 percent of the number of automated travel agent locations, 71 percent of the number of CRT terminals placed in agencies, and 71 percent of the total number of segments booked in Canada (Director of Investigation and Research, 1989, pp. 20–22). Air Canada and its affiliates were hosted on Reservec. Air Canada was also the largest airline in Canada, accounting for about 56 percent of the domestic revenue passenger kilometers (RPK) in 1986 (Director of Investigation and Research, 1988a, p. 5).

Air Canada first offered travel agencies access to its internal reservations system in 1973, allowing nonhosted carriers to have their schedules and availability displayed in 1975. From 1975 to 1983, Reservec was the only CRS in Canada.

The next largest CRS vendor, as measured by travel agent locations (18 percent) and terminals (16 percent), was Pegasus, owned and operated by Canadian Airlines International Ltd. (CAIL). CAIL was hosted on Pegasus and was the second-largest carrier in Canada, holding about 37 percent of the domestic RPK in 1986 (Director of Investigation and Research, 1988a, p. 22). Pegasus entered the Canadian market in 1984. CP Air (the predecessor of CAIL) was not satisfied that Reservec was displaying its information in a fair and unbiased fashion and decided this mode of distribution was too important to rest solely in the hands of its major domestic competitor.

SABRE, the CRS operated by American Airlines, was the third CRS vendor in Canada, entering the market in 1983. Although in 1987 it had the smallest market penetration in terms of travel agent locations (10 percent) and terminals (13 percent), it did have a higher share of bookings than Pegasus (18 percent) (Director of Investigation and Research, 1989, pp. 20–22). American Airlines has no presence in the Canadian domestic airline market, but is the largest U.S. carrier in the transborder airline market between Canada and the United States.

On June 1, 1987, Air Canada and the parent company of CAIL merged Reservec and Pegasus to form the Gemini Group Automated Distribution Systems Inc. (Gemini). The Canadian competition policy authorities became concerned about the competitive consequences of this merger in both CRS and airline markets. On March 3, 1988, these concerns led the statutory head of the Canadian competition agency, the Director of Investigation and Research (the Director), to file an application with the Canadian Competition Tribunal. The Director alleged that the merger substantially lessened competition in the provision of CRS services to travel agents and airlines, and requested dissolution of the merger by the Tribunal.

THE GEMINI CASE

The Director's Position

CRS Markets

The Director believed that the Gemini merger would substantially lessen competition in the provision of CRS services to Canadian travel agents primarily for two reasons (Director of Investigation and Research, 1988a, pp. 10–20, 1988b,c). First, the merger reduced the number of significant CRS competitors from three to two, creating a CRS that would have an overwhelming dominance of the national CRS market, holding 90 percent of the travel agent locations, 87 percent of the number of CRT terminals, and 82 percent of the total segments booked in Canada. In 368 of the 420 local markets in Canada, Gemini would have a monopoly.

Second, and most importantly, the vertical integration between Gemini and Air Canada and CAIL, and the fact that these airlines were to be hosted on Gemini, would mean that Gemini would maintain its dominant position and would, together with its parent airlines, have the incentive and ability to reduce or eliminate remaining CRS competition and prevent new entry from existing U.S. or European CRS vendors. The prospects for competitively significant entry from new nonairline-related CRS vendors was even more remote, given the large cost synergies that exist for airline-owned CRSs because airlines must operate internal reservation systems in any event.

For most travel agencies in Canada, it is critical to have complete, timely, and accurate information on Air Canada and CAIL because these are the airlines they most frequently book. In 1987, these two airlines, together with their affiliates, controlled over 90 percent of the domestic airline market and provided a significant percentage of the transborder and international airline service as well. In Canada, domestic airline service accounts for 77 percent of the total number of passengers and 60 percent of the total scheduled passenger revenues (Tretheway, 1989, p. 7). With the demise of Wardair Canada Inc. (Wardair) in 1989, Air Canada and CAIL now control over 95 percent of the domestic market.

The vertical integration between these carriers and Gemini, therefore, provides Gemini with substantial market power. If Air Canada and CAIL decide not to participate in competing CRSs, it is unlikely that these CRS vendors would remain in the Canadian marketplace because they would be deprived of the major source of CRS revenue (participating carrier booking fees for Air Canada and CAIL) and because information on these carriers, even if it could be accessed from central airline agency sources, would not be supported by the carriers to ensure completeness, accuracy, or timeliness. Air Canada's refusal to participate in Pegasus or to pay booking fees was a major factor in the poor financial performance of Pegasus and demonstrated that nonparticipation was not a remote possibility.

Even if these airlines did participate in competing systems, they could still control the scope of their participation. For example, by not providing competing CRSs with information on "seat sales" or other special discount fare classes, or not doing so in a timely fashion, the utility of the competing system would be diminished. Another example would be to restrict the functionality of competing systems by limiting the ability to offer new enhancements, such as pre-reserved seating and advance boarding passes, to Gemini.

Air Canada and CAIL could also tie the receipt of airline commissions to the use of Gemini. Such action would be a powerful incentive not to use competing systems because the major source of Canadian travel agent income is airline commissions paid by the parent airlines of Gemini. Other incentive ties could also exist, such as the offering of frequent flyer points, free tickets, or greater receptivity to special requests for clients, such as the authority to book capacity-controlled seats and fares. Even if such ties are not overt, the important relationship between these carriers and Canadian agents, and the frequent contact between the agents and the airline sales representatives, mean that some travel agents will always perceive that it is in their best interest to use the Gemini system.

In addition to the advantages flowing from vertical integration, the fact that the two national carriers are hosted in one CRS as a result of the merger provides Gemini with significant informational advantages over its competitors, even if the parent airlines of Gemini fully participate in competing systems. These advantages stem from the fact that the host system will always have the most complete, timely, and accurate schedule, fare, and seat inventory information on hosted carriers because this is the same database that the hosted carriers themselves use to keep track of their sales.

This is not true of participating carriers. For example, not all the seats available on a particular flight of a participating carrier will be displayed in a CRS because of delays in the teletype messaging systems which are used to request and confirm reservations. Delays in messages can be substantial and therefore an inventory buffer of five or more seats is usually required to prevent overselling a flight. The ability to book these last few seats, referred to as "last seat availability," is important to agencies that frequently book business travellers because these clients tend to make reservations close to departure time on heavily booked flights. The requirement for an inventory buffer may also prevent the participating carrier releasing information on deep-discount seats, except to the hosted system, because the number of deep-discount seats available is less than the level of the inventory buffer set by the participating carrier.

There can also be lags in the receipt of information. When a carrier updates its schedule and fare information, it usually updates its own database as well as sending out tapes to the *Official Airline Guide* (*OAG*) and the Air Tariff

Publishing Company (ATP), which consolidate this information with that of other carriers. It is the *OAG* and ATP tapes that are typically loaded by CRS vendors. As a result, host carrier information tends to be updated more quickly and frequently than participating carrier information. Information lags can become particularly important where fares and fare rules are frequently changed to respond to competitive conditions and travel agents must have timely information to allow their clients to capitalize on bargain fares.

Another problem that sometimes occurs is that the booking message generated by a travel agent is not received by the host computer of the participating carrier. While such "no records" problems are rare, some travel agents prefer to use a CRS on which they can make a reservation directly in the carrier's internal database and thus avoid the possibility of an irate client being denied boarding because there is no record of his reservation in the host computer. Even if the message is not "lost," long delays caused by heavy communication traffic over the teletype system can sometimes happen. By using a CRS where the requested carrier is hosted however, the travel agent will be assured of immediate confirmation of bookings or seat assignments.

While some of these informational advantages can be subtle, collectively they can have a significant impact on a travel agent's choice between competing CRSs. Many of the informational advantages resulting from hosting can be reduced or eliminated by the use of electronic direct access links which augment or bypass the slower teletype communication systems and connect travel agents to the internal database of the requested carrier. Most direct access links used today are of a "look but not book" type. Such links allow the subscriber to look at the same seat availability that subscribers to the CRS where the requested carrier is hosted to see, thus eliminating most of the last seat availability problem. These types of links, however, do not allow the travel agent to immediately decrement seat inventory over the link. In order to make a reservation, a booking request must still be sent by teletype from the subscriber's CRS to the host computer of the participating airline.

A number of CRS vendors have developed "look and book" links which do allow the booking to be immediately made and confirmed over the link. Such links remove any possibility of delays in seat confirmation or no-record problems.

In the United States, no one airline is so dominant that it can ignore distribution through all the CRS vendors. Consequently, not only do all the major U.S. airlines participate in all the systems, they all have agreed to participate in direct access links programs. This is not the case in Canada. Air Canada refused to participate in any direct access link program because it did not want to encourage the entry or expansion of rival CRS vendors into Canada, although such links would provide better information to travel agents booking Air Canada. Once CAIL became partners with Air Canada in Gemini, there became even greater incentive to deny such links in order to ensure Gemini would remain dominant in Canada.

Impact on Airline Markets

The Director was also concerned that the merger, by creating a near monopoly in the CRS market, enhanced the ability of the parents of Gemini to disadvantage their airline competitors. Denial or delay of access to Gemini would be fatal to all but the smallest Canadian carrier who could perhaps rely on direct marketing methods as a substitute for CRS distribution. Biasing the display or charging competitors very high booking fees could have equally damaging consequences for competitors. If the market power of Gemini should be used in this way, it would make new entry very difficult if not impossible. This was particularly troublesome given the fact that the Canadian domestic airline market, which has recently been deregulated, is already characterized by high entry barriers (Tretheway, 1989, pp. 18–22).

Finally, there was some concern that Gemini could make coordinated pricing between the two national carriers easier if it were used to observe each other's discount seat inventories.

Position of the Respondents

In response to the Director's position, Air Canada and CAIL (the Respondents) claimed that the Canadian travel agency market was too small to support more than one CRS on a full cost recovery basis (PWA, 1988; Air Canada, 1988). In 1987, the number of segments booked through all Canadian agencies was about the same as the number of segments booked through the smallest of the five U.S. CRS vendors, Datas II.

The Respondents believed that the nonviability of two Canadian CRS vendors was demonstrated by the poor financial performance of Pegasus in its three years of operation. By combining the operations of Reservec and Pegasus, the Respondents maintained that there would be substantial efficiency gains. More importantly, the merger was necessary to maintain a strong Canadian-owned CRS that would give Canadian airlines sufficient bargaining leverage to ensure unbiased display in foreign CRSs and ensure they could control the distribution of their product in the domestic market.

The Respondents also maintained that SABRE, the largest and one of the most highly functional CRSs in the world, would continue to grow in the Canadian marketplace and place competitive pressure on Gemini. SABRE is a low-cost producer and could treat the Canadian market on an "incremental" cost basis because the vast majority of the required investment is already recovered from their existing U.S. subscriber base.

In terms of the impact on the domestic airline market, the Respondents noted that the merger eliminated the incentive for Air Canada and CAIL, the two national carriers, to bias the display of each other's services, and thus improved the competitive position of CAIL in relation to the market leader. As to the other Canadian carriers that were not affiliated or aligned with Air Canada or

CAIL, the Respondents indicated that they had given undertakings to the Minister of Transport to not unfairly deny access or bias the display to Canadian carriers.

Consent Order

On the eve of the hearing, the Director and the Respondents arrived at a settlement which was filed with the Competition Tribunal on April 12, 1989. After seven days of hearings, including representations from a number of intervenors,[4] the Competition Tribunal issued a Consent Order dated July 7, 1989, that allowed the merger to stand, subject to a number of terms and conditions.

The Consent Order incorporates a number of provisions designed to constrain the market power that results from the fact that the two national carriers own Gemini and are hosted in it. The objective is to create a "level playing field" for all CRSs operating in Canada so that they can compete on the basis of price, service, and functionality rather than on who owns and controls the essential airline information.

The Consent Order requires Air Canada and CAIL to participate in all CRSs operating in Canada, including paying the prevailing nondiscriminatory segment booking fees of such CRSs established from time to time in North America.[5] It requires these airlines to provide complete, timely, and accurate information concerning their airline schedules, fares, fare rules, and seat availability by class to all CRSs operating in Canada, either directly or through carrier-supported central agencies, on the same basis and at the same time such information is furnished to Gemini. In no circumstances shall information concerning any restricted or special class of seats or fares offered by Air Canada or CAIL be withheld or deliberately delayed from any CRS operating in Canada.

Air Canada and CAIL are obligated to set up electronic direct access look-but-not-book links between its database and all CRSs operating in Canada at the expense of the CRS requesting it, thus removing the informational barrier of last-seat availability. The airlines must also agree to the granting of look-and-book links after June 30, 1991, further lowering the informational advantages of hosting. The link obligations only arise if the owning carriers of the CRS requesting a link to Air Canada and CAIL agree to offer a reciprocal capability to Gemini.

The Consent Order also requires that should Air Canada and CAIL provide to Gemini the capability to prereserve seats and issue advance boarding passes, such capabilities must be offered to other CRSs operating in Canada on the same reasonable terms and conditions, provided a reciprocal capability is offered to Gemini by the owning carriers of such CRSs.

Canadian Computer Reservation Systems Rules

In addition to the above provisions which concern Air Canada and CAIL, the Consent Order incorporates a set of CRS rules governing the conduct of

Gemini and its owning airlines. The CRS rules, however, are anticipated to have general application because the obligation of Air Canada and CAIL to grant direct access links arises only if SABRE and other CRSs operating in Canada agree to be bound by such rules.

The Canadian CRS rules incorporated into the Consent Order are largely drawn from the U.S. rules, although a number of changes have been made to strengthen certain provisions, particularly as they relate to the contracts between subscribers and CRS vendors. These changes are designed to reduce the barriers to entry in the CRS market and are particularly important in the Canadian context because of the overwhelming dominance of one CRS vendor which is owned by the two dominant national carriers. In addition, a number of provisions reflect the U.S. experience with the rules, and in particular are designed to prevent CRS vendors from circumventing the rules.

The tying of airline commissions or other incentives to the use of a CRS is strictly prohibited (Competition Tribunal, 1989a, 1989, s6(d)). The provision is more broadly worded than the U.S. rule (CAB, 1984b, s.255.5(d)) in order to catch all forms of incentives that are directly or indirectly conditioned on the use of a CRS in which the airline has an ownership interest and which are offered to existing and potential subscribers. The Canadian rules also require all owning carriers to indicate in writing to all travel agents who sell their products at least once each year that it is the policy of the owning carriers that airline promotions and incentives to travel agents are not conditional upon the use of a particular system.

In order to reduce the entry barrier presented by long-term contracts, subscriber contracts are restricted to a maximum three-year term (Competition Tribunal, 1989b, s.6(a)). The current U.S. rules provide for five years and this has become the standard term in that country (CAB, 1984b, s.255.6(a)). The European Civil Aviation Conference (ECAC) code also limits contract terms to three years, while both the ECAC and European Community (EC) rules permit subscribers to terminate their contract on three-months notice, provided that the contract has run at least one year (EC, 1989, Article 9, s.4; ECAC, 1989, s.13(f)). The trade-off that has to be considered in setting the contract length is that if CRS vendors do not have sufficient time to amortize their equipment, setup, marketing, and training costs, subscribers' fees will be increased substantially to cover these costs.

In order to circumvent the U.S. rule on contract length, CRS vendors included a provision in their subscriber contracts that would automatically renew or extend the contract period each time a new piece of equipment was added or deleted. In the United States these rollover provisions have been removed at the request of the Department of Transportation but have not been formally prohibited in the CAB rules. The Canadian rules contain an explicit prohibition of rollover provisions (Competition Tribunal, 1989a, s.6(f)).

The Canadian, U.S., and European codes all prevent a CRS vendor from directly or indirectly prohibiting a subscriber from obtaining or using any other system (CAB, 1984b, s.256(b); Competition Tribunal, 1989a, s6(b); ECAC, 1989, s.13(b); EC, 1989, Article 9, s.2). A gray area that may not be covered by the ban on exclusive dealing is the common practice of vendors to require travel agents to make a minimum number of bookings per terminal per month. If the minimum use level is set high enough, it can have the effect of forcing the travel agent to use only one system in order to comply with the subscriber contract.

CRS vendors maintain that such provisions are economically justified because the level of subscriber fees is based to a large degree of the level and certainty of revenues flowing from airline booking fees. Nevertheless, such provisions can raise entry barriers to CRS competition. The wording of current rule appears broad enough to prohibit minimum use provisions that lead to exclusive dealing. If such clauses are not covered by the current rules, then amendments may be necessary. In any event, the potential anticompetitive effects of minimum use provisions are lessened with the use of shorter contract terms.

A final Canadian rule designed to reduce the anticompetitive nature of CRS subscriber contracts is a prohibition on liquidated damage provisions based on segment bookings or airline revenues. Such liquidated damage provisions in the United States have made it more difficult and costly for the smaller CRS vendors to convert subscribers, particularly where they are combined with onerous minimum use provisions (U.S. DOT, 1988, pp. 131–132). The airline booking stream can easily exceed the revenue stream from the subscriber fees, resulting in a daunting potential liability for subscribers if they try to switch suppliers before the contract expires, or if they acquire another vendor's equipment and fall below the minimum use level set out in the subscriber contract. The Canadian prohibition means that vendors will have to prove in court that the loss of all or nearly all of the revenue stream from airline bookings was reasonably foreseeable by the subscriber and that the vendor cannot mitigate its damages by finding another subscriber for the balance of the contract term. In addition, the shorter contract term means that any potential liability will be reduced accordingly.

As well as provisions relating to subscriber contracts, the Canadian code contains one additional and important provision to promote CRS competition. This is the requirement that all carriers who own a CRS must allow any CRS in Canada in which it participates to issue tickets on its services, if the terms and conditions of the CRS vendor are commercially reasonable and within industry standards. This has not been an issue in the United States because no one CRS is so dominant that its airline owners can ignore participation in another CRS. In Europe, however, a major dispute arose over this issue between British Airways and SABRE. SABRE was effectively precluded from the U.K. market because British Airways refused to allow U.K. SABRE agents to print British Airways tickets (American Airlines, 1988, pp. 8–10). Denial of ticketing is a very effective anticompetitive weapon that can be employed by a CRS that dominates its home market. The European codes have so far sidestepped this issue and contain no provision in relation to ticketing.

Airline Market Safeguards

In terms of rules governing the conduct and pricing of CRS service to airlines, the Canadian rules follow very closely the U.S. rules, employing the same major precepts (CAB, 1984b, s.255.4–s.255.5; Competition Tribunal, 1989a, s.4–s.5):

a. The primary display of a CRS must not use any factors directly or indirectly relating to carrier identity. The criteria for ordering the flights on the primary display must be applied consistently to all participating carriers;
b. The same standard of care and timeliness must be applied to the loading of information from hosted and participating carriers;
c. System vendors must charge the same fees for the same or similar levels of service to all participating carriers;
d. The system vendor can not condition participation in its system on the purchase or sale of any other goods or services.

Soon after implementation of the U.S. display rules, CRS vendors attempted to circumvent them by encouraging travel agents to use biased secondary displays. The Canadian and European rules deal with this problem by making it clear that the primary display will be as useful as any other display maintained by the system vendor and that the subscriber must specifically request a display other than the primary display in order for the secondary display to be made available.

One important difference between the United States and Canadian codes is that the Canadian rules place a positive obligation on system vendors to provide access to any carrier willing to pay the nondiscriminatory fee and comply with the vendor's customary terms. This provision is particularly important in the Canadian context because nondiscriminatory access to Gemini is vital for any airline wishing to offer scheduled passenger service in Canada. A similar obligation is found in the European codes (EC, 1989, Article 3 s.1; ECAC, 1989, s.10(a)). Another distinction is that in the Canadian rules the definition of participating carrier includes hosted carriers (Competition Tribunal, 1989a, s.1(g)). This means the nondiscrimination provisions apply equally to hosted and participating carriers so that all carriers pay the same booking fees. This is important in Canada where a number of carriers not affiliated with Air Canada or CAIL are hosted carriers in Gemini.

In addition, this definition means that service enhancements which a CRS offers to a hosted carrier must be offered to all participating and hosted carriers on nondiscriminatory terms. In the United States, the rules permit a system vendor to retain such enhancements for the use of the owning carriers unless they are offered to one participating carrier, in which case they must be offered to all participating carriers on nondiscriminatory terms (CAB, 1984b, s.255.7). The Canadian rule prevents Gemini from offering an enhancement, such as advance seat selection, to certain hosted carriers, and not offering the same enhancement to the airline competitors of those hosted carriers.

The Consent Order also prohibits Gemini from unreasonably refusing to make available to travel agent subscribers any enhancements which are made available to it by participating carriers. (Competition Tribunal, 1989b, par 4.) For example, if a participating carrier offers Gemini the capability to issue advance boarding passes and is willing to meet commercially reasonable terms, Gemini cannot refuse to implement such an enhancement, even if Air Canada and CAIL decided not to develop a similar capability. This provision is designed to prevent the use of Gemini as a bottleneck to service enhancements which airline competitors to the parent airlines of Gemini may wish to pursue.

One final difference between the Canadian and other codes in relation to the airline market is the anticollusion provision. The Consent Order prohibits the sharing or exchange of commercially sensitive airline information through the operations of Gemini which would facilitate agreement to share markets or fix prices as between the two national carriers and their affiliates (Competition Tribunal, 1989b, par. 16). Unlike the general conspiracy provision contained in the Canadian Competition Act, this rule is an absolute prohibition that does not require proof that the agreement or exchange unduly lessens competition.

Enforcement

The Canadian rules have two enforcement mechanisms, one of which is unique to the Canadian regulatory regime. Breach of the Consent Order and rules by the Respondents (essentially Air Canada, CAIL, and Gemini) could give rise to contempt proceedings brought by the Director and possibly by any third party who is a beneficiary of the order (Competition Tribunal, 1989c, p. 21). Section 74 of the Competition Act provides that failure to comply with an order of the Competition Tribunal is punishable by fine or imprisonment.

The contempt mechanism is not substantially different than the U.S. or European situation where the U.S. DOT and the European Commission have the power to investigate complaints and enforce their codes through fines.[6] In the Canadian case, the Director has at his disposal all of the general investigatory powers of the Competition Act, including the power of search and seizure and oral examinations under oath whenever he has reason to believe that an order of the Tribunal has been breached (Competition Act, 1986, s.10–s.17). Unlike the European Commission, however, the Director does not have the power to impose fines himself, but must convince the Competition Tribunal that its order has been breached.

The second and unique mechanism of enforcement contemplated by the Consent Order is private enforcement. The obligation of Air Canada and CAIL to grant a direct access link to a CRS vendor arises if the recipient agrees to offer a reciprocal capability and agrees to enter into a link contract which incorporates the CRS rules (Competition Tribunal, 1989c, p. 22). The effect of this provision not only ensures that the CRS rules are of general application, but it creates an opportunity for parties to the link contracts to sue for damages or injunctive relief for breach of the CRS rules. This right of private action is important because in Canada private actions under the civil reviewable provisions of the Competition Act, which includes abuse of dominance, refusal to deal, exclusive dealing, and tied selling, are not possible.

The private right of action means that the Canadians CRS rules will be self-enforcing to some extent. The private enforcement mechanism is now operational because on September 30, 1989, SABRE entered into a link contract with Air Canada and CAIL incorporating the CRS rules.

An additional feature of the enforcement of the Canadian rules is the reporting requirements incorporated into the rules. System vendors must provide all subscribers, before entering into a contract or on renewal, a copy of the rules, and provide to the Director a report signed by an officer of the system vendor and the owning carrier indicating that the owning carrier and system vendor have complied with these rules. These provisions are designed to increase awareness of the rules among subscribers and to focus attention at the senior level of the companies concerned as to the importance of compliance. An action for noncompliance may involve the individual who signed the report as well as the company in contempt proceedings.

FUTURE OF CANADIAN COMPUTER RESERVATION SYSTEM REGULATION

The Consent Order and the CRS rules are the result of a settlement of an antitrust action between the Director and the parties to the litigation. These provisions are designed to reduce or remove the competition concerns resulting from a particular merger and are not intended to be a permanent regulatory framework for the CRS industry. The Consent Order and accompanying rules represent a compromise between the parties to the action. Although the Consent Order process allowed for input from many interested parties, the focus of the debate was on domestic competition policy issues and not other public policy issues which may be affected by the type of regulation that has been adopted.

At the Consent Order hearing, the Competition Tribunal was made aware that the Government of Canada would likely develop a permanent form of CRS regulation that would replace in whole or part the need for the Consent Order and rules. The Government of Canada has subsequently committed itself to the development of a permanent form of regulation which will be administered and enforced by the National Transportation Agency. While it is anticipated that the new regulations will be based in large part on the provisions of the Consent Order and rules, it is likely that changes will be required to reflect the experience gained under the present rules and the broader policy role of the industry regulators. In addition to domestic competition issues, for example, the new rule-makers will likely consider the impact such rules may have on the international competitiveness of Canadian air carriers.

In terms of the effectiveness of the Consent Order and rules to maintain and encourage competition between CRS vendors operating in Canada, much depends on the extent to which the direct access links and the behavioral prohibitions constrain the market power flowing from the fact that Air Canada and CAIL own and are hosted in Gemini.

Direct access links provide access to host carrier inventory when they work, but at least some carriers in the United States have alleged that these links have been frequently interrupted for anticompetitive reasons (Lenza, 1989, par 74–94). Moreover, some travel agents find that these links are not convenient to use. The success of the links in replicating the major informational advantages of the host system will only become apparent over the next few years.

Of the behavioral prohibitions, the rule against tying will be particularly difficult to enforce since the travel agent receiving the tie is benefiting from the arrangement and has little incentive to report an infraction. It is encouraging, however, that Gemini has sold a one-third interest to Covia Partnership, owners of the second-largest CRS in the United States. The addition of a third ''neutral'' owner reduces the incentive to tie because for every dollar of airline inducement given up by Air Canada and CAIL, only two-thirds will be recovered by them in benefits from their investment in Gemini. As well, SABRE in Canada has attempted on its own to encourage travel agents to report tying arrangements by offering a reward of $100,000 to any person who provides information to the Director that leads to a conviction for a violation of the prohibition against tying.[7]

In terms of the provisions relating to the distribution of airline services, the Canadian rules essentially replicate the U.S. rules. Many critics in the United States and Europe feel that these rules have failed to control abusive conduct of CRS vendors in relation to their airline competitors. (See U.S. DOJ, 1989b; British Civil Aviation Authority, 1988.) The major problem areas are display bias and booking fees. While the U.S. rules have been effective at eliminating the most blatant forms of bias, a number of airlines have complained that subtle forms of bias remain which are still having significant impacts on the display of competitors' flights. The Europeans in particular consider that the preference given to same airline or code-sharing airline (''on-line'') connections over interline connections in U.S. CRSs result in their services being given much lower screen priority although the elapsed time on these services is sometimes much shorter than competing on-line U.S. services.

The on-line issue was raised in the Gemini case by Wardair (Wardair, 1988). In the Canadian domestic market, Air Canada and CAIL have a number of affiliated or aligned carriers who provide feed traffic to the transcontinental services of the major carriers.[8] These affiliated and aligned carriers share the same designator codes. For example AC105-AC*1511 is a flight between Toronto and Victoria involving an on-line connection between Air Canada and its affiliate, Air B.C.

The Wardair intervention provided a good example of how on-line preference can be an important entry barrier to new entrants and nonaligned carriers. Due to the absolute on-line preference in the Reservec algorithm, Wardair found that its competing transcontinental point-to-point services were often not displayed in domestic itineraries that required connecting service with the affiliated or aligned carriers of Air Canada or CAIL. With feed traffic being diverted away from Wardair's transcontinental routes, Wardair found it very difficult to compete with the integrated networks of Air Canada and CAIL. This lost traffic was particularly important because Wardair had recently entered the scheduled domestic market and it needed rapid passenger growth to achieve profitability.

With the demise of Wardair, Canada is left with two national carriers, each of which has an extensive network of service provided by affiliated and aligned carriers. In order to encourage competition in the newly deregulated domestic market, small nonaffiliated carriers will have to grow and develop. While passenger convenience may support the use of on-line preference in the U.S. domestic market because of the number of connecting services, in Canada the need to encourage competition in the current duopoly has to be a strong consideration in deciding whether on-line preference should be prohibited.

Booking fees remain a major area of concern in the United States. (See, for example, U.S. DOJ, 1989b, pp. 11–14.) Critics of the U.S. rules claim that all the nondiscrimination rule has accomplished is to allow the two leading CRS vendors to set a supracompetitive booking fee level for the industry which is two times higher than the cost to them of providing the service. The U.S. Department of Justice has recently recommended that the U.S. DOT consider the abolition of booking fees, thus transferring all of the revenue generation to the more competitive CRS market for travel agent services or, in the alternative, pass on the booking fees directly to the consumer (U.S. DOJ, 1989a, pp. 43–48).

The Europeans have adopted the same nondiscrimination approach as the U.S. rules, except that their booking fee provision also requires the fee to be reasonably related to the cost of the service provided (EC, 1989, Article 10(1); ECAC, 1989, s.11(6)). One benefit of the European approach is that it reinforces the signal to CRS vendors that government regulators are prepared to regulate booking fee levels if market forces are not effective, and this provision provides an avenue for price regulation without the requirement for further administrative action to change the rules. However, any price regulation related to cost will be extremely difficult because of the problems in accurately determining the cost of providing the distribution service. Since CRS vendors and their airline owners share the same computing facilities, personnel, and software, any allocation of costs between the internal reservation system of the airline owners and the external distribution service is arbitrary.

In Canada, Gemini has chosen to follow the standard U.S. $1.85 per segment booking fee charged in the United States. Gemini has stated that it is constrained in setting booking fees because the booking fees which it receives from airlines other than Air Canada, CAIL, and their respective affiliated and alliance carriers are less than the booking fees which Air Canada and CAIL pay to CRSs other than Gemini. Consequently, any booking fee increase initiated by Gemini which triggered a similar increase by the other CRSs would result in a net economic loss to the Gemini parent airlines (Mathewson and Edsforth, 1989).

The weakness with this retaliation argument is the fact that the United States and now Europe have codes which require CRS vendors to charge the same booking fee to all participating carriers. In order to retaliate, these vendors would have to reply with an across the board increase in the United States or Europe unless they were granted an exemption from the nondiscrimination rule. The current political concern over the level of booking fees in the United States may prevent further price increases. Consequently, it is not clear what market constraints there are on the booking fees Gemini can charge, as long as they are nondiscriminatory.

From a Canadian domestic prospective, it could be argued that booking fees are not a major concern because nearly all Canadian carriers are affiliated or aligned with the parents of Gemini. Nevertheless, it will be important to consider the effect high booking fees may have on the prospects for new entry or expansion of the few remaining nonaffiliated or aligned carriers in Canada.

CONCLUSION

Regulators in the United States and, most recently, in Europe have attempted to design a code of conduct for the CRS industry which would allow these systems to further enhance the distribution of airline and related travel products to travel agents, and ultimately to the travelling public, while at the same time constraining their potential abuse in relation to airline competition.

The Canadian rules, having their genesis in an antitrust settlement of a CRS merger case, place greater emphasis on preserving competition in CRS markets. They are the only rules that mandate full participation, including direct access links, of the dominant national carriers in competing systems. By reducing the informational barriers to entry, strengthening the prohibition on tying, and mandating less restrictive subscriber contracts, the Canadian rules attempt to encourage competition among CRS vendors. This is particularly important in the Canadian context, given the dominance of one CRS vendor which is controlled by the two dominant national carriers.

In terms of protecting airline markets from abusive CRS practices, the Canadian code contains essentially the same bias and pricing rules which are now used in the United States and which are the subject of much debate as to their effectiveness. In revising the current Canadian rules, careful consideration will have to be given as to whether changes in these areas are desirable. In 1991, with less than two years' experience under the current Canadian rules, it is too early to say whether the present Canadian code will be successful in achieving all of its competition policy goals, although it is clear that competition between the CRS vendors in Canada has intensified over this period. The only certainty in this rapidly changing industry is that regulators will be constantly challenged to design codes of conduct that are effective at controlling potential abuses without stifling innovation and competitive rivalry.

NOTES

The views expressed in this chapter are those of the author alone, and do not represent the views of any department or agency of the Government of Canada. The author would like to thank Margaret Guerin-Calvert, Paul Crampton, and John Rook for their helpful comments and suggestions.

1. For a summary of the U.S. experience, see Margaret E. Guerin-Calvert (1989a).

2. The major agencies are the Air Tariff Publishing Company, which gathers airline fare information and the *Official Airline Guide (OAG),* which gathers schedule information.

3. A flight segment represents travel on one direct flight which may have intermediate stops but involves no connections.

4. Intervenors at the Consent Order hearing were the Consumers' Association of Canada, American Airlines Inc., Air Atonabee Limited, Bios Computing Corporation, Alliance of Canadian Travel Associations, and the Attorney General of Manitoba. Wardair Canada Inc. withdrew its intervention following its purchase by CAIL.

5. The Europeans have a similar principle contained in the regulations that were contained in the exemption of CRS vendors from the application of Article 85 of the Treaty of Rome. Article 11 of those regulations indicates that the Commission may withdraw antitrust immunity where a parent carrier who holds a dominant position within the common market refuses to participate in a competing CRS. Unlike the Canadian rules, however, the scope of participation is not defined; nor is there any requirement that carrier information be provided at the same time and on the same basis as it is provided to the host system.

6. Enforcement provisions of the EEC rules are contained in Articles 11 to 20. The ECAC code has no formal enforcement mechanism as yet.

7. The "Sabrewatch" program was announced by SABRE Canada in September 1989.

8. The code-sharing affiliates of Air Canada are Air B.C., Northwest Territorial Airways, Air Ontario, and Air Alliance. Air Canada also shares codes with Air Nova. CAIL code-sharing aligned carriers are Time Air, Calm Air, Ontario Express, and Air Atlantic.

10

Real Estate Multiple-Listing Services and Antitrust Revisited

John E. Lopatka and Joseph J. Simons

A multiple-listing service (MLS) is a system by which real estate brokers in an area agree to pool their listings in a central registry, disseminating information about the properties and permitting each participating broker, for a share of the commission, to sell listings of all other participants. MLSs are usually operated by the local board of Realtors, which is affiliated with the National Association of Realtors (NAR). MLSs have existed since at least the early 1900s and initially were operated manually through the use of books of compiled listings updated at periodic intervals. Today, many MLSs are computerized, and their listings are updated daily. MLSs and realty boards have been the subject of antitrust regulation since at least 1950. (See *U.S. v. National Ass'n of Real Estate Bds,* 1950.) That first exposure related to what appeared to be fairly straightforward price-fixing. In the years that followed, the scrutiny of MLSs under antitrust principles intensified, approaching something akin to public utility regulation.[1] Whether this regulation has been beneficial, however, is open to question. Proponents of regulation have assumed anticompetitive consequences when a procompetitive explanation for the various ancillary restraints associated with Realtors and MLSs was not apparent to them. No evidence that we are aware of, however, demonstrates either that the condemned restrictions caused prices to rise or that the prohibition of the restrictions has caused prices to fall. The regulatory response to MLSs may have been particularly unfortunate for small real estate brokers, who require cooperation to achieve efficiencies that large firms can achieve themselves. If antitrust intervention has made MLSs less efficient, large brokerage firms would be advantaged in that they perform many of the functions of an MLS internally. The recent growth of large brokerage firms may be a result of misguided regulation. Other detrimental effects could be that less information is revealed on MLSs, that homes take longer to sell or sell at lower prices, and that brokers in many areas would have started MLSs, but were deterred from doing so. Given these costly possibilities and the dearth of evidence of anticompetitive effects, the most appropriate response of the courts and regulators is to resist the impulse to fix something that may not be broken.

We have not yet attempted to gather sufficient data to resolve these issues. We can, however, offer theories to explain how restrictions adopted by Realtors and MLSs are efficient. These theories thus compete with the theories on which previous and current regulatory efforts have been based. In addition, we have uncovered some data that are suggestive and that raise questions as to the wisdom of existing policies.

In essence, we believe that prevailing policies fail to account fully for the fact that MLSs involve substantial economic integrations and significant network externalities. Moreover, the stuff of MLSs is information, and antitrust policy has traditionally had difficulty addressing the cooperation among firms that may be necessary to establish an efficient system of intellectual property rights. The thrust of this chapter will be to examine those factors and their significance for antitrust regulation. The first section presents a short history of Realtors and the development of MLSs. The second section sets out a brief description of the traditional ways in which the courts and antitrust enforcement agencies have analyzed MLSs and a summary of what we believe are the failings of the analysis. The prevailing economic case against MLSs is described and critiqued in the following section. In the last section, we offer alternative explanations for some common MLS restrictions.

A BRIEF HISTORY OF REALTORS AND THE DEVELOPMENT OF MULTIPLE-LISTING SERVICES

Although most states have regulations licensing real estate brokers, the term "Realtor" is the copyrighted property of the NAR and can only be used by its members. According to the NAR's historian, the use of Realtor "came into being because of the compelling need to identify to the public those real estate men who are pledged to abide by the national code of business ethics" (Davies, 1958). As with many other professions, some real estate brokers were looking for a way to distinguish themselves from other brokers who either were less trustworthy or were otherwise providing a lower quality of service. The early attempts at this differentiation involved establishing local real estate boards that promulgated and enforced codes of ethics. Eventually, these local boards became standardized under the control of a national organization, the National Association of Real Estate Brokers, the precursor of the NAR.

As reported by the NAR, the term Realtor was coined in 1915 by Charles Chadbourne, a past president of the Minneapolis Real Estate Board. He was supposedly on his way to a board meeting when he saw a newspaper headline,

"Real Estate Man Swindles a Poor Widow." The swindler was not a member of the local real estate board, yet he had "besmirched" every broker in the city. Mr. Chadbourne reportedly suggested something similar to the following: "Why could we not adopt a title which would single out our members, would imply that they are vouched for by our board as qualified and responsible, and would cement the confidence of the public in them?" (Davies, 1958). He is credited with inventing the term Realtor as well as with proposing a plan to the national association for effective administration of its use.

The early proposals for codes of ethics were aimed at what was then perceived to be a predominant cause of conflict between real estate brokers and between brokers and their clients. Most brokers had no written contracts and most of the contracts that were in writing were open listings, which meant that any agent that procured a buyer was entitled to the commission. Accordingly, there were frequent disputes over which agent, if any, was entitled to the commission. It has been estimated that up to 25 percent of commissions were lost due to "treachery of owners and buyers" (Davies, 1958).

The founders of the NAR saw two complementary responses to this problem. First, they strongly urged the use of exclusive listing contracts so that there would be no dispute over which agent was due the commission. Second, they promoted the concept of cooperative selling to provide the incentive for home owners to agree to exclusive listings. This latter concept was not necessarily embodied in an MLS system. Rather, it often consisted simply of informal cooperation among Realtors. For example, they might meet periodically for breakfast at a local restaurant. Indeed, many areas today do not have MLSs, and Realtors in many of these areas continue to cooperate informally. In addition to the national code of ethics, which governed conduct once one became a member, local real estate boards seem to have had membership requirements designed to permit only the more reputable brokers to join. Further, some local boards maintained their own educational testing requirements as a prerequisite to membership.

Competing Paradigms

Courts and enforcement agencies have typically analyzed the operation of MLSs by using one of two implicit models. First, an MLS offers enormous efficiencies in the provision of brokerage services. It therefore represents an "essential facility," and as such, the brokers who form the network cannot restrict access to it by their competitors. Any membership criteria, which by nature exclude from participation those individuals who fail to meet them, are therefore suspect. The second implicit model assumes that the rules of conduct for the MLS participants amount to an agreement among competitors to restrain competition among themselves and are therefore also suspect, if not per se illegal. Under both models the conduct is condemned unless the defendant can satisfactorily convince the court or enforcement agency that the specific restriction in question is efficiency enhancing, and even that defense may fail if the practice is deemed illegal per se. The fact that it is competitively neutral is not sufficient under these approaches to avoid condemnation.

These two paradigms fail to take into account certain principles that we believe are critical to a proper legal analysis of MLSs. An MLS represents a collective enterprise among brokers to provide services of a particular quality that could not be offered as efficiently in the absence of collaboration. Restrictions on membership and on the activities of members are essential in order to attain the desired level of quality and to distinguish members of the venture from lower-quality providers. If the founding brokers are correct in their forecast of market demand, and if they manage to provide the quality of services they set out to offer, the enterprise should succeed, and that success will attract applicants. Quality-enhancing restrictions will usually impose costs, and applicants can be expected to try to share the success without incurring the costs. They will challenge the restrictions.

This scenario is well illustrated by the facts of *Blake v. H-F Group Multiple Listing Service (Blake v. H-F Group,* 1976). In 1969, the four oldest real estate brokerage firms in the Homewood-Flossmoor area of Cook County, Illinois, formed an MLS. The president of the MLS testified that the group was formed because the firms had "had a number of problems when they were cooperating with other brokers." He complained of incidents in which brokers to whom they referred clients were unfamiliar with the homes those brokers were selling and the community in which the houses were situated. He stated that this led to his clients receiving "inadequate service" (*Blake v. H-F Group,* 1976, p. 20). The firms had no interest in joining a preexisting MLS that covered a larger territory "because they did not feel they could properly serve persons selling homes in areas outside of the immediate Homewood-Flossmoor area."

The defendants believed that to adequately serve their clients, "all of their sales personnel should be personally familiar with both the home to be sold and its surrounding area" (*Blake v. H-F Group,* 1976, p. 21). The firms placed a variety of restrictions on joining the group that were designed to ensure the quality of services offered by the members, including requirements that an applicant not employ part-time sales agents and have an office located in the Homewood-Flossmoor area. A broker, who had no office in the area and who admitted having "little personal knowledge of the area," sought and was denied admission (*Blake v. H-F Group,* 1976, p. 22). She claimed that the admission criteria violated the Illinois Antitrust Act. Fortunately, the Blake court departed from the analysis generally applied by other courts and enforcement agencies. Although the court's analysis was not especially probing, the court did affirm the trial court's judgment that the defendants' conduct was reasonable (*Blake v. H-F Group,* 1976, p. 29).

As can be seen from the *Blake* case, the context in which MLS restrictions were adopted provides suggestive evidence regarding their efficiency-enhancing nature. Two additional points regarding context are significant. First, as a general rule many restrictions were adopted at the outset of MLS formation, at a time when its members constituted such a small percentage of the market that the exercise of market power was not plausible. Given the success that the Realtors have enjoyed in many areas of the country, some may be tempted to assume that they and their MLSs became dominant instantly. That assumption, however, would be incorrect.

In California, for example, there were 15,592 licensed real estate brokers and only 1,161 affiliated NAR members in 1921. NAR California members then accounted for 7 percent of all brokers in the state. The number reached 20 percent by 1927, but declined to 10 percent by 1932. Even in the more recent past, data reported in several court opinions indicate that several MLSs were quite small relative to the local markets in question.[2] Moreover, it appears that even in the areas where MLS membership today accounts for an overwhelming proportion of licensed brokers, MLS membership originally was only a small fraction of the broker population and that growth in membership accompanied successful financial results.

Second, while there are many MLSs that are now dominant forces in their local markets, there are also many MLSs whose members only constitute a small percentage of the local market. Yet, the restrictions imposed by both are similar. Although it is certainly possible that restrictions imposed by MLSs with dominant market shares could have an anticompetitive effect or purpose, it is extremely unlikely that the restrictions imposed by MLSs with nondominant positions could have been motivated by attempts to achieve market power through either collusion or anticompetitive exclusion. If market power did not motivate the adoption of various restrictions, the next best explanation is efficiency, even if the MLS members cannot articulate one.

We do not suggest that the purposes and effects of all of the restrictions imposed by MLSs are transparent. Nor would we argue that an MLS is incapable of operating to restrict competition among brokers, return monopoly profits, and reduce consumer welfare. We do believe, however, that the traditional antitrust approach to these networks does not ask the right questions. Further, our impression, based only on theory and the type of suggestive evidence described above, is that MLSs have generally operated to enhance efficiency.

EVIDENCE OF COLLUSION IN THE RESIDENTIAL REAL ESTATE MARKET

The general economic case against MLS restrictions is derived from the argument that the market is not behaving competitively. Certain restrictions imposed by the MLS are the apparent mechanism by which collusion takes place, the case goes, and the elimination of these restrictions through the antitrust laws enables the MLS to serve its cost-reducing function at the same time that competition is unfettered.[3]

We believe, however, that the premise of the argument against MLS restrictions—that the market is performing anticompetitively—has not been established. First, although the proponents of the argument acknowledge that the structural characteristics of the industry are not conducive to cartelization, they seem unduly willing to disregard the implications of the insight. Second, the aspects of market performance that supposedly prove collusion we find ambiguous. Indeed, other characteristics of market performance, together with evidence of market structure and the history of the brokerage industry, suggest to us that the market is competitive.

The structure of the brokerage industry provides powerful evidence that price-fixing would not occur. Yet critics of MLS restrictions shrug their shoulders at this evidence and point instead to certain aspects of market performance that they assert prove cartel behavior, however unlikely that conduct would appear to be. In general, they emphasize that most brokers charge the same commission rate. This demonstrates that the industry is engaged in collusion, they assert, because (1) the difference in costs incurred to sell houses of very different values, such as a $50,000 home and a $200,000 home, cannot possibly account for the difference in compensation generated by a flat commission rate (Owen, 1977, p. 948 n.111; Erxleben, 1981, p. 188); (2) different houses that sell for roughly the same amount will not always require the same degree of effort by the brokers, yet a flat commission rate will generate the same compensation (Erxleben, 1981, p. 188); and (3) brokers possess varying degrees of competence, and in a competitive market, less-talented brokers would charge a lower rate (Owen, 1977, p. 948 n.111; Erxleben, 1981, p. 188).

We find this to be a flimsy basis on which to dismiss the evidence of market structure over time and conclude that the industry is cartelized. To begin with, the percentage of transactions that take place at the prevailing commission rate is not clear, though it certainly does not approach 100 percent. Thus, for example, Owen reported that 75 percent of all residential real estate transactions in California involved a 6 percent brokerage fee (Owen, 1977, p. 947). Even in these transactions, it is not clear whether 6 percent was merely the commission originally agreed upon or the fee actually paid, since a fee set at the time a broker is retained may be reduced at the time of sale in order to facilitate the bargain (Owen, 1977, p. 947 n.110). Further, even if 75 percent of all sales are at the same commission, that still means brokers are cheating on 25 percent of all transactions. It would seem difficult for a cartel to succeed when 25 percent of its members have defected.

Nevertheless, the proposition that a substantial number of transactions takes place at the same commission rate is undoubtedly correct. Moreover, some of these transactions surely return a greater profit ex post, particularly in an accounting sense, than others. However, differing levels of ex post returns say nothing about whether the market is performing competitively.

In this industry, a typical broker apparently quotes a standard commission at a time when he has little information about the effort that he will have to expend to facilitate a sale. The commission actually charged may then be adjusted at the time of sale. This system may in fact be an efficient way to allocate risk between seller and broker in an environment of uncertainty and to minimize the transaction costs involved in reaching an agreement on that allocation. What uniformity exists in commission rates may be no more indicative of collusion than is the prevalence of a one-third contingency fee among personal injury lawyers.

The argument that less-talented brokers would charge lower fees if the market were competitive is not compelling. Again, the factual premise has not been established. Moreover, in a typical, workably competitive market, price is determined by the marginal supplier. If the least-talented brokers require a 6 percent commission to cover their costs, one would expect more competent brokers to charge 6 percent and earn the rents associated with their unusual talent.

Furthermore, the costs incurred in selling houses will typically increase as the value of the house increases. An expensive home may have a more extensive array of features about which the broker will have to learn than a cheaper house. Wealthy buyers may demand a higher level of services from a broker and be more sophisticated negotiators than buyers of more modest means. So, for instance, a more educated broker may typically be necessary to complete the sale of an expensive house, and she may have to spend more time to do so.

In addition, wealthy buyers may expect certain amenities from a broker, such as a plush office, fine car, and the availability of service at the buyer's convenience, that a different clientele does not demand. In short, the costs incurred to cultivate the patronage of sellers and buyers of expensive houses are likely to be real and substantial.

EFFICIENCY EXPLANATIONS FOR COMMON MULTIPLE-LISTING SERVICE RESTRICTIONS

We can identify several basic explanations for MLS restrictions. First, many restrictions appear to promote the value of the MLS trademark by raising the quality of the services provided individually by the participating brokers and the inherent value of the collaborative venture. Second, many restrictions serve to prevent free-riding by members and nonmembers on investments in acquiring home seller clients, selling specific property, and promoting the MLS trademark. A third group of restrictions function primarily to reduce the transaction costs involved in the brokers' cooperative arrangement. These include the costs of exchanging information, contracting for cooperation, resolving disputes among participants, and covering the expenses of the operation. Finally, some restrictions serve to minimize a broker's expected cost of legal liability for actions of cooperating brokers, even if imposing liability would not necessarily be efficient. Below we discuss specific types of restrictions common among MLSs.

Direct Quality Parameters

In the end, a real estate seller wants to sell her house and a buyer wants to purchase the property. An MLS is a valuable tool, but the desired services are provided by individual brokers or brokerage firms. The MLS is a means by which a broker can subcontract with others to provide brokerage services, so that a seller is effectively hiring a broker and all subcontracting brokers. As the quality of the services offered by the participants in the network declines, the value of the network declines—fewer buyers will seek out MLS members, and so sellers will have less reason to hire MLS brokers. Brokers who wish to increase demand by offering high-quality services through a cooperative venture, therefore, may establish rules for participation that are designed to admit only high-quality providers.

A cluster of restrictions on MLS participation appears to be designed to help ensure that members provide high-quality brokerage services. Thus, some MLSs have specified that members must be principally engaged in the real estate business. Others allow only full-time brokers to join, or also prohibit full-time broker members from employing part-time sales persons. All of the variants of this restriction are apparently based on the wholly plausible premise that a full-time supplier of brokerage services is likely to be more skilled, more dedicated, or more knowledgeable than part-time providers.[4]

This is not to say that every MLS would want to establish this kind of restriction, though some might desist from implementing it solely out of fear of liability. The quality of part-time brokers may vary across areas. Alternatively, some MLSs may deliberately choose to offer a lower quality of services. In addition, using the percentage of a workday devoted to brokerage activities is obviously only an imperfect indicator of quality—some part-time brokers, no doubt, are highly skilled professionals. But these observations do not change the fact that this type of restriction can be an efficient way for brokers to assess quality and promote in the market a cooperative sales enterprise that meets a desired standard of performance.

Similarly, some MLSs require that an applicant for membership have been in business in the locale for a significant period of time. Some require simply that an applicant have an office within the MLS territory or have his principal place of business in the area. At least one MLS required that an applicant have no more than one office, and that office located in the MLS area. The ability to measure the worth of a house and to convince a potential seller to purchase it will generally be improved by knowledge of the community, and this type of requirement provides some assurance that brokers are knowledgeable.[5] In addition, it guarantees that an applicant will have some business record that could disclose unscrupulous conduct.

Access to Information

The quality of brokerage services rendered to sellers can be measured in part by the price obtained for the property and the time required to complete the transaction. A broker who produces a buyer willing to pay a certain price in a given amount of time provides better service, ceteris paribus, than one who produces a buyer offering less. MLS restrictions that deny access to various economic actors, such as buyers and buyers' brokers, may enhance quality by helping sellers capture a greater percentage of the available surplus from a deal.

Thus, because the transaction price will be negotiated and because the agent has better information about the market, efficiency may require a flow of confidential information from the principal to the agent.[6] By "confidentiality," we mean that the information is withheld from parties on the other side of the transaction—in other words, buyers and their agents. However, because assistance from other brokers may facilitate sale, disclosure of the confidential information to additional agents of the seller, or subagents, may be efficient. Thus, an MLS network, to function most efficiently, may have to contain confidential information to which buyers and their agents are denied access.

This is not to say that if confidential information is excluded from an MLS, and buyers are directly or indirectly allowed access, the MLS would cease to function. An MLS can serve to collect and disseminate three kinds of information: (1) information that particular, described pieces of property are available for sale; (2) information about the value that buyers are likely to place on property (which can be inferred from listing prices over time for houses described on the network or even from selling prices, if they were to be placed on the network); and (3) information about the prices that sellers are likely to accept for their property (for example, a seller must move quickly, and though he is asking $250,000 and similar houses have sold recently for $230,000, he would be willing to accept $210,000). It is the third type of information that must remain confidential.[7]

If an MLS cannot deny access to buyers or their agents, it may continue to operate by gathering and providing information about availability and listing prices, and by so doing serve a valuable function. Thus, it is not surprising that MLSs continue to operate in markets where buyers' brokers are allowed access. (See, e.g., *Market Force, Inc. v. Wauwatosa Reality Co.*, 1990.) But particularly if such an MLS allows access because of perceived legal mandates, it may not operate as efficiently as it otherwise would. Confidential information might still be exchanged among listing and cooperating brokers, but the exchange would take place off the MLS and potentially in a less-efficient manner.

Commission Rates and Splits

Long before electronic multiple listing systems were devised, the National Association of Real Estate Boards, a forerunner of the NAR, encouraged local boards to establish schedules of commissions for their members, and the local boards made compliance with the suggested charges an ethical mandate. (See *United States v. National Ass'n of Real Estate Bds*, 1950). In 1950, the Supreme Court held that the actions of a local board constituted per se illegal price-fixing but affirmed a district court judgment that the national association was not sufficiently involved in the conspiracy to incur liability (*United States v. National Ass'n of Real Estate Bds*, 1950). Later, some MLSs established commission rates and refused to list property unless the seller agreed to pay at least the established rate. (See, e.g., *Ogelsby and Barclift, Inc. v. Metro MLS, Inc.*, 1976.) Some MLSs reportedly required listing brokers to publish the commissions they would receive on each house. Some MLSs also established uniform commissions that cooperating brokers would receive, or commission "splits." Other MLSs simply published in the system the commission that a listing broker would receive and the cooperating broker's split.

An agreement to set prices among some group of suppliers in a market with inconsequential entry barriers cannot easily be explained as an attempt to earn supracompetitive profits. If an MLSs is involved, and if the MLS generates substantial cost savings for members, a requirement that all members charge the same commission is still not easy to explain as an anticompetitive arrangement if the MLS does not seriously restrict admission—any rents that the cost-saving device would otherwise generate for the participants would quickly be dissipated by new entry. There are, however, several efficiency-enhancing explanations for the typical fee-related restrictions that have been used in the brokerage industry.

A principal may want some assurance that his agent is working to sell his property. In particular, a principal may want some assurance that his agent is not working harder to sell someone else's property than his own. This is especially true because the nature of the transaction tends to induce an exclusive relationship with a single agent. The agent can promise to use his best efforts. But because the principal will of necessity have little information about the agent's efforts, such a promise would be difficult to monitor.

One alternative that may reduce the insecurity of the principal, and hence also serve the interests of an honest agent, is for the agent to guarantee that he will accept the same commission from every principal. This will tend to eliminate, though not completely eliminate, the economic incentive of the agent to skew his efforts toward any particular property. Some houses will be easier to sell than others at the listing prices, and a fixed percentage on a more expensive house will generate a higher return.[8] A uniform commission rate therefore will not guarantee that an agent will devote the same effort to selling each house. But it would at least tend to produce that effect.

The same logic would apply to a uniform commission split between listing brokers and co-op brokers. A seller may want some assurance that when his house is listed on an MLS, subagents will have little economic incentive to spend more effort to sell some other property.

A fixed commission split may be used for another, related reason. An MLS is valuable because and only because it facilitates sales. MLS membership will attract sellers as well as buyers to a broker because they expect to fare better dealing with an MLS member. The value of an MLS will increase as the number of listings on the system increases, at least up to the point where the marginal confusion cost of additional listings equals the marginal benefit. For this reason, an MLS may require its members to agree to submit for inclusion in the system all property for which the broker obtains an agency agreement, or a particular kind of agency agreement.

Comprehensive listing of property alone, however, will not facilitate sales. The MLS must also encourage agents to broker transactions involving property listed on the network, and so the MLS must ensure that members have an incentive to cooperate as subagents. To create that incentive, the MLS may have to require that listing brokers offer a sufficient co-brokerage commission. For example, if a broker could satisfy his obligation simply by listing all of his property, he could list a house and offer no commission to cooperating brokers. Such a listing would not induce other brokers to attempt to sell the house, the MLS would not facilitate the sale of that house, and the value of the MLS would decline commensurately. A fixed commission split will help ensure the utility of the network.

A guarantee of a uniform commission rate and split will be especially effective if it is enforced by some professional association of agents, for the association is more likely to obtain information about a breach of the promise than is an individual principal.

If this is the function of a fixed commission rate, however, one might ask why the relevant rule could not provide that an agent must offer every principal a guarantee that he will not accept a higher commission from a seller—in other words, some form of maximum rate guarantee. A principal who chooses to offer a commission, knowing that the agent has or may accept higher commissions, would not seem to suffer any harm. It could be that such a system would be cumbersome to implement. It could also be that such a promise could not be policed by the association as easily as one to charge a uniform commission. For example, suppose an association learns that a broker has charged one client 5 percent and another 6 percent. The broker may have promised to charge no more than 6 percent, so the broker breached no promise. But the broker may have promised to charge no more than 5 percent, in which case he would have breached his promise. The association would not be able to determine whether there was a breach without further investigation.

Alternatively, perhaps it would be inefficient for simultaneous brokerage efforts to vary based on disparate commissions. In other words, an agents' association might believe that confidence in the industry is shaken when brokers are free to devote little attention to the sale of property, for which they have accepted an exclusive agency, because the commission is small. Demand for brokerage services increases when consumers believe that the level of services rendered is invariant to the expected compensation. The courts have been hostile to this kind of argument.[9] But the argument is not necessarily wrong. If the association instituted the suspect policy when it had no market power and thereafter grew, a reasonable inference is that the policy has been efficient. And fee schedules have been used almost from the very outset by Realtors.

It is also possible that the fixed commission rate was intended to induce members to provide high quality service to their clients. In this respect, the practice would function like resale price maintenance often functions. The pre-transaction services could neither be efficiently described in a contract nor monitored if they were specified. A stipulated commission rate might then have the effect of inducing additional services. Thus, a fixed commission rate could deter a particular form of free riding—if MLS membership signified high quality, a member could free ride on the investment in establishing the value of the MLS certification by providing low-quality service at a lower rate.[10]

The certification-based free-riding argument would explain why a minimum rate would have to be specified, as opposed to a maximum rate. The argument would also suffer, however, from the same judicial hostility mentioned above. Once again, the response to that hostility is that if the practice was instituted at a time when the participants had no market power, it would not likely have had an adverse effect on competition.

The simple publication of split information clearly reduces transaction costs among brokers—a prospective cooperating broker need not contact the listing broker before deciding whether to show a listed house. The publication of the commission that the listing broker will earn on a sale also appears to enhance efficiency. A cooperating broker who is offered a particular commission but does not know the commission that the listing broker would receive will not be able to assess the deal she is being offered. For instance, if the ''co-broke'' is 3 percent, the potential cooperating broker may be far less inclined to work for the fee is she knows that the listing broker would earn 5 percent than if she knows he would earn 2 percent, if only because of the effect that information would have on her psychic utility. In other words, a subagent's decision to accept a job may be affected by the amount the agent will earn for the joint venture. That amount may indicate the amount of effort the listing broker is likely to devote to the sale of the house, which in turn is likely to affect the amount of effort the cooperating broker will have to expend. It may also indicate how difficult any sale is likely to be. If the listing broker is promised a very large commission, the proper inference may be that he and the seller expect the sale to be difficult. That kind of information will be important to potential cooperating brokers, who are being asked to invest in selling the property with no guarantee of compensation.[11]

Requirements Relating to Type of Contract Involved

MLSs have adopted various rules that either influence the type of contract entered into between the broker and the seller or establish different obligations a broker has to the MLS based upon the type of contract involved. Some MLSs have specified that only exclusive-right-to-sell listings can be placed in the system. (See, e.g., *People v. National Ass'n of Realtors*, 1981—restriction held invalid; *Murphy v. Alpha Realty, Inc.*, 1978—restriction upheld.) Less stringent variants of this requirement are that members must attempt to obtain exclusive contracts, and that members may not advertise open listings. (See, e.g., *United States v. Realty Multi-List, Inc.*, 1980—consideration of this restriction remanded to district court; *Ogelsby and Barclift, Inc. v. Metro MLS, Inc.*, 1976—restriction held invalid.) Some networks require that a member place all properties for which he has an exclusive right to sell contract on the MLS. (See, e.g., *United States v. Realty Multi-List, Inc.*, 1980; *Murphy v. Alpha Reality, Inc.*, 1978—restriction upheld; *People v. Colorado Springs Bd of Realtors*, 1984; *Guadagno v. Mount Pleasant Listing Exchange Inc.*, 1976; *Grillo v. Bd of Realtors of Plainfield Area*, 1966.)

Restrictions that deter a broker from accepting nonexclusive arrangements serve primarily to minimize the costs of disputes. An MLS functions in part to facilitate the joint provision of brokerage services by independent firms. Those services, broadly considered, include obtaining compensation from the principal for facilitating a successful sale, and brokers will be discouraged from participating in the MLS as the prospect of conflicts with other members renders their compensation less secure. An exclusive right to sell contract, by providing for the fewest contingencies that would affect the broker's right to compensation, engenders the least probability of a fee dispute between the listing broker and the seller, and hence, between the listing broker and cooperating brokers.[12]

A requirement that members list all of their exclusive contracts serves different purposes. First, it promotes the value of the MLS. A broker's membership in an MLS will tend to become more desirable to sellers as the number of listings on the MLS increases, because a rise in the number of listings will increase the desirability of the MLS to potential buyers. Second, it deters free riding by a member on efforts of the other members to increase the value of the MLS. MLS affiliation may attract a buyer to a broker. The broker may then attempt to persuade the seller to purchase a house not listed on the MLS, for which she will receive the full commission.[13] In effect, part of the investment that brokers make in promoting an MLS is to contribute listings to it. By withholding listings, a broker may be able to invest less than other members, yet share equally the value of the collective investments made.

Of course, an MLS member will typically have an incentive to persuade a buyer to purchase property that she listed on the MLS, for which she also will receive the full commission. But whenever a broker lists property, she assumes the risk that a cooperating broker will find a willing buyer first. An MLS ideally would want brokers to devote as much effort to selling any house listed in the system as to any other house, whether listed or not. A pooling requirement does not guarantee that result, but it tends in that direction.

Membership in a Competing Multiple-Listing Service

Several MLSs have prohibited members from belonging to competing MLSs.[14] This is the type of restriction that seems suspicious to an antitrust court. In fact, this restriction will tend to increase efficiency. The MLS will become more valuable to sellers and buyers as the members focus their efforts on selling property listed in the MLS. After all, the value of affiliation with an MLS, when viewed as an economic enterprise in which all participants pledge to try to broker the sale of all listed property, is a function of the commitment of the members to the enterprise. As members extend their sales efforts to property that is not listed on a particular MLS, a seller has less reason to seek out a member of that MLS.

Solicitation of Home Sellers

MLSs frequently specify that members may not solicit a seller who has entered into an exclusive right to sell arrangement with another member while the agreement is in effect. Under such a restriction, a broker may not specifically attempt to persuade a seller, while the seller has an exclusive with another broker, either to breach the grant of exclusive representation to the other broker or to give the soliciting broker an exclusive upon expiration of the contract.[15] In essence, the restriction is an imperfect attempt to establish property rights in a kind of information. It can serve to deter free riding on investments to acquire clients and to find buyers. Under a typical brokerage contract, both kinds of investment are risky—unless a sale is completed that entitles the broker to a commission under the agency contract, the broker is not compensated.

The broker can reduce this risk in various ways. For instance, he can structure the agency contract to afford some measure of protection. Thus, he can insist upon an exclusive right to sell for a substantial duration. He can also attempt to obtain agreements from those who would appropriate the value of his investments that they will not do so. The restriction on solicitation represents this approach. It is a promise by those who could appropriate the value of a contingent interest in a real estate commission that they will not free ride on the holder's investments.

If this agreement were impermissible, a broker might respond to what he perceives to be inescapable free riding on his investments in acquiring clients by limiting those investments. One of the tasks a broker will undertake in selling a house will be to disseminate the information that the house is for sale. Indeed, this is one type of information that any MLS will contain. This information, however, is valuable to both buyers and other potential brokers of the seller.

Somewhat paradoxically, then, disseminating this information could either increase or decrease the probability that the original broker will be compensated—dissemination increases the chances that a buyer will come forward, but also increases the chances that a rival broker will acquire the client upon the expiration of the exclusive if the house is not sold by then. Ideally, the listing broker would like to maximize the dissemination of availability information, but limit its use to the single purpose of attracting buyers. If a rival broker is able to free ride on the original broker's investment in identifying the seller, the rival broker can offer the seller a lower price for brokerage services. The initial investment therefore may be inefficiently low.

Alternatively, the broker may try to deny rivals the opportunity to make use of his investments. For present purposes, the original broker can treat availability information in three ways: First, he can disseminate it "privately" to a group of subagents by listing the house on the MLS. Second, he can disseminate it "publicly," by posting a "for sale" sign, running newspaper and television advertisements, mailing announcements, distributing handbills, or the like. Or third, he can disclose it to no one other than potential buyers who visit his firm's office, a strategy that might be called "nondissemination."

If participation in an MLS poses an unacceptable risk of free riding on efforts to acquire clients and sell houses, a broker may elect to forgo membership. Instead of private dissemination, then, he may choose to engage in public dissemination if the different methods of dissemination have different effects on the probabilities of attracting buyers and competing brokers. For example, the broker may believe that buyers but not brokers will drive through neighborhoods in search of "for sale" signs, whereas brokers will study MLS listings and both will peruse newspaper advertisements. Or he might conclude that all modes of public dissemination are as likely to attract brokers as is private dissemination and choose instead to expand to such a size that a policy of nondissemination becomes feasible. If the brokerage firm is sufficiently large, the broker may be able to rely on buyers to visit the office in order to discover available property, a strategy that would provide relatively great, though not absolute, protection against free riding.

If a broker avoids participating in an MLS solely because it is not allowed to protect investments in developing intellectual property, and opts instead to skew his efforts toward modes of information dissemination that lessen the risk of free riding or to expand in size in order to internalize positive externalities, the response will be presumptively inefficient. The same conclusion would follow if the lack of an acceptable system of property rights induces the broker to reduce his investments in attracting clients and selling houses or to demand additional security from sellers, such as longer contractual periods of exclusive representation or guaranteed compensation. The typical MLS antisolicitation rule therefore may allow brokers to adopt a more efficient means of brokering transactions.

CONCLUSION

The real estate MLS poses intriguing and fundamental issues of antitrust analysis. The proper economic analysis of its conduct, in light of the services it facilitates and the characteristics of the market, is far from transparent, and so airtight public policy can hardly be expected. Nevertheless, we believe prevailing doctrine is flawed primarily because it fails to recognize the efficiency-enhancing potential of restrictions on participation in the common venture.

The history of the brokerage industry suggests that the private restraints on behavior first applied to associations of brokers, and then extended to participants in MLSs, were designed to establish a high standard of quality among members of the group and to reduce consumers' costs of locating providers who met that standard. In addition, many of the restrictions that have been found to violate the antitrust laws were adopted when MLSs clearly lacked market power. This fact makes it unlikely that these restrictions were adopted for anticompetitive purposes.

The economic argument that MLSs operate anticompetitively is also seriously undercut by the structure of the market and is not proven by evidence of market performance, which is at least ambiguous. When a market simultaneously exhibits traits that make collusion singularly improbable and widespread agreements among firms for the joint provision of a service, a logical supposition is that the agreements increase efficiency. We have offered possible explanations for common MLS restrictions that are consistent with an efficiency hypothesis. The true failure of modern antitrust policy with respect to MLSs is not simply that it miscalculates potential gains and losses. Rather, it is that the analysis, by nature, fails to ask the right questions.

NOTES

The views expressed herein are solely those of the authors and do not represent the views of the Federal Trade Commission, any individual Commissioner, or the Bureau of Competition. The authors wish to thank William Page, Joseph Kattan, Thomas Ulen, and Michael Byowitz for thoughtful comments on prior drafts.

1. MLSs have been challenged under the federal antitrust laws, state antitrust statutes, and state unfair competition laws. Whatever the legal source of the attack, the fundamental claim has emanated from antitrust principles.

2. One thousand of 6,000 brokers in the county were members of the board (*Brown v. Indianapolis Bd of Realtors,* 1977); twelve of seventy-two brokers in the county were in the MLS (*Grempler v. Multiple Listing Bureau,* 1970).

3. For examples of this reasoning, see Owen, 1977, and Erxleben, 1981.

4. This kind of restriction might also stem from a concern that part-time brokers, with a smaller stake in the real estate business, might be inclined to divulge confidential information to facilitate a sale. That sort of conduct, or more generally, any conduct that is inconsistent with the agency relationship, could result in legal liability for the listing broker.

5. Limitations on the extent of brokerage operations outside of the territory of the MLS may also serve to deter free-riding on investments by the members in promoting the MLS.

6. By contrast, no similar flow would be necessary in the air travel industry because these conditions are absent.

7. The preservation of confidentiality may affect not only the quality of services a broker provides to a seller. A listing broker may be exposed to legal liability if a co-operating broker, who functions as a subagent, discloses confidential information that results in economic harm to the seller.

8. One reason that real estate brokers appear generally to specialize in particular segments of the housing market, such as expensive homes or low-cost homes, may be that sellers of low-end homes would fear that a broker who deals in high-end homes would concentrate his efforts in selling those homes, for which he will receive a larger absolute commission.

9. An ethical ban on competitive bidding among members of a professional association of engineers was found unreasonable. (See *National Society of Professional Engineers v. United States*, 1978.)

10. Notice that the free-riding argument is not that a broker charging a low commission would free ride on the transaction-specific efforts of a broker charging a high commission. Certainly a uniform commission would deter this kind of free riding, if in fact the presale efforts of the first broker were subject to appropriation by the second broker. But our argument is that a group of suppliers should be allowed to distinguish themselves in the marketplace as a source of high-quality service. If deterring transaction-specific free riding justified rate-fixing, all brokers in the market would be forced to provide high-quality service. That argument goes too far.

11. See *Murphy v. Alpha Realty, Inc.*, 1978. The court agreed with the defendant's argument that "just as the seller and listing broker are entitled to know the rate of commission involved in order to decide if they will enter into an agency relationship, potential cooperating brokers are similarly entitled to information concerning the rate of commission the listing broker is to receive from the seller and how that commission will be apportioned in order to decide whether a sub-agency relationship should be established."

12. In *Murphy v. Alpha Reality, Inc.*, the court acknowledged the basic purpose and effect of these restrictions: "Defendants justify the rule under which the MLS refuses open listings by arguing that the rule does not prohibit broker members from entering into open listings, but merely keeps such arrangements from being listed with the MLS to prevent confusion concerning which broker has earned a commission by producing a ready, willing and able purchaser. Because in an open listing the seller retains the right to employ any number of brokers as agents, the potentiality of such confusion would be enormous if such listings were listed by the MLS. In short, plaintiffs have not refuted defendants' claims . . . of reasonableness of th[is] rule . . ." (*Murphy v. Alpha Realty, Inc.*, 1978).

13. The court may have been hinting at this sort of explanation in *Murphy v. Alpha Realty, Inc.*: "Defendants assert that the rule requiring placement of all exclusive listings with the MLS prevents members from withholding desirable listings which are likely to sell quickly and thus avoid having to share commissions generated by these sales. . . . [P]laintiffs have not refuted defendants' claim . . . of reasonableness of th[is] rule . . ." (*Murphy v. Alpha Realty, Inc.*, 1978).

14. See, for example, *United States v. Realty Multi-List, Inc.*, 1980—rule abandoned prior to suit; *Ogelsby and Barclift, Inc. v. Metro MLS, Inc.*, 1976—restriction violated the Sherman Act; *Grempler v. Multiple Listing Bureau*, 1970—rule upheld.

15. See, for example, *United States v. Realty Multi-List, Inc.*, 1980—restriction upheld, court noting that it is necessary to provide brokers who disclose exclusive listings ''some insurance that the disclosure will not afford competitors an opportunity to 'steal' '' the listings; and *Murphy v. Alpha Realty, Inc.* 1978—restriction upheld.

11

Competition Issues in Electronic Data Interchange

Robin L. Allen

Electronic data interchange (EDI) is the intercompany computer-to-computer transmission of routine business transaction data in a standard format. Purchase order, invoice, and bid information are examples of data commonly transmitted through EDI networks. Purists would add that "true EDI" requires that the data be transferred "application-to-application"—that is, that it be transferred directly from one trading partner's business function computer program to another's business function program. An example is a buyer and a seller who have automated the purchasing process: The buyer's purchase order program would utilize purchase order data as input and then keep track of pending and filled orders while the seller's accounts receivable program would keep track of invoices sent and payments received (Ferguson and Hill, 1989). Such purists would say that customers simply entering purchase order data into a seller-provided terminal directly connected to the seller's automated invoicing and inventory system is not an example of true EDI since there is no business application on the customer side. Purists make this distinction to emphasize that EDI can achieve much more than simply increasing the speed and lowering the cost of processing (even though these are significant accomplishments in and of themselves): it can fundamentally change the way business is transacted.

EDI has generated much enthusiasm in the business community. For example, proponents claim that in ten years EDI will be as "commonplace as the telephone" ("EDI Gains," 1989) and that it is "one of the top ten technologies of the 1990s" (Winkler, 1990). Certainly, the growth of EDI has been impressive: Third-party providers of EDI network services in the United States have increased sales from $11.3 million in 1985 ("EDI Gains," 1989) to $145 million in 1989 and sales are projected to be $252 million in 1990 and $1 billion in 1993 ("Third Parties," 1990).

A Gallup poll conducted in the first half of 1989 probably gives the best available picture of current and anticipated use of EDI: Of the 1,504 respondents representing firms with average sales of $1.16 billion and median sales of $180 million,[1] 17.0 percent were using EDI, 5.4 percent were planning to adopt EDI in 1989, 5.7 percent were planning to adopt EDI in 1990, 52 percent had no EDI plans for the next two years, and 19.9 percent did not know. In addition, the firms currently using EDI were asked how many current trading partners they had and how many they planned to add in 1989 and 1990. The average number of current trading partners was 12.6 with a median of 4.2. The average and median figures for number of planned new trading partners in 1989 were 21.1 and 4.0 respectively, and 33.1 and 10.0 respectively for 1990. The firms were also asked what percentage of non-EDI documents they were planning to convert to EDI within the next three years. The average respondent planned to convert 36.1 percent of non-EDI documents and the median respondent planned to convert 27.5 percent of non-EDI documents (Masson and Hill, 1989). This suggests a growing role for EDI in many firms and industries.

Unlike the three other electronic services networks (ESNs) discussed in this book—computer reservation systems (CRSs), automatic teller machines (ATMs), and multiple-listing services (MLSs)— EDI has no "antitrust past"—that is, there has been no antitrust litigation involving EDI networks. Furthermore, it is unlikely that there will be much antitrust litigation in EDI's future. This lack of current and expected litigation may be explained by a crucial difference between EDI networks and the three other electronic service networks: in the three other ESNs the firms that use the network services also provide the network services. However, in EDI there has been a strong trend toward using *third parties* as providers of network services.[2] The fourth section of this chapter presents specific antitrust issues that have arisen in airline CRS networks, real estate multilist networks, and banking ATM networks and explains why third-party ownership of EDI networks should prevent these antitrust issues from arising in EDI applications. As a background to this discussion, the next two sections of the chapter present (1) an explanation of the basic components of EDI and (2) a discussion of the historical development of EDI, including three case histories.

THE BASIC COMPONENTS OF ELECTRONIC
DATA INTERCHANGE

In addition to the necessary computer hardware, there are three basic components to a workable EDI system: (1) a transaction message standard, (2) translation software, and (3) a communication system.

Transaction Message Standards

A transaction message standard is a set of rules for translating one or more types of standard business documents into electronic messages. These standards may be generic, industry-wide, or proprietary. Generic standards such as ANSI (American National Standards Institute) X12 are broadly formulated so as to accommodate the messaging needs of a wide variety of industries. Industry-wide standards are tailored to the special needs of their industries. Some industry standards are created specifically for an industry while others are based on a subset of a generic standard. UCS (Uniform Communications Standard), a standard used for the grocery industry, and ORDERNET, the standard used for the pharmaceutical industry, are examples of standards specifically created for an industry, while the electrical and chemical industries are examples of industries that chose to adopt the ANSI X12 standard (Sokol, 1989). Proprietary standards are created by one firm to use with its trading partners. GM and Sears are examples of firms that have developed proprietary standards.

The set of rules composing a transaction message standard can be divided into two categories: format rules and usage rules. Format rules describe how the business data must be formatted. Usage rules describe the conventions to be used for commonly used terms (e.g., CA for case), the interpretations of data fields that may be ambiguous, and in the cases where the standard is derived from a generic standard, which set of data items will be used.

Translation Software

The purpose of translation software is to take data stored in the in-house format, convert it to a standard format, prepare the data for transmission, and then send it to the EDI communication system.

Communication System

Computer-to-computer communication may be accomplished via direct telecommunications links between trading partners or indirect telecommunications links through a third party "value-added network supplier" (VANS). VANS are companies that act as communications intermediaries between EDI trading partners. Some of the services VANS provide (which can be selected cafeteria-style by subscribers) are electronic mailboxes, translation, and services that allow trading partners to communicate even though they transmit data at different speeds and/or have different communication protocols. In 1989, the three largest VANS in the United States by percent of industry sales were GE Information Services (18 percent), Sterling Software (11 percent), and BT Tymnet (9 percent) ("Third Parties," 1990). However, the market may drastically reconfigure, since such large corporations as AT&T, MCI, Sears, and IBM are entering or becoming more involved in the market.

Firms choose to participate in EDI networks for one of two reasons: Either they believe they will realize efficiencies or their trading partners believe it will produce efficiencies and thus make it a condition of doing business.[3] These efficiencies range from the straightforward—savings from reducing expenditures on postal and courier services, in-house keying and file-clerk services, and paper—to the more subtle. For example, because EDI allows a firm to know more precisely the timing of deliveries, it may now decide to reduce inventories through "just-in-time" ordering.

HISTORICAL DEVELOPMENT OF ELECTRONIC DATA INTERCHANGE

In this section I describe the historical development of the two major facets of EDI: the methods of communication and the infrastructure by which communications take place.

Standardizing Electronic Data Interchange

Even before EDI was technically feasible, trade associations and governments were working to standardize routine business documents in order to benefit from the resulting efficiencies. One of the earliest efforts was made by a UN committee on trade development which organized a working party for the simplification and standardization of trade documents in the early 1960s (Warner, 1989). In the United States, the first formal work on standardizing business documents began in 1968 with the establishment of the Transportation Data Coordinating Committee (TDCC) (Ferguson and Hill, 1989). The TDCC was also the first organization to publish actual EDI standards, in 1975 (Notto, 1989). The grocery industry followed suit in 1982, with its own industry-specific standard, the UCS (Sokol, 1989). However, during the time when the transportation and grocery industries were developing their own industry standards, other industries followed less deliberate paths. For example, ORDER-NET, an EDI standard developed by Informatics General for communications between drug manufacturers and wholesalers, became the de facto industry standard because Informatics General was the first entrant into EDI for the drug industry (Sokol, 1989). During the 1970s and early 1980s, there was *no* standard for the automotive industry; all of the major automakers used their own internal data formats in communicating with their suppliers (Sokol, 1989).

In the late 1970s, it was recognized that having industry-specific EDI message standards could impede the proliferation of EDI, because industry-specific standards often are inadequate or come into conflict with other standards when an attempt is made to add another layer of the vertical production and supply chain to an EDI system. For example, ORDERNET may be perfectly adequate for communication between drug manufacturer and wholesaler, but if the drug manufacturer wishes to use EDI to communicate with its suppliers, such as chemical, paper, and metal manufacturers, it may find that these industries already have other standards, or that ORDERNET is not flexible enough to allow efficient communications with these industries. Therefore, in 1979 the American National Standards Institute (ANSI) established a committee to develop uniform standards for cross-industry EDI (ANSI, 1987). This set of standards, known as ANSI X12, was first published in 1983, and it continues to be updated (Ferguson and Hill, 1989). By 1989, ANSI X12 had achieved widespread acceptance as the cross-industry standard. In addition, many industries recently adopting EDI are choosing ANSI X12 as their standard and then developing guidelines for industry-specific use. Some of these industries are the electrical, chemical, metals, paper, office products, and apparel industries (Sokol, 1989).

Development of Electronic Data Interchange Networks

In general, EDI is introduced to an industry via proprietary ordering systems (Sokol, 1989).[4] As more trading partners start communicating electronically, the industry tends to go to a more efficient industry-wide system that offers many more functions than the ability to send and receive purchase orders. Not all industries follow the same pattern. It is instructive to study the development of EDI networks in particular industries.

The Grocery Industry

The grocery industry established bar coding in the early 1970s. This standardization turned out to be a key event in the movement to EDI in the grocery industry, for two reasons. First, it created a standard numbering system for items sold in the grocery industry, and second, it created the organizational structure as well as the background experience for performing a complex cooperative task such as industry-wide EDI (Norris, 1989).

Not long after bar coding was established, grocery manufacturers and distributors began discussing the possibility of computerizing the data exchange taking place between them (Norris, 1989). In 1976, an official committee representing the grocery manufacturers and distributors was formed to study this issue, and in 1978 a request for proposals (RFP) for a data transmission network feasibility study was issued.

The feasibility report, issued in 1980, made a number of recommendations, including the recommendation that the network be open—that is, that trading partners be free to select their own VANS. This recommendation was made for two main reasons: (1) with an open network, there is no need to select and then regulate the monopoly network operator; and (2) with an open network, users can reap the benefits of price and nonprice (innovation and services) competition (Norris, 1989). According to the director of the study, closed systems are simpler and more efficient than open systems, but ''the flexibility of the open systems approach plus the opportunity it affords for networks to compete and innovate provided more than offsetting advantages, above and beyond the monopoly supervision problem'' (Norris, 1989).

By 1982, the network was operational (Norris, 1989). Many of the original companies that used EDI chose not to use VANS. However, as of 1989, VANS were used by almost all of the wholesale and retail sectors of the grocery industry (Sokol, 1989).

Hospital Supply Companies and Hospitals

The roots of EDI for the hospital supply companies' exchange of business documents with hospitals can be traced to 1976, when American Hospital Supply (acquired by Baxter Travenol in 1985) instituted Analytical Systems Automated Purchasing (ASAP), a system in which purchase order data was transferred over teletype machines (Gardner, 1989). By the mid-1980s, Johnson & Johnson, Abbott Laboratories, and Baxter offered their own proprietary systems for PC-based purchase ordering.[5] More recently, each of these systems has recruited other hospital supply vendors to join their systems to make them more attractive to customers.

The current situation is not very satisfactory to hospitals: it is inconvenient and expensive for hospitals to have three different PC-based systems, each dedicated to purchasing. Furthermore, the current technology is really just computer-based purchase ordering, not a true EDI network, and therefore does not offer the opportunity to exchange other business documents (i.e., requests for bids, shipping notices, and invoices) electronically and does not allow for the more efficient application-to-application transfer (Bone, 1989).

However, Baxter, Abbott, and Johnson & Johnson have not been anxious to move to a true EDI network because they now enjoy a direct connection to their hospital subscribers whereas the other vendors on the host system are reached via more circuitous routes. If Abbott, for example, has to be reached through a VAN there will be an extra charge (which amounts to approximately $.20 more per purchase order) to make the telecommunications connection. In addition, the direct connection to hospital subscribers puts the three systems at an advantage over the other vendors on the system: If "City Memorial" is already placing an order through Baxter, it may decide to order a few more items from Baxter to take advantage of the direct connection, rather than bother to make an additional and more circuitous connection with another vendor.

Not surprisingly, it has been the hospital side of the industry that has spearheaded the drive for a "true EDI" system. A taskforce of multihospital buying groups, alliances, and group purchasing organizations has been formed to develop a formal business plan for a hospital supply–hospital EDI network (Gardner, 1989). In October 1989, this task force issued a request for information to eight VANS, ten software vendors, and several vendors of other types of services necessary to create a network ("Coalition to," 1989). As of January 1990, no definite plans had been made for the structure of the network. However, the taskforce is leaning toward choosing multiple VANS (perhaps two or three) rather than one, even though the "volume discounts" will be largest if only one bidder is selected. This is because the taskforce is concerned that past experience from other industries has shown that sole VANS can become complacent and that the industry is eventually harmed by higher prices and less innovation.

The Pharmaceutical Industry

The roots of EDI communications between ethical drug manufacturers and wholesalers can be traced to 1971 when Bergen Brunswig (a drug wholesaler) began sending purchase data electronically to Eli Lilly (a drug manufacturer). In line with the technology of the day, the system worked as follows: Bergen Brunswig's purchase order data were punched onto 80-column cards and read into the computers of Management Horizons Data Systems (MHDS), a firm that sold computing services. The data were then transmitted over phone lines to an Eli Lilly computer where an identical set of cards was created to be used as input for processing the purchase order (Bone, 1989; Sokol, 1989). Over the next few years MHDS began serving other industry clients (Sokol, 1989).

In 1975, Informatics General Corporation (the acquirer of MHDS) suggested the idea of an industry-wide clearinghouse for electronic purchase orders to the National Wholesale Druggists' Association (NWDA). NWDA sent out an RFP to several VANS and Informatics was selected. During the first years following Informatics' selection as the industry-designated clearinghouse, ORDERNET (the name given to Informatics' electronic clearinghouse) served virtually all the pharmaceutical manufacturers and wholesalers who used EDI. In recent years, as more commercial VANS have begun operation, ORDERNET has lost some market share, although it still has the largest market share of all the VANS serving pharmaceutical manufacturers and distributors. As of 1986, the EDI usage level in the pharmaceutical industry was the highest for any industry—a 99 percent penetration rate among drug wholesalers and a 90 percent penetration rate among drug manufacturers (Sokol, 1989).

Today, EDI in the drug industry is primarily used for purchase ordering, invoicing, and a set of electronic transactions designed to deal with a specific business practice in the health care industry having to do with the distributor serving as a billing intermediary for drug discounts negotiated between hospitals and manufacturers (Sokol, 1989).

ANTITRUST ISSUES

Antitrust concerns regarding the three other ESNs discussed in this book fall into two broad categories. In the first category are cases in which some network participants also sell services to other network participants and disputes arise over the fees charged. In the second category are cases in which antitrust concerns have been raised out of fear that actions taken by network participants may harm consumers who use network services but are not participants in the networks (e.g., home-buyers who use an MLS are consumers who use network services but are not participants in the network).

To date, there have been no litigated antitrust cases involving EDI. In fact, the author was not able to find even any *allegations* of anticompetitive conduct by EDI participants. Certainly, it is quite unlikely that cases would arise in EDI similar to the situations described above, simply because EDI networks generally do not fit either of the two prototype complaints. On the one hand, it is rare for EDI network participants to buy and sell network services to each other, and on the other hand, the users of EDI network services also are network participants. Therefore, to the extent that EDI antitrust concerns arise, they would generally arise in a different context than previous cases.

The actual institutional framework of EDI is not very conducive to antitrust litigation, for two reasons: First, because both the sellers and the buyers belong to EDI networks, there is a large group of network constituents that have the incentive to oppose attempts made by the other side of the network to use it for anticompetitive purposes. Second, in EDI networks (more exactly, true EDI networks, not proprietary purchasing systems), there are formal organizations that exist to which both the buyers and the sellers belong that govern the networks. Therefore, if one side of the network behaves anticompetitively, it will be relatively easy for the other side to respond—that is, there is a natural forum within which the offended party(s) can act to protect its interests.[6] In addition, just as the mere presence of an antitrust authority may deter anticompetitive behavior, the fact that there is a well-organized group to oppose anticompetitive behavior may have a similar effect.

Below I illustrate the differences between policy problems posed by EDI networks and other types of ESNs by comparing the practices and structures that have been the foci of regulatory and antitrust concern regarding MLSs, CRSs, and ATM networks with the most similar characteristics of the three EDI networks examined in this chapter.

Proprietary Networks as a Barrier to Entry/Expansion: Airline Computer Reservation System Networks and Hospital Supply Purchase-Ordering Systems

Airline CRS networks have been the subject of much antitrust interest. Probably the most prominent antitrust concern relates to the CRS as a possible barrier to entry by de novo competitors or as a barrier to expansion by incumbent competitors in the market for air travel. This concern reflects a perception that agents using a CRS sell a disproportionately large number of tickets for the airline that owns the CRS (U.S. DOJ, 1989a).

It is important to note that CRSs are seller-owned. However, in the case of EDI networks there are not that many seller-owned systems; in most of the systems where there is vertical integration, it is the buyer that owns the system (Gardner, 1989). In addition, proprietary systems are rapidly becoming the EDI equivalent of "high button shoes." This is because proprietary systems have limited capabilities relative to true EDI systems. That is, proprietary systems generally offer only purchase-ordering capabilities whereas true EDI systems offer more functions and greater efficiency (assuming a large-enough scale). Therefore, proprietary ordering systems generally are viewed as the first stage of an industry's development toward true EDI.

The hospital supply industry uses seller-owned ordering systems and is similar in some respects to the CRS industry, where travel agents are alleged to book disproportionate numbers of flyers on the host CRS's airline. Recall that in the discussion of network development in the hospital supply–hospital EDI it was explained that hospitals order more from the host ordering system than they would otherwise because it is inconvenient to switch to ordering from another company when a hospital is already communicating with the host system.

However, whatever anticompetitive effects flow from the advantages of system owners in the hospital supply industry, it is unlikely that this will remain an issue much longer. As mentioned in the third section of this chapter, there is a movement led by the hospital industry to convert to a true EDI system. In such a system all orders are deposited in mailboxes, and the ordering process is neutral. According to Garren Hagemeier of the Federation of American Hospital Systems, the desire for neutrality is a contributing factor in this movement toward true EDI, although not the most salient factor.[7]

In addition, there is no reason to believe that the hospital supply–hospital industry is unique among EDI-using industries in its move to an open network. In particular, there are three reasons why it is unlikely that EDI will not lead to proprietary networks like the airline industry CRSs. First, for historical reasons, switch-over costs to an open system are much lower in EDI than for CRSs. Airline CRSs developed out of an extensive and complex internal reservation system already in place. In EDI, in general, there is no analogous internal, computerized order-processing system. While a few firms did have some in-place systems before VANS were available, these systems, for the most part, were not nearly as extensive or complex as airline internal reservation systems. In fact, most firms have considered adopting EDI in the era since third-party VANS were available. Such firms have either decided to use VANS or have designed their systems to be compatible with VANS (e.g., use the standard language, format, and software).

Second, to the extent that it is true that airlines enjoy host system advantage, they will be less interested in changing to a third-party system. However, in EDI, the buyers are more sophisticated (firms rather than airline ticket buyers) and the information transmitted is less complex, thus limiting host system advantage, to the extent it exists in EDI at all. Finally, as mentioned earlier, buyers who use EDI networks can and do organize to make sure their interests are represented. In contrast, it is hard to imagine that airline ticket buyers will similarly organize to convince the airlines that they should switch to an open network.

Trade Association Rules as a Device to Exclude Competitors: Real Estate Multilist and Electronic Data Interchange Standard-Setting

Potential home-buyers prefer to deal with brokers who have access to a large inventory of homes. Home-sellers prefer to deal with a listing broker who has a large number of agents. Although there are a number of ways that a real estate brokerage firm can accommodate these buyer and seller preferences, the most common method is to participate in an MLS. The possibility that MLS membership requirements may be used to exclude discount brokers from MLS has been an antitrust concern (Erxleben, 1981).

Is it likely that a similar issue may arise with EDI? That is, should there be concern that EDI networks will institute rules or standards that will make membership and entry (or continued viability) difficult for "aggressive" competitors? Available evidence on the degree of EDI network exclusivity shows that the networks are trying to remain as open as possible. Two examples: (1) According to attorney John F. Donelan, Jr., who provides legal counsel on EDI to the transportation industry, the Data and Computer Systems Committee (D&CS) of the Transportation Data Coordinating Committee "has long endorsed the principle that EDI standards should be open to and freely usable by all parties. It has traditionally declined to endorse standards which incorporate information in which one or some few parties have a proprietary or controlling interest." In support of the committee's position, Donelan (1987) cites two Supreme Court decisions (a 1961 decision, *Radiant Burners v. Peoples Gas Light & Coke*, 364 U.S. 656; and a 1982 decision, *American Society of Mechanical Engineers v. Hydrolevel Corporation*, 456 U.S. 556) that found against firms who used trade associations' standard-setting powers as an opportunity to harm innovative competitors. Donelan also points out that the D&CS tries to make sure that the trade association's standard-setting power is not abused by a subset of members by making sure that all meeting and subcommittee meetings are open to all interested parties (Donelan, 1987). (2) When the grocery industry formulated its rules governing access to the industry network, it mandated that a VANS must support EDI transmissions even when only one of the two trading partners is its customer. According to Phyllis Sokol, author of *EDI—The Competitive Edge*, this rule was instituted "to assure [sic] that every company wishing to do EDI would have the ability to do so without restrictions by their [sic] trading partners or third-party agents" (Sokol, 1989).

As mentioned earlier, there is less likelihood that firms could get away with such abuse of a trade association because the relevant downstream or upstream part of the industry that would be affected is not likely to allow such an abuse of market power.

Perhaps the most difficult issue in this area is not exclusivity but inclusivity; it is possible that making rules (such as described in the grocery example above) that facilitate inclusivity by subsidizing small firms and/or encouraging less-efficient technology may not be in the best interest of the network.

Anticompetitive Uses of Network User Fees: Automatic Teller Machines, Proprietary Purchase-Ordering Systems, and Value-Added Network Suppliers

One of the major antitrust issues in ATM banking networks is whether it is considered price-fixing when the member banks decide on a fee schedule for interchange transactions. In particular, certain banks that have a large depositor base, a large number of ATM cards, but operate a small number of ATMs would be concerned that these fees are set too high. (Banks that have a small depositor base, a small number of ATM cards, but a large number of ATMs would think the fees too low.) As mentioned earlier in this section, it is unlikely that a similar issue will arise in EDI, because it is rare for a firm to buy EDI services from competitors. It is much more likely that the firms will transmit directly or through VANS. Only in the case of a proprietary purchase-ordering system that serves its competitors could such a situation arise. Even this situation differs from the ATM situation. In ATMs there is one fee that is agreed upon as the interchange fee. In the case of proprietary systems, there is usually more than one system available to users and prices are set unilaterally. However, it seems unlikely that there is much to be concerned about in the case of proprietary systems. First, these systems are considered to be a temporary first stage of EDI. Second, to the degree that there is a perceived abuse of market power, this may just serve to quicken an industry's move to a true EDI system.

Probably the most serious competition problem is not related to the potential for market power abuse by network members but rather to the difficult question of optimal network design. Recall that industries have to decide whether they will have a closed or open network, and if they choose an open network, how many VANS will be selected. These industries implicitly decide how to trade off the economies of scale from fewer VANS (e.g., the fewer VANS, the fewer the interconnection charges) for the additional competition from more VANS (e.g., price and innovation competition). This decision is complicated and a wrong decision could prove to be costly.

CONCLUSION

EDI has rapidly evolved from its beginnings in the early 1970s. In its most primitive stage EDI usually consists of a proprietary purchase-ordering system that uses an in-house data format. From the standpoint of an industry, proprietary purchase-ordering systems have two major drawbacks: they are inefficient (there may be a different hardware and software package and a different data format for each proprietary system) and their capabilities are limited. (Generally they transmit only one or two types of electronic documents and they do not allow for application-to-application transfers.) These drawbacks are overcome when an industry moves to a "true EDI" system. This evolution also has implications for the possibility that EDI can be used to successfully engage in anticompetitive activity. The first stage (proprietary ordering systems) offers the greatest possibility for successful anticompetitive activity because of the exclusive vertical link EDI establishes between particular companies. However, the second stage of EDI development, the "true EDI" stage, attenuates opportunities for antitrust harm because the vertical link is dissolved—third-party value-added network suppliers (VANS) take over EDI responsibilities and/or the vertical link is rendered neutral because all EDI communications are direct (no company uses its competitor's network services). At this stage, the only realistic opportunities for diminution of competition are of the more traditional variety—the third-party network service suppliers may obtain market power. Even this possibility can be attenuated because in many industries a trade association can make deliberate choices about the number of competing VANS that will serve the industry.

NOTES

The views expressed are the author's and do not necessarily reflect the views of the U.S. Department of Justice. I wish to thank Garren Hagemeier and Albert Smiley for helpful comments.

1. The sales figures represent only 1,010 of the 1,054 firms. About one-third of the surveyed firms did not provide figures.

2. For example, a recent survey showed that almost 85 percent of new EDI users are purchasing third-party network services (Payne, 1990).

3. In the latter situation it is almost always the case that it is a large business making the adoption of EDI a condition of doing business with its smaller trading partners.

4. More accurately, a proprietary ordering system should be described as "partial EDI" since it is not "application to application."

5. Much of the information presented in this section of the chapter was provided by Garren Hagemeier in a phone interview with the author in January 1990.

6. Recall that one of the traditional economic justifications for government-funded procompetition legal activity is that the transactions costs of private antitrust activity (i.e., consumers banding together to sue sellers for violations of the antitrust law) are prohibitive. EDI networks are an example of a situation where the costs are not prohibitive.

7. The most important factors are efficiency and the enhanced capabilities of a true EDI network.

References

Adams, J., & Yellen, J. (1976). Commodity bundling and the burden of monopoly. *Quarterly Journal of Economics, 90,* 475–498.

Adelman, M. A. (1955). Concept of statistical measurement of vertical integration. In G. J. Stigler (Ed.), *Business concentration and price policy* (pp. 281–330). Princeton: Princeton University Press.

Air Canada. (1988, April 22). Response to the Director's application. *D.I.R. v. Air Canada, Competition Tribunal CT-88/1.* Ottawa, Canada.

American Airlines. (1988a, May 30). Request to intervene. *D.I.R. v. Air Canada, Competition Tribunal CT-88/1.* Ottawa, Canada.

———— (1988b, January 11). *Complaint Against British Airways PLC.* U.S. Department of Transportation, Docket 45389.

———— (1989, April 20). Submissions in respect of the draft consent order. *D.I.R. v. Air Canada, Competition Tribunal CT-88/1.* Ottawa, Canada.

American National Standards Institute. (1987, July). *An introduction to electronic data interchange.* Data Interchange Standards Association, Alexandria, Va.

American Society of Travel Agents. (1983, June 21–23). Testimony of the American Society of Travel Agents. *U.S. House of Representatives, Airline Computer Reservation Systems: Hearings before the Subcommittee on Aviation of House Committee on Public Works and Transportation.*

Antonelli, C. (1988). *New information technology and industrial change: The Italian case.* Norwell, MA: Kluwer Academic Press.

Aspen Skiing Company v. Aspen Highlands Skiing Corporation, 472 U.S. 585 (1985).

Association of Retail Travel Agents. (1983a, June 21–23) Testimony before U.S. House of Representatives. *Airline Computer Reservations Systems: Hearing Before the Subcommittee on Aviation of House Committee on Public Works and Transportation.*

Avmark Aviation Economist. (1987, May). *Computer Reservation Systems,* p. 21.

Ayres, I. (1985). Rationalizing antitrust cluster markets. *Yale Law Journal, 95,* 109–125.

Bain, J. (1956). *Barriers to new competition.* Cambridge: Harvard University Press.

Baker, J. B. (1988, Spring). The antitrust analysis of hospital mergers and the transformation of the hospital industry. *Law and Contemporary Problems, 51,* 93–164.

Baxter, W. F. (1983). Bank interchange of transactional paper: Legal and economic perspectives. *Journal of Law and Economics, 26,* 541–588.

Bell, D. (1973). *The coming of post-industrial Society: A venture in social forecasting.* New York: Basic Books.

Berkey Photo, Inc. v. Eastman Kodak Company, 603 F.2d 263 (2d Cir. 1979), *cert. denied* 444 U.S. 1093. (1980).

Besen, S., & Saloner, G. (1989). Economics of telecommunications and standards. In R. Crandall & K. Flamm (Eds.). *Changing the rules: Technological change, international competition, and regulation in telecommunication* (pp. 177–220). Washington, DC: The Brookings Institution.

Besen, S. M. & Johnson, L. L. (1986). *Compatibility standards, competition, and innovation in the broadcasting industry* (R-3453-NSF). Santa Monica, CA: Rand.

Blair, R., & Kaserman, D. (1983). *Law and economics of vertical integration and control.* New York: Academic Press.

Blake v. H-F Group Multiple Listing Service. 345 N.E. 2d 18 (Ill. App. Ct. 1976).

Bone, R. W. (1989). Electronic communications at Bergen Brunswig. *EDI Forum, 1,* 41–43.

Borenstein, S. (1989). Hubs and high fares. *Rand Journal of Economics. 20,* 344–365.

Bremner, B. and Rothfeder, J. (September 10, 1990). Dow Jones' $1.6 billion baby is hardly a bundle of joy. *Business Week,* pp. 60–62.

British Civil Aviation Authority (1988, March). *Submission to the House of Commons Select Committee on Transport.* London, England.

Broadcast Music, Inc. v. Columbia Broadcasting System, Inc. 441 U.S. 1 (1979).

Brown v. Indianapolis Board of Realtors. 1977-1 Trade Cas. (CHH) par. 61,435 (S.D. Ind. 1977).

Brynjolfsson, E., Malone, T. W., & Gurbaxani, V. (1988, December). *Markets, hierarchies and the impact of information technology* (Working Paper No. 2113-88). Cambridge: Sloan School of Management, MIT.

Brynjolfsson, E., Malone, T. W., Gurbaxani, V., & Kambil, A. (1989, December). *Do firms get smaller with information technology?* (Working Paper). Cambridge: Sloan School of Management, MIT.

Butters, G. (1977). Equilibrium distributions of sales and advertising prices. *Review of Economic Studies. 44 (3),* 465–491.

Carlton, D. (1984). Futures markets: Their purpose, their history, their growth, their successes and failures. *Journal of Futures Markets, 4,* 237–271.

———— (1991, October). The general theory of allocation and its implications for marketing and industrial structure. *Journal of Law and Economics,* forthcoming.

Carlton, D., & Klamer, M. (1983, Spring). The need for coordination among firms, with special reference to network industries. *University of Chicago Law Review, 50,* 446–465.

Cash, J., Jr., & Konsynski, B. R. (1985, March–April). IS redraws competitive boundaries. *Harvard Business Review,* 133–142.

Caves, R., & Bradburd, R. (1988). The empirical determinants of vertical integration. *Journal of Economic Behavior and Organization, 9*, 265–279.

Chandler, A. D. (1962). *Strategy and structure: Chapters in the history of the American industrial enterprise.* Cambridge: MIT Press.

—— (1977). *The invisible hand.* Cambridge: Harvard University Press.

Civil Aeronautics Board. (1982, December 16) *Competitive Marketing of Air Transportation,* (Docket 36595).

—— (1984a, March 1). *Notice of proposed rulemaking-airline computer reservation systems* (EDR-466, Docket 41686).

—— (1984b, July 27). *Final Rule* (EDR-466).

Clemons, E. K. & Row, M. (1988). McKesson Drug Company: A Case Study of Economost—A Strategic Information System. *Journal of Management Information Systems, 5(1),* 37–50.

Coalition to develop plan for industrywide EDI. (1989, October 27). *Modern Healthcare,* p. 12.

Comanor, W. C. (1985). Vertical price fixing, vertical market restrictions, and the new antitrust policy. *Harvard Law Review, 98,* 983–1002.

Competition Act. R. S., c. C-23, s. 1; 1986, c. 26, s. 19. Ottawa, Canada.

Competition Tribunal. (1989a, July 7). Computer Reservation System Rules. *D.I.R. v. Air Canada, Competition Tribunal CT-88/1.* Ottawa, Canada.

—— (1989b, July 7). Consent Order. *D.I.R. v. Air Canada, Competition Tribunal CT-88/1.* Ottawa, Canada.

—— (1989c, July 7). Reasons for the Consent Order. *D.I.R. v. Air Canada, Competition Tribunal CT-88/1.* Ottawa, Canada.

Continental Airlines et al., v. American Airlines and United Airlines. (1986). U.S. District Court, Central District of California, cases CV86-0696 ER(Mex) and CV86-0697 ER(Mex).

Copeland, D. and McKenney, J. (1988, September). Airline reservations systems: lessons from history. *MIS Quarterly. 12 (3),* 353–370.

Cournot, A. A. (1927). *Researches into the mathematical principles of the theory of wealth* (N. Bacon, Trans.). New York: Macmillan. (Original work published 1838.)

CRS—bound by politics. (1988, August). *Airline Business,* pp. 22–27.

David, P. (1986). Clio and the economics of QWERTY. *American Economic Review, 75,* 332–337.

—— (1987). Some new standards for the economics of standardization in the Information Age. In P. Dasgupta & P. Stoneman (Eds.). *Economic policy and technological performance.* Cambridge: Cambridge University Press.

Davies, P. (1958). *Real estate in American history.* Washington, DC: Affairs Press.

Davis, S. M. (1987). *Future perfect.* New York: Addison-Wesley Publishing Company, Inc.

Delta Airlines. (1986, June 16). Third Party Complaint. U.S. Department of Transportation Docket 44094.

Director of Investigation and Research. (1989, April 19). Agreed statement of facts. *D.I.R. v. Air Canada, Competition Tribunal CT-88/1.* Ottawa, Canada.

——. (1988a, December 7). Amended application. *D.I.R. v. Air Canada, Competition Tribunal CT-88/1.* Ottawa, Canada.

—— (1988b, May 20). Reply. *D.I.R. v. Air Canada, Competition Tribunal CT-88/1*. Ottawa, Canada.

—— (1988c, March 3). Application. *D.I.R. v. Air Canada, Competition Tribunal CT-88/1*. Ottawa, Canada.

Dixit, A. K., & Stiglitz, J. E. (1977). Monopolistic competition and optimum product diversity. *American Economic Review, 67,* 297–308.

Donelan, J. F., Jr. (1987, December 11). Electronic data interchange: Legal considerations bearing on the establishment of industry-wide EDI standards. *National Industrial Transportation League Reporter,* Circular No. 87-34, pp. 1–12.

Drucker, P. F. (1988, January–February). The coming of the New Organization. *Harvard Business Review,* pp. 45–53.

Eads, G. (1970). *The local service airline experience.* Washington, DC: Brookings Institution.

Economides, N. (1989a). Desirability of compatibility in the absence of network externalities. *American Economic Review, 79,* 1165–1181.

—— (1989b, August). *Variable compatibility without network externalities.* Unpublished manuscript.

Economides, N. & Salop, S. (1991). Competition and integration among complements, and network market structure. (Working Paper). Stern School of Business, New York University.

EDI gains wider acceptance. (1989, November). *Computer-Aided Engineering,* pp. 12–13.

EDI network services. (1990, March 5). *Network World, 7,* p. 9.

Erxleben, W. C. (1981). In search of price and service competition in residential real estate brokerage: Breaking the cartel. *Washington Law Review, 56,* 179–215.

European Civil Aviation Conference. (1989, March 7). *Code of Conduct for Computer Reservation Systems.*

European Community. (1989, June 2). *Regulation 6085/89 of the Council of the European Communities as a Code of Conduct for Computerized Reservation Systems.*

Farrell, J., & Saloner, G. (1985). Standardization, compatibility, and innovation. *Rand Journal of Economics, 16,* 70–83.

—— (1986). Economic issues in standardization. In J. Miller (Ed.), *Telecommunications and equity* (pp. 165–78). Amsterdam: North-Holland.

Faulhaber, G. R., Noam, E. M., & Tasley, R. (Eds.). (1986). *Services in transition.* Cambridge, MA: Ballinger Publishing Company.

Ferguson, D. M., & N. C. Hill. (1989). Electronic data interchange: A definition and perspective. *EDI Forum, 1,* 5–12.

From foreign desk to foreign exchange. (1988, July 23). *The Economist,* pp. 63–64.

Gardner, E. (1989, March 17). A direct line between buyer and supplier. *Modern Healthcare,* pp. 26–28.

Gorman, J. A., Musgrave, J. C., Silverstein, G., & Comins, K. A. (1985, July). Fixed private capital in the United States. *Survey of Current Business,* 36–47.

Gort, M. (1962). *Diversification and integration in American industry.* Princeton: Princeton University Press.

Grempler v. Multiple Listing Bureau. 266 A.2d 1, 3 6–7 (Md. Ct. App. 1970).

Grillo v. Board of Realtors of Plainfield Area. 219 A.2d 635, 639 (N.J. Super. Ct. 1966).

Grip-Pak, Inc. v. Illinois Tool Works, Inc. 694 F2d 466 (7th Cir. 1982), *cert. denied*, 461 U.S. 958 (1982).

Guadagno v. Mount Pleasant Listing Exchange, Inc. 1976-2 Trade Cas. (CCH) par. 61,065 at 69,799 (N.Y. Sup. Ct. 1976).

Guerin-Calvert, M. E. (1989a). Vertical integration as a threat to competition: Airline computer reservations systems. In L. White and J. Kwoka, Jr. (Eds.), *The antitrust revolution* (pp. 338–370). Glenview, IL: Scott, Foresman, and Company.

———— (1989b, April 21). Affidavit. *D.I.R. v. Air Canada, Competition Tribunal CT-88/1*. Ottawa, Canada.

———— (1989c, March 10). Affidavit. *D.I.R. v. Air Canada, Competition Tribunal CT-88/1*. Ottawa, Canada.

Harris, L. (1988, June 29). The 1988 Louis Harris Survey. *Travel Weekly. 45 (no. 57)*, p. 15.

———— (1982, May). Travel agent survey. *Travel Weekly*, p. 56.

Huber, G. P. (1984, August). The nature and design of post-industrial organizations. *Management Science, 30*, 928–951.

Illinois Brick Co. v. Illinois. 431 U.S. 720 (1977).

International Civil Aviation Organization. (1988, December 9). *Study of computer reservation systems* (AT-WP/1564). Toronto: ICAO.

Is your company too big? (1989, March 27). *Business Week*, pp. 84–94.

Johnston, R., & Lawrence, P. (1988, July–August). Beyond vertical integration—the rise of the value-adding partnership. *Harvard Business Review*, pp. 94–101.

Joskow, P. L. (1985, Spring). Vertical integration and long-term contracts: The case of the coal-burning electric generating plants. *Journal of Law, Economics and Organization, 1*, 33–80.

———— (1987, July). *Asset specificity and the structure of vertical relationships: Empirical evidence*. Unpublished manuscript. MIT, Cambridge.

Kambil, A. (1989). *The impact of information technology on vertical integration: Empirical examination and policy implications*. Unpublished master's thesis, MIT, Cambridge.

Katz, M. (1989). Vertical contractual relations. In R. Schmalensee & R. Willig (Eds.), *Handbook of industrial organization* (pp. 655–722). New York: North-Holland.

Katz, M., & Shapiro, C. (1985). Network externalities, competition, and compatibility. *American Economic Review, 75*, 424–440.

———— (1986). Technology adoption in the presence of network externalities. *Journal of Political Economy, 94*, 822–841.

Kauper, T. (1988, August 19). Opinion of the arbitrator, in the matter of the arbitration between First Texas Savings Association and Financial Interchange, Inc. (*Reprinted in Antitrust & Trade Reporter* (BNA), 1988, August 25, *55*, 340–373).

Keene, P. (1988). *Competing in Time: Using Telecommunications for Competitive Advantage*. Cambridge, MA: Ballinger Publishing Company.

Klein, B., Crawford, R., and Alchian, A. (1978). Vertical integration, appropriable rents, and the competitive contracting process. *Journal of Law and Economics. 21(2)*, 297–326.

Koopmans, T., & Beckmann, M. (1957). Assignment problems and the location of economic activities. *Econometrica, 25*, 53–76.

Leland, H., & Meyer, R. (1976). Monopoly pricing structures with imperfect information. *Bell Journal of Economics, 7*, 449–462.

Lenza, A. M. (1989, November 22). Affidavit. Comments of SystemOne *Direct Access System, Inc.* U.S. Department of Transportation Docket 46474.

Levine, M. E. (1987, Spring). Airline competition in deregulated markets: Theory, firm strategy, and public policy. *Yale Journal of Regulation, 4,* 393–494.

Levy, D. T. (1985, August). The transaction cost approach to vertical integration: An empirical examination. *Review of Economics and Statistics, 67,* 438–445.

Lippman, S. A. and McCall, J. J. (1976). The economics of job search: A survey. *Economic Inquiry. 14,* 155–189.

Loeb, M., & Magat, W. (1979). A decentralized method for utility regulation. *Journal of Law and Economics, 22,* 399–404.

Lyle, C. B. (1987, January). ICAO looks into possible abuses in computer reservations system services. *ICAO Bulletin, 42,* 25–31.

Machlup, F. (1962). *The production and distribution of knowledge in the United States.* Princeton: Princeton University Press.

Malone, T. W., & Smith, S. A. (1984). *Tradeoffs in designing organizations: Implications for new forms of human organizations and computer systems* (Working Paper No. 1541–84). Cambridge: Sloan School of Management, MIT.

Malone, T. W., Yates, J., & Benjamin, R. (1987, June). Electronic markets and electronic hierarchies. *Communications of the ACM, 30,* 484–497.

Maloney, M., McCormick, R., & Tollison, R. (1979, October). Achieving cartel profits through unionization. *Southern Economic Journal, 42,* 628–634.

Market Force, Inc. v. Wauwatosa Realty Co. 706 F. Supp. 1387 (E. D. Wis. 1989), aff'd, 1990–2 Trade Cas. (CCH) par 69,094 (7th Cir. 1990).

Maskin, E., & Riley, J. (1984, Summer). Monopoly with incomplete information. *Rand Journal of Economics, 15,* 171–198.

Masson, D. J., & Hill, N. C. (1989). The state of U.S. EDI: 1989. *EDI Forum, 2,* 15–24.

Mathewson, G. F., & Edsforth, J. (1989, March 3). Affidavit. *D.I.R. v. Air Canada, Competition Tribunal CT-88/1.* Ottawa, Canada.

Mathewson, G. F., & Winter, R. (1986). The economics of vertical restraints in distribution. In J. Stiglitz & G. F. Mathewson (Eds.), *New developments in the analysis of market structures* (pp. 211–236). Cambridge: MIT Press.

——— (1984, Spring). An economic theory of vertical restraints. *Rand Journal of Economics, 15,* 27–38.

Matutes, C., & Regibeau, P. (1988, Summer). Mix and match: Product compatibility without network externalities. *Rand Journal of Economics, 19,* 221–234.

Miller, M. W. and Winkler, M. (1988, September 22). A former trader aims to hook Wall Street on—and to—his data. *Wall Street Journal,* pp. 1, 26.

Mitchell, R., and Heywood, P. (March 3, 1985). Detroit tries to level a mountain of paperwork: All-electronic communication with suppliers could save $200 a car by 1988. *Business Week,* pp. 94–96.

Monteverde, K., & Teece, D. (1982a, Spring). Supplier switching costs and vertical integration in the automobile industry. *Bell Journal of Economics, 13,* 206–213.

——— (1982b, October). Appropriable rents and quasivertical integration. *Journal of Law and Economics. 25(2),* pp. 321–328.

Morrison, S. and Winston, C. (1989). Enhancing the performance of the deregulated air transportation system. *Brookings Papers on Economic Activity: Microeconomics,* pp. 61–112. Washington, DC: Brookings Institution.

Murphy v. Alpha Realty, Inc. 1978-2 Trade Cas. (CCH) par. 62, 388 at 76,311, 76,314, 76,315 (N.D. Ill. 1978).

National Bankcard Corp (NaBANCO) v. VISA, U.S.A. 779 F.2d 592 (11th Cir. 1986).

National Society of Professional Engineers v. United States. 435 U.S. 679 (1978).

Ng, Y., and Weisser, W. (1974). Optimal pricing with a budget constraint—the case of the two-part tariff. *Review of Economic Studies, 41,* 337–345.

Norris, R. C. (1989). The ADL Grocery Report revisited. *EDI Forum, 1,* 44–48.

Notto, R. W. (1989). EDI standards: A historical perspective. *EDI Forum, 1,* 120–128.

Ogelsby & Barclift, Inc. v. Metro MLS, Inc. 1976-2 Trade Cases (CCH) par. 61,064 at 69,796, 60,797 (E.D. Va. 1976).

Owen, B. (1977). Kickbacks, specialization, price fixing, and efficiency in residential real estate markets. *Stanford Law Review, 29,* 931–967.

Payne, R. (1990, March 26). Take a close look before getting on the wire. *Computerworld,* pp. 81–82, 86.

People v. Colorado Springs Board of Realtors. 692 P.2d 1055, 1059 (Colo. 1984).

People v. National Association of Realtors. 1981-1 Trade Cas. (CCH) par. 64,102 at 76,649 (Cal. Ct. App. 1981).

Phillips, A. (1987). The role of standardization in shared bank card systems. In H. L. Gabel (Ed.), *Product standardization and competitive strategy* (pp. 263–282). Amsterdam: Elsevier.

Pindyck, R. S., & Rubinfeld, D. L. (1976). *Econometric models and economic forecasts,* New York: McGraw-Hill.

PWA Corporation. (1988, April 22). Response to the director's application. *D.I.R. v. Air Canada, Competition Tribunal CT-88/1.* Ottawa, Canada.

Rey, P., & Tirole, J. (1986, December). The logic of vertical restraints. *American Economic Review, 76,* 921–939.

Rise and rise of America's small firms, The. (1989, January 21). *The Economist* (U.K.), pp. 67–68.

Rosse, J. (1978). The evolution of one-newspaper cities. In H. Kirkwood (Ed.), *Proceedings of the symposium on media concentration* (2, 429–471). Washington, DC: Bureau of Competition, Federal Trade Commission.

Salop, S. C. (1979, Spring). Monopolistic competition with outside goods. *Bell Journal of Economics, 10,* 141–156.

———. (1990). Deregulating self-regulated ATM networks. *Economics of Innovation and New Technology, 1,* 85–96.

Salop, S. C., Scheffman, D. T., & Schwartz, W. (1984). A bidding analysis of special interest regulation: Raising rivals' costs in a rent-seeking society. In *The political economy of regulation: Private interests in the regulatory process* (pp. 102–127). Washington, DC: Federal Trade Commission.

Scherer, F. M. (1983). The economics of vertical restraints. *Antitrust Law Journal, 52,* 687–707.

Schmalensee, R. (1981). Monopolistic two-part pricing arrangements. *Bell Journal of Economics, 12,* 445–466.

Simon, H. A. (1961). *Administrative Behavior* (2nd ed.). New York: Macmillan.

Sokol, P. K. (1989). *EDI: The competitive edge.* New York: Multiscience Press.

Spence, A. M. (1976, June). Product selection, fixed costs and monopolistic competition. *Review of Economic Studies, 43,* 217–235.

Spengler, J. (1950, August). Vertical integration and anti-trust policy. *Journal of Political Economy, 58,* 347–352.

Stalk, G., Jr., & Hout, T. M. (1990). *Competing against time: How time-based competition is reshaping global markets.* New York: Free Press.

Stevens, R., Martin, R., & Warren, W. (1987, September–October). ATM nonadopters: How valuable are they? *Banker's Magazine,* pp. 51–53.

System One Direct Access, Inc., Continental Airlines, Inc., and Eastern Airlines, Inc. (1989, November). Comments. *Computer Reservations Systems (CRS) Regulations before the U.S. Department of Transportation* (Docket 46494).

Telser, L. G. (1960). Why should manufacturers want fair trade? *Journal of Law and Economics, 3,* 86–105.

Texas Air Corporation. (1989). *1988 Annual Report.*

——— (1990). *1989 Annual Report.*

Third parties, EDI shape enterprise internetworks. (1990, January 8). *Network World,* pp. 1, 27.

Trans Data Corporation (1987a). *ATMS and debit cards: Strategy and promotion* (Research Rep.). Salisbury, Md.

——— (1987b). *National directory of shared ATM/POS networks* (1987 ed.). Salisbury, Md.

Tretheway, Michael. (1989, March 10). Affidavit. *D.I.R. v. Air Canada, Competition Tribunal CT-88/1.* Ottawa, Canada.

Tucker, I. B., & Wilder, R. P. (1977, September). Trends in vertical integration in the U.S. manufacturing sector. *Journal of Industrial Economics, 26,* 81–94.

United Airlines v. Austin Travel. (1987). U.S. District Court, Southern District of New York, 681 F. Supp. 176.

United States v. National Association of Real Estate Boards. 339 U.S. 485, 489, 495 (1950).

United States v. Realty Multi-List, Inc. 629 F.2d 1351, 1355, 1357 n.7, 1359, 1369 n.33, 1387 (5th Cir. 1980).

USAir et al., v. American Airlines and United Airlines. (1984). U.S. District Court, Central District of California, case CV84-8918 ER.

U.S. Department of Justice. (1983, November 17). *Comments and proposed rules on computer reservation systems.* (EDR-466, Docket 41686, filed with the Civil Aeronautics Board).

——— (1985, December 20). *1985 report of the Department of Justice to Congress on the airline computer reservation system industry.* Washington, DC.

——— (1989a, June 22). *Justice opposes merger of airline computer reservation systems* [Press release].

——— (1989b, November 22). *Comments of the U.S. Department of Justice filed in advance notice of proposed rulemaking-computer reservation system regulations before U.S.D.O.T.* (Docket 46494).

U.S. Department of Transportation. (1988, May). *Study of airline computer reservation systems.* Washington, DC.

Wardair Canada, Inc. (1988, June 1). Request to intervene. *D.I.R. v. Air Canada, Competition Tribunal CT-88/1.* Ottawa, Canada.

Warner, T. (1989). Why in the world—EDIFACT? *EDI Forum, 1,* 129–132.

Weitzman, M. L. (1979). Optimal search for the best alternative. *Econometrica 47(3),* 641–654.

Wilde, L. L. and Schwartz, A. (1979). Equilibrium comparison shopping. *Review of Economic Studies, 46,* 543–553.

Wildman, S. S. (1989). A model of supply and demand for information in a competitive market. Unpublished manuscript.

Williamson, O. E. (1975). *Markets and hierarchies: Analysis and antitrust implications.* New York: Free Press.

——— (1981). The economics of organization: The transaction cost approach. *American Journal of Sociology, 87,* 548–575.

——— (1985). *The economic institutions of capitalism.* New York: Free Press.

Winkler, C. (1990, January 8). Proceed with caution. *Computer Systems News, 449,* 27.

Index

Page numbers in italics indicate references in figures and tables.

About the Contributors

ROBIN L. ALLEN is an economist with the Antitrust Division of the U.S. Department of Justice. Allen's major areas of expertise are industrial organization and health economics. Dr. Allen was a Victor H. Kramer Fellow at the University of Chicago Law School in 1986–1987.

RICHARD ANNAN is a Senior Commerce Officer with the Bureau of Competition Policy, Consumer and Corporate Affairs, Canada. He has worked in the area of merger review for the past three years, including being responsible for the Gemini case that resulted in the current Canadian computer reservation system (CRS) rules.

DENNIS W. CARLTON is Professor of Business Economics in the Graduate School of Business, the University of Chicago. He has also been a member of both the Law School and the Department of Economics at the University of Chicago, and has served on the American Economic Association's Advisory Panel to the Census. Co-editor of the *Journal of Law and Economics,* Associate Editor of *Regional Science and Urban Studies* and of the *International Journal of Industrial Organization,* Dr. Carlton is the author of numerous articles and the co-author of a leading textbook in industrial organization.

NICHOLAS ECONOMIDES is an Associate Professor of Economics in the Leonard Stern Graduate School of Business at New York University. Past positions include Visiting Professor of Economics at Stanford University and Associate Professor of Economics at Columbia University. A Research Associate in both the Center for Telecommunications and the Center for the Study of Futures Markets at Columbia University and a recipient of grants from the National Science Foundation and the Council for Research in the Social Sciences, Dr. Economides is widely published in academic journals, including the *American Economic Review,* the *Rand Journal of Economics,* the *Journal of Economic Theory,* the *European Economic Review,* and *Regional Science and Urban Economics.*

RICHARD J. GILBERT is Professor of Economics, Director of the university-wide Energy Research Group, and an Affiliate Professor in the School of Business Administration at the University of California–Berkeley. He has taught as a Visiting Fellow at the University of Cambridge and the University of Oxford. An Editor for the *Journal of Industrial Economics* and a past Associate Editor for the *Journal of Economic Theory,* Gilbert has published in numerous scholarly journals, authored books, and served on the review panel of the National Science Foundation.

MARGARET E. GUERIN-CALVERT is Assistant Chief of the Economic Regulatory Section of the U.S. Department of Justice's Antitrust Division, where her areas of expertise involve network industries as well as work in competition advocacy, mergers, and regulatory reform in numerous regulated industries. Prior to taking her current position, Dr. Guerin-Calvert was a Senior Economist at Economists Incorporated, an economics consulting firm specializing in microeconomic analysis of antitrust and regulatory issues. She also served as an economist at the Board of Governors of the Federal Reserve System. A former Adjunct Lecturer at the Institute of Policy Sciences at Duke University, she has published articles and papers in a number of major economics journals.

AJIT KAMBIL is a Ph.D. candidate in management information technologies at M.I.T.'s Sloan School of Management. He has worked at Arthur D. Little Inc. and at Intelsat on market research for new telecommunications services.

JOHN E. LOPATKA is Professor of Law at the University of South Carolina, where he teaches antitrust and economic analysis of law. Previously, he was Assistant Director for Planning in the Bureau of Competition of the Federal Trade Commission (FTC). Before joining the staff of the FTC, he was Associate Professor of Law at the University of Illinois College of Law.

ROGER G. NOLL is Morris M. Doyle Professor in Public Policy at Stanford University. Prior to teaching at Stanford, he was Institute Professor of Social Sciences and Chairman of the Division of Humanities and Social Sciences at the California Institute of Technology from 1965 to 1982. Noll also was Senior Staff Economist for the Council of Economic Advisers and a Senior Fellow at the Brookings Institution. Recipient of the first National Association of Education Broadcasters' Book Award and the author of six books and more than 100 articles, he has been an active member of several government advisory councils.

STEVEN C. SALOP is Professor of Economics and Law at the Georgetown Law Center. He has taught at M.I.T., the University of Pennsylvania, and George Washington University, and has held a variety of positions in the Bureau of Economics at the Federal Trade Commission, including Associate Director for Special Projects, Assistant Director for Industry Analysis, and Deputy Assistant Director for Consumer Protection. Dr. Salop was also an Economist with the Office of Economic Analysis at the Civil Aeronautics Board and an Economist at the Federal Reserve Board. He is a prolific author and the Associate Editor for the *Journal of Economic Perspectives*.

JOSEPH J. SIMONS is an attorney with the New York firm of Wachtell, Lipton, Rosen, & Katz. Prior to joining the firm, he was the Associate Director for the Bureau of Competition at the Federal Trade Commission and an Adjunct Professor of Law at the Georgetown University Law Center. In 1991 Mr. Simons was named to the *Crain's New York Business* list of "forty-under-forty" leaders in New York City.

STEVEN S. WILDMAN is Associate Professor of Communication Studies at Northwestern University and Director of Northwestern's Program in Telecommunications Science, Management and Policy. He has been the Ameritech Research Professor at Northwestern University and an Ameritech Research Fellow, Senior Economist at Economists Incorporated, and Assistant Professor in Economics at the University of California–Los Angeles. A former consultant to the RAND Corporation, Dr. Wildman is the coauthor of *International Trade in Films and Television Programs* and numerous articles dealing with economics and communications.